# IT SHOULDN'T HAPPEN TO A MANAGER

Also by Harry Redknapp:

Always Managing
A Man Walks On To a Pitch

# HARRY REDKNAPP

WITH JEREMY WILSON

# IT SHOULDN'T HAPPEN TO A MANAGER

HOW TO SURVIVE THE WORLD'S HARDEST JOB

EBURY
PRESS

1 3 5 7 9 10 8 6 4 2

Ebury Press, an imprint of Ebury Publishing
20 Vauxhall Bridge Road
London SW1V 2SA

Ebury Press is part of the Penguin Random House group of companies whose
addresses can be found at global.penguinrandomhouse.com

Penguin
Random House
UK

First published by Ebury Press in 2016

www.penguin.co.uk

A CIP catalogue record for this book is available from the British Library

HB ISBN 9781785034565
TPB 9781785034589

Printed and bound in Great Britain by Clays Ltd, St Ives PLC

*For all the brilliant and not so brilliant players*
*I've managed in my long career*

# CONTENTS

# PROLOGUE: THE BEAUTIFUL GAME

It was my first match as Jordan manager and the scene inside the Amman International Stadium was just about as far removed from how it all started for me in football as you could imagine. We were preparing for a World Cup qualifier against Bangladesh when all the players suddenly got in a circle, laid down their shirts and said their prayers before kick-off. It was all rather different to being on the touchline with my dad, sharing a cheese roll while we watched East London Boys in Mile End Park, but an experience I would not have missed for the world. We all got stuck in with the prayers, including me and my assistant Kevin Bond. We didn't really know what we were doing, what we were saying or what we were singing but it felt important to all be together before the match.

We had an incredible few weeks with Jordan in March 2016, beating Bangladesh 8–0 and then losing 5–1 against Australia in the qualifiers for Russia in 2018. Australia were obviously on a different level – they had drawn with Germany and only narrowly lost to England – but the people in Jordan were so special. It was wonderful to get to know Prince Ali bin Hussein a little bit. I first met him at the 'Football for Peace' game in Greenwich in 2015. His father was the great King Hussein of Jordan, who people idolised, and his sister is married to Sheikh Mohammed, who is now the ruler of Dubai. She's a lovely person and sends me messages about horse racing.

My son Jamie always said that I would drive my wife Sandra mad if I was around the house too much when I stopped managing full-time but, honestly, I have loved it. I enjoy waking up in the morning thinking, 'I haven't got any aggravation today.' After 32 years of sleepless nights, it can be quite nice when my biggest decision of the day is whether to have a cappuccino or a latte with my mate Mervyn at the café down the road from my house in Bournemouth. I'm definitely more relaxed and it is not difficult to stay busy. Football is still my life. I love going to watch the games every week with BT Sport and spending time with people like Rio Ferdinand, Steve McManaman, David James and Paul Scholes. My experiences in football now stretch more than 60 years and my obsession for the sport has never wavered. I have met some of the most incredible characters and been lucky enough to play with, manage and compete against some of the greatest players in the history of the game. When I saw a list the other day of the managers who have worked in the Premier League, I was genuinely shocked to see that only Sir Alex Ferguson and Arsène Wenger had clocked up more games and that no one had managed more clubs in the division since it was relaunched in 1992.

Having managed a few of the modern stars of the game – people like Luka Modrić, Frank Lampard, Rio Ferdinand and Gareth Bale – it is strange now to think that my first memories of watching football with my dad remain so vivid. They go all the way back to iconic players like Tom Finney and Duncan Edwards. My dad had been a prisoner of war and would be there, with his flask, at every game he could get to. Like me, he was sports mad. We used to stand over a big manhole cover two hours before kick-off on Highbury's North Bank and I can still picture the band playing and everyone cheering when the girl twirled her baton with ribbons in the air. Then waiting for the half-time scores and filling them in by letter in the programme. In his later years, my dad would get the train to see Jamie play for Liverpool. Jamie would pick him up at the station and my mum would always have sent a cheese roll for him and Steve McManaman, who would also get a lift in the car.

It will become evident through this book that almost everything has changed, especially for a manager, and yet what strikes me even more powerfully is how it is still the same things that ultimately make the difference. I have surprised myself with how many new stories I have remembered when I have thought back over the many different sides to my profession. I have also recalled some of the more famous stories and moments of my career. The passage of time does sometimes give you a different perspective. I really hope people enjoy reading some of the stories as much as I have enjoyed reminiscing. I also truly hope that there is something in this sort of guide to football management, Harry-style, that might help people on their own journey in whatever capacity that might be. I have tried to tell it as it really is for those people on the touchline who, every Saturday, place their ambitions and sometimes livelihoods in the hands of 11 players. Football management is a very demanding job and there are a million things now that can sidetrack you and cloud your judgement. Yet the very best managers have always shared one quality. They never allow the basic simplicity of this most brilliant and beautiful sport to be dislodged from the forefront of their thinking.

# CHAPTER ONE

# THE IMPOSSIBLE JOB?

It was more than four years after most people might have expected but, following England's shocking defeat to Iceland at Euro 2016, the Football Association did finally give me a call. Dan Ashworth, the technical director, asked if he could come down to Bournemouth for a coffee. I never realistically thought that I had a chance of the job, even if I would still have loved to be involved, but Dan was a nice guy and it was a relaxed chat. I am not really one for interviews. I know that some managers now have professional training and deliver presentations when they get in front of a chairman or directors. It can work because the game is increasingly being run by academics who have never set foot inside a dressing-room. They can be baffled with bullshit about a ten-year plan, or whatever, as if that is going to inspire a group of footballers on a Saturday afternoon. I'm not into all of that. I wouldn't even know how to turn on an overhead projector. I just sit there and talk to someone. This is me. This is what I am. This is what I do. This is what I think. It was always just a chat anyway, with Dan, rather than an interview. They wanted my thoughts on the national team and why we keep failing when we get to tournaments, but also on how we can get more English coaches involved at Premier League clubs.

I very much share the concern about the opportunities for British coaches, but I don't feel that is at the heart of England's failure. The problem in summer tournaments is not somehow linked to our work on the training ground. I love coaching players, but that is not the really important part of the job with England or any international team. They are all very good players already. Man for man, we had a better squad at Euro 2016 than Portugal. The England job is not about standing on the side of a pitch and teaching Harry Kane or Wayne Rooney how to finish. David Beckham had learned to cross like he did by the time he had joined Manchester United at the age of 16, let alone broken into the England team. These players have been practising every day of the week for their clubs and so the difference at international level is made by creating an environment in which you get the best out of people. The manager needs to make international football something for the players to look forward to and enjoy. There needs to be a clear system and identity to your play that is geared towards the strengths in your squad. And, above all, the players need to feel relaxed and confident. It really is not much more complicated than that, but England have consistently failed to find those basic ingredients.

I cringed when I read about England players saying that they couldn't talk to the media, or that they had bodyguards with them even while walking through secure areas inside a stadium at Euro 2016. It's no wonder everyone seemed so uptight. I spent some time at St George's Park, which is the base for all the national teams, in the summer of 2015 when I helped to coach an England team of people who had been homeless. I had my concerns about the environment straight away. Not with the facilities. They are fantastic – absolute state-of-the-art – but it takes much more to win football matches. I know that from my time at Portsmouth when we did not even have hot water in the showers for much of the year. My worry about St George's Park was whether there would be enough there over longer blocks away to occupy players and build team spirit. I thought it was a bit cold and sterile. A golf course would have helped. You don't want them sat in their rooms, bored out of their brains, thinking, 'If we lose this game, the press are going to slaughter us all.' I recently watched Alan Shearer's film about Euro '96, and something that really came across was the fun that they had. Everyone could see the tension and fear in the England team at Euro 2016 during the Iceland game. If you feel under too much pressure in anything you do, your mind slows down and your decision-making is affected.

I really do have the greatest respect for Roy Hodgson's career and sympathy for what he would have gone through after the tournament, but once we went behind to Iceland, we looked like we were gone. It seemed they were thinking, 'what's going to happen tomorrow?' The fear seemed unbelievable. That is the last place you want to be in. Roy is a good person and that Iceland game certainly should not ruin his life or define his career. He'll come back at another club and, as tough as it has been, I think he got off quite lightly compared to previous managers, when you remember that we did not win a game at the 2014 World Cup. People like Graham Taylor got destroyed, but I am pleased the reaction recently has been more measured. After a setback like that, you don't want to buy a newspaper, put a radio on and see what people are saying. Eventually it dies a death. You ride the storm and it is soon time to move on with the new manager.

I felt that we were well equipped to play a more defined system with three at the back at Euro 2016 – something we could still do going forward. I would have liked to have seen John Stones starting and being encouraged to step out with the ball. I would also have not given up so quickly on John Terry, who still had a huge amount to offer after retiring from international football in 2012 when he was only 31. We were all over the show against Iceland but, in Kyle Walker, Nathaniel Clyne, Danny Rose and Ryan Bertrand, we had some of the best attacking full-backs in the tournament. They would have been ideally suited to playing as wing-backs. It was a system that was used by Chris Coleman's Wales and also Italy under Antonio Conte.

Roy takes the ultimate responsibility but it was certainly not just down to the manager. So much blame is placed at the door of managers and, with the exception of the people who actually make their living in the dugout, it suits everyone else in football to have it that way. Yet how many people were talking about Kyle Walker and how he let someone run off him before Iceland's equaliser? You rely on players doing their jobs, and Roy would probably have told Kyle a hundred times, 'Be careful, their favourite move is a long throw and a flick on for the runner to peel off behind.' But Kyle was still asleep and lost his man. What can you do sat there on the touchline if you have been telling the player that all week?

There have also been plenty of other disasters before this one. The FA have let us down over previous years. Brian Clough was not just the greatest manager that England never had but, in my opinion, up alongside Sir Alex Ferguson, Bill Shankly and Sir Matt Busby as the greatest manager of all time. I loved watching the *I Believe in Miracles* film about him and, more than ever, it made me think, 'How did he never get a chance?' Terry Venables was excellent and we somehow lost him after one tournament. The same with Glenn Hoddle, who I thought was the last England manager to really have us playing with an identity.

I was pleased to see Sam Allardyce appointed and shocked at how he subsequently lost his job after only 67 days. He had worked hard all his life for it and, while he made a mistake, I can't say I agree with entrapping people. It must have been devastating, especially as, for all the backlash after Euro 2016, it was a good time to take the job. We might have been at an all-time low but we have great senior players and some very exciting young talent like Stones and Marcus Rashford. I spoke to Ryan Giggs about Rashford at the end of the 2015–16 season and he said that everybody at Manchester

United is convinced that he is the real deal. Good players always give you a chance, just as I found when I took over a squad at Tottenham Hotspur that were somehow bottom of the Premier League in October 2008.

As well as Sam, some people from the *Telegraph* tried to snare me at the same time. They set me up to go and meet with some people. They were supposed to have had a Chinese owner wanting to buy a club and, if he bought the club, he would like to get me involved. That was the story. So I turned up and, for three hours, I was bored out of my brains. If anyone looks at the whole tape, time and time again, I told them not to get involved with buying players. I told them that it was a bad investment and that he would be better off buying a lower division club and building it up. That was the only advice I kept on giving them.

It was an absolute load of nonsense. If that was the best they could get out of three hours of sitting with me and trying to set me up, it was pretty sad. When the bill for the food came up, the four of them even got up and left me to pay. The *Telegraph* rang me on the Wednesday before publishing the story on the Friday night and, all week, I was thinking, 'Did I say something wrong? Have I said something that night?' My wife was saying, 'You must have said something Harry,' but I had shot down in flames everything that they said to me. They made me and Sandra ill all week with worry. I had Sandra crying. It was wrong what they tried to do.

The FA's selection process was also very different in 2016. Dan Ashworth, David Gill and the chief executive Martin

Glenn made the decision to appoint Sam. David Bernstein, Alex Horne, Adrian Bevington and Sir Trevor Brooking, who together appointed Roy, had all already left the FA. Five people were interviewed this time and, as well as me, they got advice from other people in the game, including Sir Alex Ferguson. I think Alex's endorsement of Sam would have been important given that David Gill was his chief executive at Manchester United. It was hard not to notice the difference from 2012, before Roy was appointed. Alex, as well as most other people in football, was saying that I should get the job. We had reached the Champions League quarter-final with Tottenham in the previous year and had been in the mix for the Premier League title for much of the season. On that occasion, however, Alex's endorsement just ended up with a letter to Manchester United from the FA which asked him not to speak about me or the vacancy.

I was delighted that the FA did initially appoint another English manager in Sam but I could not give them much help on how they encourage others to get more experience in the Premier League. It is one of the biggest challenges facing our game and it comes down to the club owners. The 2016–17 season has started with just four English Premier League managers. It is the 25th season of the Premier League and it has still never been won by an English manager. I am certain that it is not down to a lack of quality but we are stuck now in a vicious circle. It all contributes to a very difficult decision for the higher-profile and recently retired British players about whether they pursue management or a job in the media.

It is easy to say that they should serve their apprenticeship and work in the lower leagues, but how many people reading this would turn down a better paid, easier and less time-consuming job? It was very different in my time because no player was earning enough money to just pack up. Now let's say you're Frank Lampard, Rio Ferdinand or Steven Gerrard. You have been earning £200,000 a week. Are you going to go and take a job in the lower leagues for £50,000 a year? Are you going to be there all day and have to put up with the same pressures as higher up the pyramid, as well as a chairman who is probably double busy and telling you who should and shouldn't play? When you have been used to training in the morning, having a massage, lunch and then going home, are you suddenly going to stay at the training ground until 6pm before watching a lower-division or non-league game trying to pick out a player on a free transfer? I know people can say, 'The salary is not important because they've got enough money,' but it's still the aggravation of it all. Are they really going to go and suddenly have to work 14 hours a day for £50,000 a year rather than three hours for £200,000 a week? So, unless those boys manage a big club straight away – and I think Stevie G, Rio or Frank could all be fantastic one day at a Liverpool, Manchester United or Chelsea – will they learn the ropes lower down? If not, will they be ready if they do get that opportunity? You can hardly blame them if they end up in the television studio for a few days a week on a couple of million a year. It all leaves the English system at risk of losing a lot of great football brains.

For those who do follow the coaching route, usually out of necessity, the only way to create a Premier League opportunity if you are British is by taking a club up. Maybe former players like Rio, Frank and Stevie G would be an exception but I am not convinced. The only one I can see definitely getting a big job is Eddie Howe at Bournemouth, but I think he is a one-off because he has done such unbelievable work and his teams play such great football. Eddie was also in the frame for England after Euro 2016 but was only 38 and it was too early for him. He will be perfect in a few years' time, and I think he'll get the chance when he is ready. For the rest, I worry. I don't know how you get your opportunity for one of the big jobs if you are the manager of Rochdale or Peterborough. I don't even know how you get your chance if you are a manager like Sean Dyche or Steve Bruce, who has consistently delivered. I was the last English manager to get the opportunity at what you might now call one of the 'big six' Premier League clubs. We exceeded all expectation at Tottenham by twice finishing in the top four – something that the club had never previously done in the Premier League – but where did it get us? It got me the sack and, in more than four years since, no Englishman has managed another of those teams.

I would love to see a system where they change all the managers that finish in the top half of the Premier League and they have to swap jobs with those in the bottom half. I'd love to see if there's any difference. I think that people would be surprised.

Put Sean Dyche in at Manchester City and see if he can't win the league. I'm sure he could. Stick José Mourinho or Pep Guardiola at Burnley or Hull City. They would still need a miracle and could easily get relegated. It's a bit different when you are told, 'OK, here's £200 million to spend on some players. You're taking over Manchester City and, oh, you've already got Sergio Agüero, David Silva and Yaya Touré.' Or, 'Here's £100 million. Go and buy Paul Pogba.' You haven't got to be a genius, really, to put together a decent team. In fact, you've got to be an idiot not to. I've been at both ends and I know. I had to be clever when I took over just about the worst team I have ever seen at Portsmouth in 2005 and try to keep them up, but I did not really have to be that bright a few years later at Tottenham to turn around a squad with Luka Modrić, Gareth Bale and the rest. Why can't Steve Bruce manage Manchester United one day? He was a great captain for them. He has gained huge experience as a manager in winning four promotions to the Premier League as well as going within a whisker of winning the FA Cup at Hull, but he has not even been on the radar when the job comes up. The owners want a sexy name and they are not looking at English managers.

It was something I talked to Dan Ashworth about but, even in the time since I left full-time management at QPR in February 2015, it feels like it is getting more difficult. In the Championship, where the opportunities have generally been greater, Sheffield Wednesday, Huddersfield, Fulham, Queens Park Rangers, Newcastle, Aston Villa, Reading, Nottingham

Forest and Wolves all started the 2016–17 season with non-British managers.

The opportunities for British managers both domestically and in Europe might be more limited but they do exist further afield. The money that people are earning in China is incredible. Sven-Göran Eriksson is out there managing and, if you have no ties, it's a great place to go and make a fortune. I value life in Bournemouth with Sandra, my children and grandchildren too much. We love it where we live. You can see that in the jobs I have taken and turned down over the years. I'd miss our two bulldogs, Lulu and Barney, as well. I have never wanted to be only coming home one day a week. It's not a life I want to live but, equally, I could never not be involved in football.

What was perfect for me was the three months I spent at Derby County at the end of the 2015–16 season. That came totally out of the blue when the chairman, Mel Morris, asked if I would like to come and help out Darren Wassall. I said straight away to him that I would not do it unless Darren wanted me to come in, but he was fantastic about it. I met him and he said, 'No, Harry it would be great. It would be a big help to me.' I loved working with him and the coaching staff. I would love to have got promoted with them but we just had one bad day to Hull City in the first leg of the Championship play-off semi-final. We played badly and they scored with a shot that took about two deflections. I had missed the buzz of a matchday. I would not want to be doing it full on every day of the week, but a couple of days with a young manager would be great. I think I could be a big help as a sounding board and then, on a Saturday, by being around, watching the game and having a chat at half-time. Gerry Francis has been doing that for years with Tony Pulis and goes everywhere with him. I would enjoy that sort of role and feel like I would have a lot to offer.

# CHAPTER TWO

. . . . . . . . . . . . . . . . . . . . . . . . . . . . . . . . . . . . . . . . . . . . . . . . . . . . . . . . .

# MANAGING UPWARDS

Knowing when to shut up in front of a chairman or owner has never been a strong point of mine but, whenever I have regretted a run-in, I would take some comfort from the knowledge of Barry Fry's extraordinary experiences of boardroom interference.

Even now, when Barry recounts such tales to me, they can send a tear down my cheek in laughter but also a small shiver up my spine. There was Keith Cheeseman at Dunstable United, who ended up spending time in jail for various financial crimes. And then there was Stan Flashman, the 20-stone ticket tout who sacked Barry seven times but then kept on reinstating him during nine rollercoaster years together at Barnet.

Stan would ask Barry for the team every Friday and withhold his wages until after the match if he did not agree with the selection but, for sheer barmy interference into a manager's running of the dressing-room, you would have to go some way to top the story about a player called Harry

Willis. He was a very good striker at Barnet but, after they lost a game at home, Big Stan came steaming into the dressing-room. He was a terrible loser and totally unpredictable. He started threatening the players. He turned to Willis: 'I am going to rip up your contract. You ain't ever playing for the club again.' He then tore up his contract, even though his little gesture meant nothing as it was just a copy that was held by the club. But he did not stop there. 'If I ever see you come anywhere near this building, I am going to get you done in. I'll break your legs with a cricket bat.'

This was not totally unusual. Stan had once even promised to have Barry encased in a motorway bridge. Barry would often tell Stan that 'he did not know the difference between a goalline and a clothes-line' and they had come to blows before. Mostly, though, Barry knew how to handle him. That was not the case for the poor lad Willis, however. He had never heard anything like it. Barnet were due to play the following Monday night but Willis rang Barry on the morning of the game. 'I'm not coming,' he said. 'I'm scared of Stan. He will get me done in. I know what he's like. He's mad.' He was one of Barry's best players. Barry begged him and eventually went to meet him on the morning of the game to explain that Stan was definitely not coming. It was not easy but, in the end, Barry just about persuaded him on the condition that Stan would be nowhere near the ground. So Willis turned up but Barry told him to come in via the back door just in case Stan had someone watching the front door. No one quite knew what Stan might do from one minute to the next. Poor Willis was looking over his shoulder constantly but still played the game and scored a hat-trick in a 5–2 victory.

Barry was in the dressing-room immediately after the game when the telephone went in his office. He took the call and it was Stan: 'What was the score?'

'We won 5–2,' said Barry.

'Well done. Willis didn't play, did he?' asked Stan.

'Yeah, he played,' said Barry. 'He was brilliant, Stan. He got three goals.'

There was a pause, before Stan replied, 'I told you, Barry. That's how you motivate players.'

I first came across Stan when I was going to games with my dad, and he would come along the queue at all the big matches selling tickets. No matter what anybody says, virtually every player sold their tickets back in that era. You were earning £15 a week and, for the big games, the ticket touts would come on a Friday outside the ground. The players got half a dozen tickets so, through selling them on to people like Stan, they would sometimes match their wages. And Stan was not the first chairman to want to manage the team himself – although dishing out death threats is hardly standard practice, interference has got much more common these days. The aggravation is no different even lower down the leagues with owners who might not have any money. It is why my main advice to any young manager is to think especially carefully about the first job they take. Getting a difficult chairman or owner is obviously never ideal but better later in your career when you have at least had the chance to establish yourself. I had a chat with Ryan Giggs after he left Manchester United following the appointment of José Mourinho and, even for such a great player and bright lad, there are few guarantees. The natural instinct is to jump at the first opportunity that comes along, especially if it is in the Premier League, but it is vital to resist that inclination if the circumstances that you are walking into are wrong. Steve Bruce's situation at Hull City before the 2016–17 season was a case in point. He is a very experienced manager and obviously felt that he would need a miracle to keep the team up. He had lost three key defensive players at the start of the season to injury and the club had not brought any players in. It was a nightmare. He must have been sitting there thinking, 'I'm going to get relegated again. The club is up for sale. Do I need another relegation?' Sometimes you have to be realistic.

Taking that first job is the most important decision you will make. If you go into a club with no potential or no prospects of being successful, then the chances are that it will be your last job. Quick judgements are unfairly made in football and good people are written off hastily. I saw that at Southend United with two of West Ham United's most legendary players, Bobby Moore and Alvin Martin. Bobby knew the game inside and out. I will always believe that he could have been West Ham's greatest manager if he'd have ever got his chance. Instead, he took a job with no money, no players, and sadly he didn't make it. Then he had to spend the rest of his life hearing people say, 'Yeah he was a great player, great captain of England, but wasn't a manager.'

Well, he never had a chance because he went to a club with a rubbish team. Southend then came to Alvin 11 years later. I remember telling him that people would judge him quickly but he thought that he would do well and dived in when there was, again, very little prospect of being successful. Suddenly that was the end of Alvin as a football manager. Yet maybe if he had stayed at West Ham and moved on to the coaching staff, he would have ended up with the job when I left.

I said to Ryan Giggs, 'Wherever you go, you've got to make sure that you've got a chance to be successful otherwise you will be written off. Like with Bobby, people will be very quick to say, "Ryan Giggs, fantastic footballer, but wasn't a manager." You have to be as sure as you can that you make the right choice.'

That invariably means a chairman or owner with a bit of ambition who will give you an opportunity. You obviously don't want someone who is telling you exactly which players to buy and sell or who wants to pick the team. That sort of thing soon gets round and you have to do your homework. I have even read of chairmen, such as Sam Hammam at Wimbledon, trying to give themselves a say on team selection written into a manager's contract. I also remember Dave Bassett telling me how Sam's kids were jumping all over the coach. Dave asked him to stop them, to which he apparently replied, 'Bassett, I own this club. If I want my kids will jump all over you.'

You have to run a mile from serious interference on your team decisions because there are only two outcomes. Give in once and they will be trying to pick the team every week.

Ignore them and, unless you win just about every game, your days are numbered anyway. It is an impossible situation and, as the profile of owners has changed, it has certainly got more common. You also have to be sensible about how you handle your chairman or owner. That is something I impress upon young managers following my own mistakes. I was never one for trying to push myself into a director's world. Boardrooms did not interest me and, when we played away, after the game I'd just go into the manager's office for a glass of wine or a cup of tea then go home. Someone like Arsène Wenger is very different. He goes to all the board meetings at Arsenal and even does a quick walk around the directors' box at the Emirates before home games. I have seen it for myself at some Champions League games and find it amazing that he can be so relaxed.

I would keep my distance from the boardroom and often snap when I was younger if I thought they were talking rubbish. I'd say things like, 'You haven't got a clue. What do you know about football?' It has probably cost me a few jobs. I am certain that was the case at West Ham after I accused the chairman, Terry Brown, of not being able to 'fucking add up' over how much we had spent. I also totally lost it with him once when it was suggested that I was only playing Frank Lampard, who is my nephew, so that he could collect appearance money. It was nonsense – we can all see how good Frank became – but I should not have talked to him as I did. I've never spoken to Terry since I left West Ham but I have got no problems with him and we got on very well, mostly.

Looking back on it, I was probably a bit too big for my boots at times. My wife Sandra would regularly warn me about this and, in hindsight, there were times when I was wrong. Sandra used to say, 'You should be more respectful, Harry, you're an employee.' I just had a short fuse with directors who I thought did not know what they were talking about. I found it hard to just sit and go, 'Yeah, yeah, yeah.' I know that Gordon Strachan was similar when he was younger and lasted only one board meeting at Southampton before it was agreed that it was better for him not to attend again. Bobby Moore's treatment at West Ham – when he should have been in the front row of the directors' box but was instead asked to leave one match because he did not have a ticket – also only hardened my feelings towards some of the hierarchy.

At Southampton, the chairman Rupert Lowe was a real character; a complete toff. He would go on about near-post corners and offer to demonstrate how to take one successfully. It would end up with me saying, 'What do you know about football? You played hockey, didn't you? How do you know how to take a near-post corner?' He would then come back with something like, 'I'll bloody take them better than those idiots, Harry.' It is quite funny looking back and, whatever anyone says about Rupert, he did a lot of good things for Southampton. He organised the stadium for the club and played a massive part in developing an academy that has produced so many great players. He deserves some credit and, as time went on, I did get on better with chairmen and owners. I didn't have any problems at Tottenham Hotspur with Daniel Levy and, for all the mistakes that have been made, I genuinely think that Tony Fernandes at QPR is a lovely guy and brilliant man to work for. I hope he sticks in there and the club succeed under him. You also have to remember, ultimately, that it is their club and their money. It is natural for them to want to be involved in the football side, and I was always happy to explain what I was doing and talk through any issues that might concern them. I also did not mind them visiting the dressing-room 20 minutes after a game. What I didn't like with some chairmen or owners was seeing them only when we won and not if we had lost. I would say, 'Either come in all the time or not at all. It's great to see you – no problem at all – but it is no good just walking in when we win. I can't walk into the dressing-room when we win and not when we lose. We are all part of it and we have got to be together.'

Some chairmen are obviously far more hands-on than others. Milan Mandarić at Portsmouth was like that. He was the worst loser you have ever seen. He made it very difficult for Tony Pulis and Graham Rix before me, but our relationship was different. I had just turned down a very good job at Leicester City and had been managing in the Premier League at West Ham. I had never set out to get the job at Portsmouth so I would never be exactly tip-toeing around him. To an extent, I think he quite liked that. He'd just walked all over everybody in the past. I was different to anyone he'd had before. We had our ups and downs but we also laughed. We'd have a row and then we'd have a drink. He had very strong opinions and I loved his company but, if he came out with a load of nonsense, I'd just say, 'What do you effing know?' Then we'd have a massive argument, but we still always had a lot of respect for each other. We also shared some of the very best and most enjoyable highs I have ever experienced in football. We were actually similar in many ways. If we thought something, we would usually just come out and say it. Milan's story and how he helped pioneer the Silicon Valley boom in the 1970s after leaving Yugoslavia for the United States is incredible. He was Businessman of the Year in America but loved his football and was one of the first hugely wealthy overseas owners in England.

It was all very different when I started out as a player at West Ham. The chairman, Mr Pratt, owned a little wood-yard 20 yards from the ground. We only ever called him 'Mr Pratt'. If he spoke to us and if he said 'hello' you had done well. Along with the chairman, all the administration of a football club was overseen be a secretary who also, typically, was not a football person but would sit with their glasses perched on the end of their nose quoting rules at you. The secretary would draw up the registrations, contracts and liaise with the Football League on fixtures. A big change occurred when the chief executives came in – they were more outgoing and higher profile and would work between the chairman and secretary. Clubs were all owned by local businessmen who were also fans. Bob Lord at Burnley, for example, was the local butcher who had made good. He would drive around in a Rolls-Royce but really cared for the club and its players. The vast majority of Premier League owners now are billionaires, usually from abroad, who have generally been very successful in their own fields but have had no previous connection to the club. They mostly do love football but are obviously also in it for kudos and the investment. A millionaire is not enough any more. They have to have billions and, while you probably would not like to know how some of them have made their money, they generally only know winning.

Others also have large egos and want to be the star attraction. You see it in how some of them come into a club and instantly start taking pictures off the wall of great ex-players and managers. It sounds ridiculous but it happens. Some don't want to know about the past. I don't know if it was his decision or a mistake but, at Portsmouth following the takeover by Sacha Gaydamak in 2006, they had a makeover of the boardroom and 14 oak chairs that dated back to the mid-1800s and originally used on the HMS *Warrior* warship were dumped in a skip. These were chairs that Winston Churchill and Field Marshal Montgomery had supposedly sat on during the Second World War. Happily they did end up being recovered and were subsequently featured in an episode of *Antiques Roadshow*.

Many owners buy a club and, straight away, they are asking, 'Why isn't my team top of the league?' They don't realise or care that while they are spending £40 million on players you might be competing with clubs who are spending £250 million. They have not all got money to spend on players, and you have to accept that when you take a job, but you do want to be able to look at it and say, 'Yeah, I've got a chance here of improving this team.' It is no good thinking that the best you can do is halfway, or the status quo, because, even if you do that, you are probably still suddenly gone in a year's time. When another job comes up, the chairmen will be looking at guys who have been promoted or finished in the top six rather than guys who finished in the middle or near the bottom, however tough their job. But if you make a success in that first job, you are up and running. You are on the ladder and at least one more chance will follow.

Did I follow all this advice? Not really. Nothing was planned and, as with so much in my career, I can be grateful to Ron Greenwood. He gave me a first taste of coaching when he insisted that we all have afternoon jobs at West Ham and I went to the old Pretoria School in Canning Town four afternoons a week. I came from the same background as the kids. It was a tough school and I loved it. We would split £20 a week three ways for those 12 hours that would almost always end with a game in the old gym. My first coaching with adults was when I was playing in Seattle with Jimmy Gabriel. People seemed to enjoy the sessions I was putting on and I felt quite at ease with it.

Bobby Moore came out and liked what I was doing and immediately said that, whenever he got a job, he would like me to work with him. We ended up at Oxford City in the Isthmian League. I would drive the 200-mile round trip there from Bournemouth and, as the owner wanted me in every day, I would sit and basically waste a day in the Portakabin until the players arrived of an evening for training. They would have been working all day and so getting them off for an away game would always be a problem without an understanding boss. Bobby would usually arrive about 5.30pm. We would train in the park in Oxford when it was light and then, once winter came in, we would use the ground under the floodlights. It was a great experience and, because I loved being with Bobby, something I thoroughly enjoyed. It would be midnight by the time I got home but, after nine months whizzing up and down the motorway, the pistons blew out on my little old Ford Fiesta 950 and it was time for both of us to find a different challenge.

I did take my coaching badges while at Oxford and completed what remains the only formal coaching qualification I have. To get the full badge, it was two weeks at Lilleshall. There would be 70 people on those courses. Half of them would be ex-footballers, and it was the best fortnight of your life. At the end of each day, we would all go up to the pub in the village. Frank Clark would bring his guitar and a few beers and a big sing-song with Frank and Norman Hunter would ensue. You would have teachers overseeing the course who mostly had not been professional players. There would be a lot of laughs because you would have all these managers and ex-players challenging the teachers. I remember Charles Hughes, who was the FA's director of coaching, telling everyone that the reason Brazil were so good was the beaches. That was where they were learning their skills. Jim Smith then piped up and asked

28

why, if that was the case, Torquay, Blackpool, Scarborough, Brighton and Bournemouth were not top of the league. I also remember Larry Lloyd, the great Nottingham Forest centre-back, taking a session on crosses. He had just won two European Cups and he was showing us how to head balls away and get into position when the teacher stopped him and said, 'No, you don't hit it like that,' then started questioning his heading and telling him a completely different technique. Lloydy was in his thirties by then: 'I've just won two European Cups, headed 400 balls this year out of my box and you're telling me the way I'm heading the ball is wrong.' He slaughtered him. We also once got hold of the teacher's notebook to see what was in there. His wife has written him out a shopping list: four pounds of potatoes, three pounds of cabbage and some pork chops.

It wasn't exactly hard to get your coaching badges back then. To pass, you would take three training sessions and, at the end of the fortnight, there would also be a written test. I passed the practical element but I failed the written part about the laws of the game. I had left school at 14 and writing and exams were never really my thing. It was all questions like, 'What's the maximum and minimum width of the pitch?' So I had to re-sit the exam a few months later in Southampton at the Hampshire Football Association. I arrived and got chatting to the fella in charge and he was a great guy. He could see that it was all a bit silly and turned to me. 'I'll leave you on your own to take the test,' he said. Then he left the rulebook on the table and off he disappeared. He had left all the answers out for me. I had two hours to complete it and, yes, I did manage to pass this time.

Today it has become mandatory for every Premier League manager to have the Pro-Licence qualification. They work at it now for three years and it covers all sorts of areas, from psychology and media management to tactics and sports science. It's a long process and, even then, once you've passed, there are few guarantees. Football management is impossible to recreate and there is no substitute for actually doing the job. Luckily there would be no extra exams or tests. They gave me, Sir Alex Ferguson and a few others an exemption from the Pro-Licence out of respect for how long we had already been managing.

I had ten chairmen in my first managerial job at Bournemouth but, at the start, it did not look like I would last nine days let alone nine years. The story is worth re-telling. Mr Walker was my first chairman and made me the caretaker manager after he'd had a fall-out with Dave Webb. We were playing Lincoln away, who were top of the old Third Division, and just about every match that weekend had already been called off by the Friday night. There was snow and frost everywhere. Yet when we got up on the Saturday morning, we were still told that the game had a chance of going ahead. They had built about eight fires on the pitch in an attempt to thaw it out. It didn't do much good. When we got there we could see that you might have one area that was a bit better but the next fire would be 30 yards away and the rest of the surface in between was still frozen. We had a big extra problem. The only boots we had with us had long nylon studs. The Lincoln players had these little pimpled moulded boots which were perfect. It was a disaster. We were 9–0 down with about 25 minutes still to go. I always remember us then getting a corner and our kitman, John Kirk, shouting at the players to push up. I shouted even louder, 'No, fucking get back. We are not going to win this one 10–9.' We hung on to lose 9–0 but I was sure that I would not last, especially when we then got beat 5–0 by Leyton Orient. Two away games. Goals for: 0; goals against: 14. The chairman, though, was willing to keep me on and things started to pick up when we beat Oxford United 3–2 and then went to Gillingham and won 5–2. Alec Stock, who was a Bournemouth director at the time, told me that there would be a board meeting the next day. 'Well done, you have turned it around – I'm sure they will make you manager on a permanent basis, but some advice: have a think and write down what you want. A bit of petrol money. Your telephone bill paid for. Those sort of things.' So I went home and prepared this list. Petrol money. Telephone bill. I think I might have been planning to try for a second-hand club car as well but, whatever money they offered me, I would have been happy.

So what happened? Mr Walker invited me in and said, 'Harry, you have done a good job but I have just sold the club and I couldn't guarantee your position. Good luck.' And that was it. I had been sitting there thinking that I would be manager and, 15 minutes later, they had sold the club. I was clearing bits and pieces off my desk when Brian Tiler, who would become managing director, walked through the door with a fella called Anton Johnson. Anton was right up there with the biggest characters I have ever come across in football. He already owned Rotherham, would later buy Southend, and was a proper lad from Essex – great fun and larger than life. He wore a big full-length fur coat and arrived in a battered old Rolls-Royce. He had a mate with him called Harry who was wearing a chauffeur's hat. Anton was the new owner. Brian said that they were planning to bring in Don Megson as manager but that they wanted me to stay as his assistant. I had nothing else to do and we needed the money. We had two kids. Sandra did a bit of hairdressing but, otherwise, we had no income.

Meggy eventually stayed for seven months and we had some fantastic times. Anton took us all to Portugal for a week at the end of the 1982–83 season. We had never been anywhere with Bournemouth before. The lads could not believe it even if, when we got there, we ended up in the wrong place to start with – we were walking up this long dusty road in the middle of nowhere to find our villas. We had met a honeymoon couple on the plane going out there. The kid had his hair all dyed and was talking to all the players, challenging them to some betting on the European Cup final and then the FA Cup final replay which were being played on consecutive nights. He was, 'Harry, I'll have the pick for the FA Cup and you can have the European Cup.' Manchester United were playing Brighton in the FA Cup final replay and a very good Hamburg team were in the European Cup final. I was thinking, 'What's the point, we'll end up level.' But then he said, 'I'll take Brighton in the FA Cup and leave you the choice in the European Cup. £100 a game? Do you want that, Harry? Are you scared?' I have never been happier to have a bet in my life and, fair play, he came knocking on the door of the villa I was sharing with Anton and Brian Tiler with the £100 both mornings.

Tragedy was to strike some years later when myself and Brian were involved in a car accident while travelling through the night from Rome to watch the England v. Cameroon quarter-final at Italia '90 in Naples. Brian died and it was a miracle that I survived. He was a wonderful director to work with and he taught me about managing people as well. Young managers can get into situations when they are not sure of how to handle something and having an experienced person to talk to and take the pressure off is invaluable. Brian knew when I was on the verge of a blow up. He knew if the owner had said something I didn't like and knew how to handle me. He would be, 'Get your gear, Harry, let's have a day's racing or a game of golf.' To have a buffer like Brian, who understood the game, was invaluable in managing my relationships with the various Bournemouth owners. Brian was unique in many ways in that sort of boardroom position because he was a former player himself and had been captain of Aston Villa. He would give me a lift if I was down and was someone who I could confide in. Peter Storrie was similarly important later in my career at West Ham and Portsmouth.

For all the advice people want to give you, management can often feel quite lonely. Neil Warnock used to say that Simon Jordan was great for him in keeping his mood up at Crystal Palace if he ever felt like packing it in. Whoever has worked at Peterborough since Barry Fry moved into a director of football role in 2006 has been lucky to have someone like him working with them. The best chairmen are those who can also sometimes motivate the manager. You don't want them interfering where they are not wanted but you do want to feel their support. I only wish Brian could have stayed with me throughout my career. The pressure from above has only increased in football and his was the sort of role that could really still help young managers today.

# CHAPTER THREE

. . . . . . . . . . . . . . . . . . . . . . . . . . . . . . . . . . . . . . . . . . . . .

# FINDING PLAYERS

The 'Ron Manager' character on *The Fast Show* was based on Alec Stock, one of my early mentors at Bournemouth. He had been a captain in the army and was one the poshest people I have ever met. He was also very astute and, without any warning, would sometimes deliver a pearl of wisdom gathered from 35 years in management that ranged from Yeovil Town in the Southern League to AS Roma in Serie A. My desk was a particular mess when he once dropped into what passed for an office at Bournemouth. I was embarrassed and began straightening the papers but he just looked at me like I was daft. 'Harry,' he said. 'You will never get the sack for having an untidy desk. It's just if you lose games and buy bad players.' He was right then and he remains right today. A lot of people like to let you think that there is some kind of complex formula for football management but it ultimately boils down to knowing a good player and how they can fit into your team. That is not to say that your tactics and preparation don't matter, but the starting point is the quality of your players and how skilfully you build your squad.

Magic wands have simply never existed in football, but what has changed dramatically is how players are identified and assessed. A talent pool that once barely spread beyond the vicinity of your local area now includes literally every part of the globe. Clubs now have entire departments dedicated to spotting and assessing talent, which has changed completely the process of scouting players. As soon as one of the recruitment people suggests a player, you can go into a room and watch a video of him for several hours. It can be the most obscure club in the world but, within two minutes, the player can be up on the screen. You can have highlights or see an entire match.

A manager would get ridiculed years ago if they admitted buying a player on the basis of a video but, in many cases today, he is recruiting a player he has never seen live. The key difference now is that you are not just watching some video that an agent or the selling club has prepared. Your own scouting department has the technology to decide what you watch and show you the good and the bad. It is a fantastic resource. You will also get every statistic imaginable. I would always look at their goals, assists, height and pace but, beyond that, I can't say that I found the rest of it useful. Other statistics can sound important but they have no context if you can't see what the opposition are doing or you have no idea what job the player has been asked to do for their team. For example, a manager might have asked a player to hit balls into the channel as a means to relieve pressure and get throw-ins higher up the pitch. This player might be doing exactly what is wanted for their team – and you would be able to see that if you are watching the whole game – but his pass-completion stats at the end will be useless. Yet that doesn't mean he could not be a very accurate passer of the ball under a different manager with different instructions.

Most clubs these days have a director of football, sporting director or head of recruitment. It can work well if the boundaries are clear. At some clubs, the manager is hardly involved in picking the transfer targets, but I don't see how that works if he is then asked to pick the team, motivate them and decide the system. The manager needs help and cannot be an expert on players everywhere in the world but, for me, he should still have the final say on who is bought. I would always still jump in the car or get on a plane to watch a player in person if I could. I'd learn more than from any number of videos or statistics. You get a feel just from the warm-up and how they carry themselves. You have the view of the whole pitch and see everything in relation to the rest of the game. You can watch everything they are doing off the ball as well as on it. How well do they concentrate? What areas do they take up out of possession? Do they talk much? Do they organise those around them? What runs do they make? How do they move? Maybe it is just what I have become used to but, even if you have a video of an entire match, you don't get that wider perspective in the same way. A camera just follows the ball. When I watch a game in person, I can relate everything that the player is doing to the other 21 people on the pitch. I went to Lille to watch Eden Hazard three times when I was Tottenham manager and, although we spent several hours speaking to him at a hotel in Paris, it was mega money and we could not quite persuade him once Chelsea reached the Champions League – by somehow beating Barcelona and Bayern Munich to win it in 2012. You could immediately see that there was something special about him and, as a winger, he is almost a throwback in many ways. He has that ability to go from standing still to suddenly accelerating, which is something that is quite rare, but which a lot of the best wingers could do. He reminded me a little bit of the great Jimmy Johnstone at Celtic. Like Jimmy, Hazard would also slow people down but still keep the ball and then suddenly go and leave the full-back for dead. We had no doubts that he could develop into one of the world's best players.

Driving the length and breadth of the country to watch matches when we were not playing was as much a part of my daily routine as taking training in the morning. Days that stretched 16 hours or more were common. The only games that were shown on television when I started at Bournemouth were the one or two featured fixtures each week on *Match of the Day*. There was only one way to see players: get to the games yourself. The directors' boxes would be full of managers and scouts at every match. It was so important that it was not unheard of for managers to miss their first team on a Saturday in preference for watching a particular player at another game. You might have had a scout who recommended a player or had your card marked about someone but sometimes you were just watching people that you did not know for the first time and then backing your judgement.

It meant that you got to know the lower leagues and that is why it remains such a challenge to start there. If Gary Neville or Rio Ferdinand takes a League One job, will they know if there is a centre-half at Rochdale or Bury who can do the job? They wouldn't have a clue to start with but they'd have to learn quickly or find someone who does know the ropes if they want to be better than the people down there. You chat to someone like Paul Dickov and he will give you chapter and verse on every team in the lower leagues. It was the same learning curve when I went to Oxford City in the Isthmian League – suddenly you were working in what felt like a whole new world. We could not walk in and know more about all the teams than old Billy Smith down the local market, who played in the league for 12 years, managed for 15 and is friends with half the players. You have to get to know players and learn what you are looking for when you watch them. It is a grounding that I would still believe is invaluable even now if I was trying to weigh up a player we might buy, an opponent or even while assessing one of my own players during a game.

My generation all trod that path. Sir Alex Ferguson was at East Stirlingshire, St Mirren and Aberdeen for 12 years before Manchester United. Sam Allardyce was at Limerick, Preston, Blackpool and Notts County before taking Bolton into the Premier League. I loved that part of management. Get in your car. Drive to a game. Find a player. We took Tony Pulis from

Newport to Bournemouth after an eight-hour round trip in the pouring rain. Stuart Morgan, who had been a manager at Weymouth and worked with me at Bournemouth, was an invaluable help with the non-league scene. I signed Efan Ekoku on his say-so. I went to see Ekoku on a Tuesday night and no one could have played worse if they had tried. I don't think he did a thing right for 90 minutes. I turned to Stuart and said, 'Are you sure?' There was another club interested and we needed to make a decision. Stuart said, 'I'm telling you, Harry, he is different class. His pace is electric. He has got a big future. If he is no good you can sack me.' I said, 'We will, don't worry,' and took the gamble. We sold him to Norwich City for £800,000 and Stuart went just about everywhere with me since.

Another of my favourite signings came straight out of non-league. It was a beautiful sunny Bank Holiday Monday in 1986 but I had decided to go to Nuneaton for a game. Sandra was unimpressed. 'Really? Why? Who's playing?' It was England non-league against the Welsh non-league, and that was where I found Carl Richards. He was an incredible athlete from Enfield and, after the game, I waited for him next to the old hut where the players would file out. I was hiding behind the shed so no one saw and I called him over as he left. He thought Bournemouth were in the Isthmian League but was up for joining us once he realised we were professional. He would drive me mad with his laid-back attitude in training but was great for us. 'Wait for the real games,' he used to say. He also prompted one of my biggest mistakes when, at a time when his attitude was causing me maximum frustration, he suggested a mate of his come down for a trial. I said no. It later transpired that this pal was Ian Wright.

Efan, Carl and Wrighty were proof of something I learned quickly. The gap between the divisions, and even from non-league all the way up to the Premier League, is not necessarily as wide as people think. Yes, there might be a gulf in quality if you look across an entire team but there are also individuals who get stuck at a certain level when it is the people around them who are making all the difference. It works both ways. There are players you might take out of the Premier League and put them in the lower divisions but they will not be any better than the lads who are there. I have seen it with people who dropped down from clubs like Liverpool, Arsenal and Spurs, where they have won big trophies, but you think, 'They are not as good as my players.' There are also people lower down that just need an opportunity to play with top players. It's a much easier game then. If you play at the Palladium your performance is going to be better than at the working men's club up the road. The whole place makes you step up and perform better. Football is similar. People always say the FA Cup is a leveller, but sometimes it is more about the chance to play on a decent pitch in front of 30,000 people.

Look at Stuart Pearce. He did not suddenly go from non-league standard at Wealdstone to probably the best left-back in the world. He just got noticed by Bobby Gould at Coventry and was given a chance. I remember listening to Bobby talk about it. He said he was only there 10 minutes and Stuart lifted the outside right-back into the fifth row of the crowd. He thought, 'He'll do me,' and went home. Les Ferdinand was similar. When I took Matty Holmes from Bournemouth to West Ham, people were saying, 'West Ham?' but I knew he could play. He was fantastic and was sold to Blackburn for £1.2 million. Linvoy Primus also made the step up quite late in his career, as did José Fonte, who has gone from League One to winning the European Championship with Portugal in the space of five years. We now also have the examples of Jamie Vardy and Charlie Austin who have risen up to the Premier League after playing non-league until quite late into their careers. The players are still out there and, even with all their added resources, scouting departments have missed a trick by becoming obsessed with foreign players at the expense of the domestic market. Just look at Dele Alli. He was in the MK Dons team that thumped Manchester United in the League Cup in 2014 but not one United scout seemed to notice and it was Tottenham who got an absolute bargain at £5 million for him during the January window in 2015.

As much as possible, you also make enquiries to try to find out about the character of a potential signing. That was obviously easier with a British player and, as you gained experience, you would find that you usually know someone, somewhere who can help. If not, I might ask Jamie to find someone who knew the player. When Brian Clough signed Kenny Burns, his due diligence even involved sending his assistant Peter Taylor to observe him at the local dog-track in Birmingham. He wasn't a big gambler and so Clough signed him. Asking people who you trust is the key as there are plenty of players out there who do not have very good ideas. You might even directly ring up the player's manager for an opinion. That manager might be desperate to get rid of the player but, even if he has been a problem, there is an unwritten code that you are honest. You can't all be screwing each other over, really – as managers there remains this sense that you are all in it together – and a player's reputation does get known inside the game quite quickly. You could never say to someone, 'Yeah, he's a great lad, take him,' when you know he is a shit. It wouldn't be right and would come back on you anyway.

One example is when I went to watch Pierre van Hooijdonk at Celtic when we were in desperate need of a striker at West Ham United. It was my third full season and we were in real danger of going down. He had scored 32 goals the previous season but was still for sale. At half-time I passed Tommy Burns, who was then the Celtic manager, in the stands. He just shook his head and went, 'Not for you, Harry.' It was something he didn't really have to do and will always stick with me as I had not asked him his opinion. He could easily have kept quiet to try to get rid of him for £5 million, but he didn't. Tommy Burns might have saved my career, really. Van Hooijdonk ended up at Nottingham Forest and scored only one goal in eight games and they went down that season. I changed tack. I was also interested in Dean Holdsworth at Wimbledon but, frankly, I found Joe Kinnear impossible to deal with. He wouldn't answer the phone or return a call. Eventually I met

Joe in a Chinese restaurant a hundred yards from where he lived in Mill Hill and he said, 'Ring me tomorrow.' I did and it was the same. Someone else would answer the phone. 'Yes, I'll put you through.' Pause. 'Oh, sorry, he's not here, just left.' It worked out for the best because, for the same cost of van Hooijdonk, I took Paul Kitson and John Hartson. We were 18th at the time but they got 13 goals between them in the last 14 games and, with one or the other always scoring, we lost only one game in eight weeks and finished 14th.

I could never give someone a duff character reference for a player but I was once less than honest with Tottenham chairman Daniel Levy when he asked my advice. I was at Portsmouth and Glen Johnson had been with us on loan from Chelsea the previous season. Daniel called me and asked me for my opinion of Glen as they were looking to sign a right-back. He was available for a great price at £4 million but what Daniel did not know was that we were also in for him and hoping to get a deal done the next day. So I gave him a bit of a thumbs-down. I told him that Glen had been a good player for Portsmouth but that he wasn't at Tottenham's level. Glen would probably have been upset with me at that time if he found out but it worked out for everyone. He helped us win the FA Cup that next season and then got a big move to Liverpool while Daniel took Kyle Walker instead.

My attitude to Daniel and Tottenham was also hardened after they got one over us a few years earlier for Michael Carrick. It was a done deal that he would join us at Portsmouth for £2.5 million from West Ham. It was a ridiculously cheap fee for a player of his class. I had even met Michael at his house with Peter Storrie, the Portsmouth chief executive, and Michael's agent David Geiss. He was coming down the M3 to do his medical and sign the contract when, just as he passed Fleet Services, he received a phone call from Tottenham. Daniel had got wind of the deal and knew that I had managed Michael at West Ham. He trusted my judgement and made a counter offer. I knew that was it. Sometimes you can still persuade a player even when a bigger club comes in but Michael had a house two minutes from their training ground in Chigwell and I knew he liked living in the area. Jacques Santini, who was the Tottenham manager at the time, didn't seem to have a clue who he was, and Michael did not start playing regularly until Martin Jol came in. I think they just took a gamble on him based, in effect, on my recommendation. Tottenham then sold Michael to Manchester United for £18.5 million and so made about £16 million on him in two years. Even that has turned into a bargain for United and, 12 years on, one of the first things that José Mourinho did after replacing Louis van Gaal was to give Michael a new contract.

When you were buying from abroad, it became increasingly difficult to find out much about the character of someone, and we all had some problems. When I was at Portsmouth they had a total nightmare up the road at Southampton with their £3.2 million record signing Agustín Delgado. He had come over from Ecuador with a teammate, Cléber Chalá. Delgado was OK but kept disappearing, while Chalá did not play a single game. The local *Daily Echo* newspaper carried a back-page mugshot of Delgado under the headline, 'Wanted: Have you see this man?' Delgado once turned up to a training session 45 minutes late with an interpreter, who was wearing ankle socks and cycling shorts, but also expected to join in for a trial.

We famously had Javier Margas from Chile at West Ham United. He had been excellent in the 1998 World Cup but could not settle. His wife returned home and, in what was like a scene from a film, he jumped out of the first floor of the hotel he was staying in when I came into the reception to meet him. He grabbed his passport and some money and, even though he was under contract to us, he fled to the airport. He took the next flight home and never played for West Ham again. Marco Boogers lasted even less time after being sent off for a high tackle on Gary Neville. It was a time when we did not think enough about how foreign players would settle outside of football when they came to England. Today, all clubs have staff to help with that transition.

Having players on trial can be a great way of learning about them and seeing their character up close. Kolo Touré, for example, ended up at Arsenal after a trial in which he clattered Arsène Wenger with a late challenge in a five-a-side match. Touré thought there was no way he would be signed and all Wenger's staff were wondering what would happen as the manager sat in his office with an ice-pack on his ankle. Arsène just said, 'I like his desire. Tomorrow we sign him.' Touré went on to be part of the great 'Invincible' Arsenal team of 2003–04. Andrés D'Alessandro was one of my most important signings but he only came to Portsmouth because I had remembered him from a trial at West Ham several years earlier. I had first seen him playing for the Argentina Under-21 team against England at Craven Cottage in February 2000. He was little with skinny legs and funny little feet that pointed outwards but, against a good England team that included Jamie Carragher and Frank Lampard, he was on another planet. I asked Frank after the game and he laughed: 'I was scared to go near him. Every time anyone did, he nutmegged them. I've never seen anything like it.' So we chased after him and the agent let him come over to West Ham for two weeks to train. He was fantastic. After one session, Paolo Di Canio said to me, 'This is a world class player in the future.' He was only 19 but at £5 million the chairman, quite understandably, pointed out that we had Joe Cole coming through and other priorities. Yet I never forgot about him and, when I returned to Portsmouth for the second time in 2005, we really were in a terrible mess. We were in desperate need of a spark and I thought, 'I wonder what ever happened to that little Argentinian kid?' He was at Wolfsburg but I got hold of someone who made contact and they eventually agreed to a loan with an option to buy him for £5 million.

D'Alessandro arrived on a Monday morning and we were playing Bolton at home the following night. Big Sam was their manager. He had got a few big brutes in his team. There was also something wrong with the pitch. It was just a mud heap. It had come up in lumps like a ploughed field and you couldn't play football on it. Anyway, I walked in on the

Monday morning with this kid, who my assistants Joe Jordan and Kevin Bond had never seen. I said, 'I'm going to play him tomorrow.' They looked him up and down. He was 5 feet 7 inches and still had skinny little legs with feet that poked out to the side. 'Against Bolton? On that pitch. You're kidding Harry, aren't you?' said Joe. I said, 'He's a different class. Wait till you see him play.' One of our players – I think it was Azar Karadas – also recognised him from an international game he had played with Norway when he was younger. He just turned to the other lads and said, 'He's the best player I have ever played against.' Anyway, D'Alessandro played the next night against Big Sam's Bolton and, although we only drew, he was the best player on the pitch by a million miles. He also changed the whole atmosphere of the club at a time when I was under huge pressure. It was make or break for me as well. I had gone to Southampton, come back to Portsmouth and there would be a little group of fans behind the goal at away games still with a 'Judas' banner. In the year since I had gone, they had sold most of the best players. They had got rid of almost every one of my great lads. Dejan Stefanović, who had luckily stayed, told me I was crazy. 'This is the worst team I've ever seen in my life,' he said. And he was the captain.

Our signings changed everything that January. As well as D'Alessandro, we also brought in Pedro Mendes, Sean Davis and Noé Pamarot from Tottenham. I had really wanted Pedro but Daniel Levy would only give us Pedro if we took the other two. It was one of his three-for-one offers. We had something like that before when we tried to take Darren Anderton back to Portsmouth. The deal had looked likely to be done until Daniel decided he would only let Darren go if we took a few more players off his wage-bill that he didn't want. We walked away that time but we needed players in 2006 and so I took Davis and Pamarot. The first problem, however, was that they kept going down with cramp to begin with because they weren't match fit. They had been bombed out by Tottenham and they were not all training with the first team. Davis and Mendes had not played a competitive match since the previous autumn. When they cramped up, I was thinking, 'What? Oh my God. It's over. These are my big hope.' Yet they just needed some match-time and, once we beat Manchester City at home on 11 March, we took off and finished the season by taking 20 points from the last 10 games to stay up by one place. We had been beaten 5–0 by Birmingham in the January and had been as much as eight points behind at one stage. The 'Harry Houdini' headlines were flattering but I was under no illusion. Better players made the difference.

Of all the teams I built, I take particular pride from those at Portsmouth. It was different at Tottenham, where we already had great players and it was more about repairing confidence, but, like at Bournemouth and to an extent West Ham, the success at Portsmouth was about judgement and recruitment. It also showed how one or two pieces in the jigsaw can complete the picture and allow the rest of the team to play. At Bournemouth there was a striker called Trevor Aylott who could hold the ball up and bring others into the game, as well as the centre-back John Williams. In my first spell at Portsmouth it was Paul Merson and Arjan de Zeeuw. Portsmouth had been fighting relegation in the five or six years previously and no one thought promotion was on the cards before the 2002–03 season. I remember my mate rung me up and said, 'I'm going to have a bet on Portsmouth at 33–1 for promotion.' I told him not to even think about it. 'Don't waste your money,' I said. 'We haven't got a prayer. If we can finish halfway I will be happy.' But that was before Merse arrived three days before the season. Steve Kutner, his agent, wasn't sure if he would come but I spoke to Merse. 'I'll make you captain, play you off the front two,' I said. 'That will do,' he said, and his presence turned the club around.

After escaping relegation the second time around, we then built a really powerful team that won the FA Cup and was up challenging in the top half of the table for far less money than people realised. It is rubbish to say we spent big money at Portsmouth or somehow just bought success. We were very good at picking players, getting value for money and making them want to play for us. Sol Campbell was a unique free transfer – an absolute monster of a defender and a fantastic player. We were offering him half of what he was on at Arsenal but, after a coffee together, he fancied it. He just walked away from Arsenal and a massive amount of money. We paid about £1 million for David James. Again, the wages were decent but not crazy. Sylvain Distin and Hermann Hreidarsson were free transfers. Lassana Diarra had fallen out with Arsène Wenger and was the buy of the year. We got him for £5 million before selling him to Real Madrid for almost £20 million. We also brought in Niko Kranjčar, Glen Johnson, Sulley Muntari and Jermain Defoe, all of whom we later sold for a profit.

Kanu was another signing who was unbelievable value. We hardly paid him any dough but he just wanted to play, and the story about his first few weeks at Portsmouth is one of my favourites throughout my whole career. I have told it a few times but what people did not know was that I had joked to my staff about pretending to lose the registration forms if he turned out to be no good when we invited him down for a training match. We need not have worried. I had rung him on the Monday before the 2006–07 season started because we did not have a striker. Svetoslav Todorov had an injury and could not play 90 minutes. I was going to play a centre-half up front. We were just kicking names around when I said, 'What happened to Kanu?' Tony Adams had played with him at Arsenal: 'Leave off, Harry, he's got to be 45 by now. I spoke to the physios at Arsenal. He's finished.' I got a number and called him. 'What you been up to, big man? Have you been training?' He replied, 'Er, I went for a run in the park one day.' I said, 'Well done. Come down tomorrow. Bring your boots.' My staff were, 'Harry, he hasn't trained. He's not done a pre-season. We can't just play him in a training game.' I stuck him in and, for 60 minutes, he was out of this world and scored two goals. We gave him a contract there and then until the end of the season but, after scoring four goals in the first three games, we found out what can happen if you haven't trained for several months. We were on our way back from Middlesbrough and, when we got back to Bournemouth airport, he was slumped down with the luggage. He looked up at me and said, 'I can't move.' We were, 'C'mon, big man. C'mon, King. The coach is here.' He said, 'I can't, gaffer.' His body had gone into shock. So we ended up all lifting him into a wheelchair and then pushing him out of the airport. We then all lifted him again onto the coach back to Portsmouth, from where the kit man had to drive him all the way to north London where he lived. He even had to carry poor Kanu into his bed.

I know that I became synonymous with transfer deadline day in my later years but the reality was that it was usually a nightmare because I had been brought into a club in trouble. The experience at Tottenham, where we had such a good squad already, was far preferable. Yet even then, Daniel would always be in the market for late deals. I already knew what he was like because, when I was at Portsmouth, he would ring me up at 9.30pm or 10pm on deadline day to see what was going on. I remember we had all gone to an Italian restaurant one transfer window at about 10pm thinking that was it for the night when Daniel was on the phone. 'Do you want Charlie Adam?' he said. I was just about to dig into my pasta. I asked, 'How are you going to find him and get him down here in the next two hours?' He couldn't get that one done but he really did deliver for me in 2010 when, out of the blue at about 4pm on deadline day, he called. 'I have a present for you,' he said. 'We can get Rafael van der Vaart on loan. Would you be interested?' I was: 'Of course, I'd love to.' He could not get him on loan in the end but he did get him for a great price at

£8 million after a possible move to Bayern Munich had broken down. Rafa was fantastic and one of the players who, within 18 months, had pushed us into the position of Premier League title contenders. January 2012 was the one time that I was encouraging Daniel to spend because, with Rafa, Gareth Bale and Luka Modrić, I felt we were only two top players short of winning the league. We had a very, very good team but Daniel had made up his mind and seemed reluctant. We ended up with two free transfers in Ryan Nelsen from Blackburn and Louis Saha from Everton. They had both been good players in their prime but were well into their thirties and not sufficient to maintain our momentum and we ended up fourth.

As well as spotting players, knowing when it is time to say goodbye is also an important part of the job. That could be because of age, form, finances, attitude or simply because the team itself is evolving and moving up or down a level. I was initially surprised that Paul Merson wanted to leave after inspiring our Portsmouth promotion in 2003. He had got back into the Premier League, but he was such a clever lad in many ways. He knew football inside out and I think he looked at it and thought, 'I don't want to play in the Premier League, it's too quick for me.' I was also thinking, 'I'm not going to get away with him in the Premier League.' I had played him in a position where he had no responsibility. In the Championship I'd just let him play where he wanted to play. He'd have a walkabout when we didn't have the ball. But after promotion I was thinking, 'We aren't that good in the Premier League that we can suffer having one player who is not going to work when we haven't got the ball.' So I was quite happy to let him go. Merse had done the job. He'd got us promoted.

I have lost other popular players for the wider good. At West Ham we sold Julian Dicks to Liverpool and used the money to improve the squad. Graeme Souness began by describing him as 'the little fat geezer' but, even at the age of 40, couldn't resist the physical challenge of facing him in training. The money was also too good to turn down when Sven-Göran Eriksson at Manchester City came in for Benjani on deadline day in 2008. We loved Benji at Portsmouth and I sometimes see him again now at Bournemouth games as he has moved back down to the south coast area since retiring. His work-rate was incredible but he was the sort of player who was liable to put a few balls down the M27 when he was practising his finishing. Anyway, we told Benji about the interest from Manchester City and he was unimpressed. 'I like it here, boss, I'm happy,' he said. We were, 'No, no. You should go. Manchester. Big club. Big chance. You'll love it.' We had to pretty much shove him out of the door and, even when he got to the airport, he didn't get on the plane. One plane went, then another. I rang him and said, 'Benji, what are you doing?' He eventually got on the last plane and arrived in Manchester at about 10.15pm. We completed the deal at literally one minute before the window closed. They loved him at City as well. He was a great lad. But £9.5 million! Only Sven could have paid that much for him.

# CHAPTER FOUR

# AGENTS AND CONTRACTS

Sign a player today and you sometimes need to find a bigger office just to accommodate all the people who are brought along to do the deal. Agents, advisors, lawyers, PR experts, uncles, aunts and mates. The player usually barely opens his mouth during negotiations. It is quite a contrast to the signing I still rank as perhaps my best, way back in 1986 when I was managing Bournemouth. John Williams was playing in the old Third Division for Port Vale but they were skint and we had become aware of his qualities. He was available for just £20,000 and I spoke to their manager John Rudge. 'He'll get you promoted and he is a fantastic fella,' he said. The day he signed was quite close to Christmas but I remember that it was sunny. It was one of those bright but cold days. John pulled in at Dean Court and had a lady in the car with him. I greeted them and invited them into the ground. The girl did not move.

I looked at her and said, 'Come in.'

John was, 'No, no. She's all right. She'll stay in the car.'

I said, 'You can't stay in the car. Come on in. We'll be an hour or two.'

He said, 'No. She'll stay in the car.'

I said, 'Don't be silly. You can't. C'mon on. Have a cup of tea.'

So she came into the office and, as were going through his wages, his contract and bonuses, I said to the girl, 'What do you do?' She said, 'I'm a nurse.' I said, 'That's brilliant. There's a new hospital opening up the road. I'm sure we can help get you a job.'

So this small-talk carried on and she was also party to all the chat about his salary, his contract, our ambitions and where he was going to live. The three of us even all went for a walk along the beach, which was something I would always try to do with potential signings on a nice afternoon, and he would lates say that I had made it feel like the French Riviera. John moved down to Bournemouth the next week and so I asked him about the girl who he had brought down. Did he want us to ask about jobs at the hospital for her? It was then that he told me that he only met her a few days before driving down and she would not be joining him in Dorset. He'd gone out, met her in a nightclub in the Potteries and brought her straight to Bournemouth for a little holiday. It was quite handy for me, though, because I had it on him whenever he stepped out of line: 'If you don't behave, I'm going to tell your girlfriend about the day you signed.' He would be, 'Don't do that, don't do that,' and would get back on track. John came in for the last

26 games of a 46-match season and the only match we lost was the one that he missed through suspension.

The girl who John had brought along when he signed his contract only wanted a cuppa and a biscuit, which is a bit of a difference to the £20 million that was reportedly paid to the agent who accompanied Paul Pogba to complete his world-record transfer to Manchester United. Entire deals can hinge on the cut that the agent is getting, and that is a regular reason for delaying transfers. You can be talking about millions of pounds. The players do not generally get involved in any way, shape or form. They let the agents do everything. Why the players put up with it is anyone's guess but the power that agents have over some of them is scary. It can feel as if the agent's demands are more important than the player's. That would be unthinkable years ago. The player would be, 'Hang on, I want to sign for this team. That's where I'm going. You ain't stopping me. Don't get greedy, otherwise I'll just do the deal myself.' The reality now, however, is very different. In some cases, if there are three or four clubs in for a player, the agent will successfully push the deal to the place where they are receiving the best fee. It always bothers me if a player seems excessively influenced by his agent. It would make me question if I really wanted him. I would think, 'If you are so weak that you have got to rely on an agent for everything, how are you going to make decisions on the pitch or set an example off it?'

How does all this happen? The agents get into their players' heads when they are younger. They offer to do lots of simple things for the players which they could – and should – very easily do for themselves. The players then end up leaning on people who really do not provide the best support. Footballers are easy-going. All they usually know is turning up for training and playing on a Saturday. When it comes to anything else, they are mostly happy to rely on their agents without even realising that they have become overpowered in some of their most important career decisions.

I have even experienced a player making threats in relation to his agent's fee. I would stress that I got on great with Lassana Diarra. He was a nice lad but he had a very strong personality. His agent was owed money by Portsmouth and he came to see me before a big game. 'The club owe my agent,' he said. 'They haven't paid any of his fees. Unless he gets the money before Saturday, gaffer, I'm not playing.' I said, 'What do you mean you're not playing?' He said, 'I'm not playing. He looks after me. He's been my agent since I was 16. If he doesn't get his money before Saturday I won't play.' And he wasn't joking either. So I had to go to Peter Storrie, the chief executive, and say, 'Look, he ain't going to play unless the agent gets paid.' And they had to sort it out. I don't know the ins and outs of what the agent was or wasn't owed but it showed the leverage that they can sometimes have over you as a manager.

The power was all with the clubs previously, even if it did go too far that way. When I was a player, you just had an appointment with the manager at the end of each season to find out what would be happening. If you stayed on you were happy. If you got a £1-a-week rise, you were delighted. If you got a £5-a-week rise, you thought that you had won the pools.

Managers were not questioned or challenged. Brian Clough, inevitably, had his own unique methods for dealing with players who tried to defy him. There was a youth-team player who dared to ask for a pay rise and Cloughie's response was to inform him that if he did not like the original offer he would have to take off the club tracksuit he was wearing and walk home in his pants. He was also capable of great generosity if a player had impressed him. Mark Crossley tells a story of being summoned to sort out his contract. When he arrived, Clough was in the sauna and shouted for him to get a towel. He then produced a blank piece of paper for him to sign. 'Trust me or clear off and play for Barnsley,' he said. Crossley just agreed and, to his surprise, Clough promptly doubled his weekly wages from £750 to £1,500 a week out of appreciation for his faith.

Pat Nevin also stands as proof that an intelligent player can sometimes outwit a chairman in a way that an agent might never manage. Nevin was just 19 when he was called into Ken Bates's office at Chelsea to sort his contract. Ken clearly expected to have the upper hand. He put Pat on the spot and asked him what he expected. Unsure what to say, Pat requested £500 a week. Ken stormed out of the office without saying a word and clearly expected, upon his return, for Pat to have lowered his demands. Pat, though, simply had a look through the desk drawer and found some of the other players' contracts. Realising he was actually worth a bit more, he upped his demands. He also admitted what he had done to Ken, who was so impressed by his enterprise that he gave him exactly what he wanted.

When Larry Lloyd was renegotiating his contract, Clough found out that his washing machine was broken down and arranged for another one to be delivered to his home. The twist was that it had been taken direct from the laundry room at the City Ground. Archie Gemmill negotiated a television and carpets from Nottingham Forest for his front room, but even that does not match the sweeteners that helped to secure Paul Gascoigne's move from Newcastle United to Tottenham Hotspur in 1988. He had verbally agreed to sign for Sir Alex Ferguson at Manchester United when he got a call from Tottenham. They offered to buy a house for his mum and dad. His dad's request for a garage was also met. Then his sister came on to make sure a sunbed got thrown in too.

Although agents had been gradually creeping into the game during the 1980s, it wasn't until the 1990s that they became common. Today things have escalated to the point where they are fighting over players. It can be difficult to work out who controls the players, while the agents bad mouth each other to the clubs. It becomes like selling a house that someone else once had on their books. They all want a percentage. Then they come on to the club and complain, saying things like, 'I mentioned him first and I'm entitled to X amount.' It has become very aggressive. When you hear how nasty it can get, you genuinely wonder if it will end up with someone getting hurt or even killed over some deal or other.

Agents have also changed things completely when you are trying to get a deal done because, even if you think you have an agreement with a player, they will be pushing him to other clubs to see if there is something better out there. It has made it even more difficult to keep a transfer deal secret, although that has never been easy. I even experienced it to a small extent myself when I was a young schoolboy player who was being chased by several London clubs. Charlie Faulkner was the scout then at West Ham. I remember that he always carried a shiny cigarette lighter with him. He was also astute and good at his job. He signed John Sissons at a time when every club wanted him. John had played for England Schoolboys two years running and only lived about 15 minutes from him. Charlie had not immediately persuaded him to sign but was so determined to beat the opposition that he put a telephone in the Sissons's neighbour's house and paid her bill. If anyone knocked on John's door who looked like a scout, she would ring Charlie up and he would go over and interrupt them to make sure he did not sign the contract. As repayment to the woman who lived next door to John, Charlie would cut the grass and also bought her a washing machine.

Malcolm Allison was also incredibly resourceful with his thinking when he gave Tony Book his first professional contract by signing him for Plymouth Argyle from Bath City. Knowing that the directors might not go along with a 30-year-old, he simply doctored his birth certificate by two years from 1934 to 1936. It resulted in what became one of the most incredible transfers in football history because Malcolm was completely vindicated and Tony won every domestic trophy with Manchester City before being appointed their manager after retiring at the age of 40. He went from non-league to being voted joint Footballer of the Year with Dave Mackay in the space of just five years. Yet Tony, who rates Malcolm as the best coach in English football history, would have finished his career at Bath if Malcolm had not gone there for a little spell between jobs and spotted him.

That was back in 1964 but one thing that has never changed is that no deal is complete until you have that contract signed. Every manager will have their own stories of transfers that have fallen through at the last minute. Peter Odemwingie famously turned up at Loftus Road in a car on transfer deadline day before the deal had been agreed between the clubs. He had to be refused entry to the stadium and, although he got a lot of stick, it was just unfortunate. We all thought the deal would be completed earlier in the day so he'd driven down to London. The big mistake he made was coming to Loftus Road itself. It happens a lot that players wait in a hotel nearby while the clubs are negotiating. The first time a player hears about a possible transfer is not when a manager or the chairman tell him. He already knows because his agent has talked to him. 'This is what they'll pay you, this is what they'll give you, blah blah ... ' It's all done. They are way down the road before the clubs negotiate, although things can suddenly change at any moment.

It is nothing new and Brian Clough certainly had no concern about etiquette or any rules when he made a bold attempt to take Bobby Moore to Derby County in 1973.

He got Bobby's number from the journalist Nigel Clarke, who ghost-wrote his column in the *Daily Mirror*, and arranged a meeting. Bobby was concerned about where he would fit in with Roy McFarland and Colin Todd, to which Cloughie responded, 'I'll put you on the pitch and get those two to learn from you.' Cloughie then suddenly turned up unannounced at West Ham and, after persuading someone to let him have a look around the place, met Ron Greenwood and tried to do a deal. Ron would not have any of it and Bobby ultimately joined Fulham the following year, but there is a lovely additional detail in Matt Dickinson's *Bobby Moore: The Man in Full* biography that I did not know. Apparently Cloughie gave Bobby a little package many years later. Inside was a tablecloth made of Nottingham lace for Bobby's wife Tina and a handwritten note: 'It was a tragedy we could never get together.'

Cloughie had rather more luck when he took Ian Woan from under our noses in 1990 on the basis of no more than an awareness of our record at Bournemouth for uncovering non-league diamonds and reading on Teletext that we were close to a deal.

That was a lesson: once you have made up your mind, you do the deal as quickly as possible and you try not to let anyone know about it. With Shaka Hislop at West Ham, we signed the deal in January for the end of the season when he was still at Newcastle. He signed a bit of paper and we put it in a desk drawer. It was kept quiet until the end of the season, and we had Shaka on a free. You worry constantly until these deals are done. I even took matters into my own hands sometimes and have been known to use a different name for a player in a trial match so as not to alert other clubs.

Finding out about a potential transfer can also of course work the other way, and I have pulled off some completely unexpected coups. Eyal Berkovic had seemed likely to join Tottenham in 1997 after arriving at Heathrow to meet them. We also went to Heathrow and my hopes were not high. Tottenham were paying him more. They were probably seen as a bigger club than West Ham and, as a Jewish lad, I wondered if there would be an additional pull given the large Jewish following at Spurs. Gerry Francis met Eyal on behalf of Tottenham and was honest with him. 'You're going to be in my squad,' he said. 'I can't guarantee which position you're going to play. It's up to you to get in the team.' That left me an opportunity and so, when it was my turn, I told him just exactly what he wanted to hear. 'I'm going to build my team around you,' I said. 'I'm going to play you as a number 10 and I just want you on the ball. Everything is going to come through you. Make us play.' His eyes lit up and I kept my word. We did play him in that position and he was an amazing footballer for us.

It showed that, although some players are only bothered about the bottom line financially, others can be swayed both by knowing how much you want them and how you might use them.

We did, however, once buy a player at Portsmouth who I was not really trying to sign. David Nugent was a good player and had scored goals in the Championship but I also had one or two other strikers I was looking at. The owner, Sacha Gaydamak, was keen on an English striker and so I agreed to meet Nugent. I didn't try that hard to persuade him to come but, about four or five hours later, I got call to say that he wanted to play for Portsmouth even though he had other clubs in for him. We ended up taking him, but I think my instincts were right. He has had an excellent career but, at the time, we were pushing up towards the top half of the Premier League and he has never been quite so prolific at that level.

One story that has gone down in folklore on the after-dinner circuit but merits retelling here – partly because it still makes me smile; and also because Barry Fry still uses it regularly – involved how we signed Mark Newson at Bournemouth. He was at Maidstone United but Tottenham were ready to pay £250,000, which would have been incredible money for a non-league club. I had seen him playing for Tottenham reserves, behind closed doors when he was on trial, and he was the best player on the pitch. Maidstone knew I was interested but there was obviously no way we could even consider the sort of money that Tottenham were willing to pay. I had given up but then I got an anonymous call out of the blue. 'Harry, I hear you are after Mark Newson,' said the caller. 'Yes,' I replied, 'but he is off to Spurs.' 'Just marking your card, Harry,' said the voice on the other end of the line, 'but he's not on a contract. The contract is still in the draw. He's on the dole.

He can go anywhere. He is not registered.' So, the next morning, I rang Mr Young at the registrations department of the Football League and had it confirmed.

I then invited Mark down to Bournemouth. We went to have a pizza with Brian Tiler, the managing director. He said, 'I think Tottenham are going to sign me, Harry.' I said, 'Yes, but you're not going to get in their team. You've got to be realistic. You've got a chance to come here. I'm going to make you captain. I want to build a good team next year and you're going to be important. You're going to play every week.' He said, 'Well, let me think about it.' I said, 'No, you can't. Sign before you get on the train home. You've got to sign today. I can't let you go.' I think we gave him £200 a week. 'Come in and play,' I said. 'You'll love it here. Play. If you do well, I'll sell you in 18 months and you can go to Tottenham.' He went for it.

I then rang Barry, who was the manager of Maidstone, and told him the news. He started calling me every name under the sun and was making all these threats to me. 'I tell you now, Redknapp, you've had it. If you have done that, I will get the boys to come down and blow your fucking legs off.' I said, 'Unlucky, Barry, you should have had him on a contract.' I wasn't remotely worried about Barry letting off steam in the heat of the moment and couldn't take his threats seriously. The phone went again five minutes later and it was Barry's chairman, Jim Thompson. 'Harry,' he said, 'I'm so sorry Barry has spoken to you like that. I do apologise. We don't do things like that at Maidstone. He's out of order.

Please accept my apologies but, look, we made a mistake, you have been very clever. Let's come to a gentlemen's agreement, sort a fee and get it sorted.'

I said, 'There is no fee. He wasn't on a contract and we have signed him.' He said, 'You dirty bastard.' His language was worse than Barry's. I thought that would be the end of it but, next day, three fellas turned up at Bournemouth from Maidstone. It was Barry, the chairman and another great big geezer. We spotted them through the window. So, me and Brian Tiler called a car to pick us up on the other side of the stadium. We bolted straight across the pitch and got into our getaway vehicle. Barry has since claimed that they had made the 280-mile round trip simply to ask for anything, even a friendly. Mark was excellent for us. He was my captain in the season we won the league and played for another few years before we ended up selling him to Fulham for £300,000. Barry says now that he would have done exactly the same thing and that he laughed about it the next day. I also, at least partially, made it up to him a few years later when I tipped him a 40-1 winner during a day out we had together at Ascot.

It was obviously easier back then for a manager to deal directly with a player, and people often ask what I really think of agents. The truth, like any walk of life, is that you have your good and bad. No one has a problem with players having someone to represent their interests, and there are some good lads out there, but the problems start when an agent cares more about his own interests. Some of the stronger players will have the agent in their proper place and decide themselves what they think is fair, but it is frightening how rare that is. The players typically get signed up by agents when they are 12 or 13 now. They are signing dozens and dozens of these kids, hoping that one comes off, not bothered about those who don't. The players are often only a money-making machine for them. I have known agents who have persuaded players to buy specific houses and then, almost certainly without the player's knowledge, been paid a cut by the builder. I would doubt that more than 10 per cent of agents are interested in the players as people. And a player rarely sees them once they are retired or need help.

Sadly there are a lot of ex-players struggling. There is an extraordinary statistic that 50 per cent of all Premier League footballers go bankrupt within five years of retiring. How can that happen if the agents are looking after these players and advising them so well? I know players who are really good people who have been badly advised and lost everything because of investments that they were encouraged to make. I would like to see an agency set up that really looks after the players. The players should also make more use of the Professional Footballers' Association. I often used Mick McGuire, who was the deputy chief executive and a brilliant negotiator. He would do a better job than most agents – who cost millions – and he would charge you a flat fee of £1,000. People might find it hard to believe that footballers can get into such financial difficulties when they have been earning so well but it's all simple enough, really. Most have no income when they stop playing and, if you have been living consistent with earning, say, £2 million a year, any savings will very soon disappear. Footballers have usually got a big house, a big mortgage, a big car, kids at private schools and a certain lifestyle that involves not thinking twice about a nice holiday, a flash watch and a bet on the horses. They start eating into their money and, even if they have saved a bit, it does not take long to get into trouble.

The managers used to deal directly with the agents far more often, and they were always offering you players. They would tell you about how great their player was and, even if they had some off-field issue, how they had settled down. You could be offered hundreds of players over one transfer window. That has changed now. These days agents mostly bypass the manager and go to the owner, chairman, chief executive, a head of recruitment or director of football. The agents are not interested in the manager because they know that they are usually just passing through. The chairmen mostly love it. They get a nice bottle of wine or hamper at Christmas. They also like having someone phoning them up to say, 'I've got a very good player for you,' even if most of the ones they are trying to flog are useless. I've also known agents get straight on the phone to the chairman for a moan. 'Your manager has left my player out, the training is rubbish, this is rubbish, that is rubbish.' If a player is trying to force your club to accept a bid for them, there are also some agents who will encourage them not to train properly, be disruptive or down tools completely and refuse to play. It is totally out of order but it does happen and, again, you have to wonder about the character of a player who accepts this advice.

I liked player contracts that were incentivised, but it needs to be for results rather than just appearances. If you are paying someone £50,000 a week and they want appearance money or goal bonuses, you have to ask what they are being paid their 50 grand for in the first place. I'm especially into performance incentives for lads on smaller wages. If you do well, you should earn well. I think that applies to coaches as well and, when I accepted my advisor's job at Derby County for the final months of the 2015–16 season, I made it clear that I did not expect a penny from the club unless we at least reached the play-offs. The chairman offered me a wage and I said, 'If we don't finish in the top six, I don't want any money.' I was confident we would make the play-offs.

Historically, the manager's wage was slow, to keep pace with players' when things really took off for them but, after people like Arsène Wenger came in and were suddenly earning bigger money, it did change quite dramatically. Managers are generally still not paid anything like the players but, at the top end, they are earning very well. There are also usually bonuses in their contracts – for staying in the league, getting promoted, qualifying for Europe or winning something. It is also common for players and managers to accept a relegation clause. For managers, there is usually a cut of 50 per cent or a third, although that was something QPR failed to prepare for with the players when they were relegated in 2013. The problem is that players are often in a position to refuse. If they are on £80,000 a week, they are unlikely to accept a relegation clause lowering their salary to £30,000 if they have a guaranteed three-year-deal elsewhere. That can be a problem in a lot of transfers, especially if you are asking a player to take a step down, and leaves relegated teams lumbered with contracts they are struggling to afford. QPR were naïve initially with agents and paid a heavy price for very average players. It tied them into situations that became difficult to reverse at any sort of speed, but they have since been able to rebuild.

The management of player contracts has become a science in itself at some clubs. I have heard of Arsenal using analysts from Harvard University to help them compute value and decide the best moment and level to make offers to players. It does not surprise me because getting this aspect right can really now strongly influence a club's chances of success.

# CHAPTER FIVE

## YOUTH POLICY

It is more than 50 years since England have played in the final of a major international tournament and, whenever I watch matches involving young kids, I feel like I get a small insight into why.

'Boot it!'

'Clear it!'

'Pass!'

'Hit it!'

'Get rid of it!'

'Don't be greedy!'

Don't get me wrong, there are some brilliant coaches and volunteers who give up their time to organise grassroots football, and the game would be dead without them. I, for one, will be forever indebted to Albert Chamberlain, an old docker, who started off our little team on the Burdett Estate in the East End of London where we grew up. He saved our bacon. Yet more and more in youth football today you see people living out some sort of José Mourinho fantasy on the touchline. Some of them just pollute the atmosphere and are part of a footballing culture in this country that has seriously held us back. I know some instruction can help at the right time, but do you think Lionel Messi was getting shouted at and pressurised when he was taking people on and playing matches for hours on end on the streets of Rosario? Or George Best in Belfast? Or Diego Maradona in Villa Fiorito, the shantytown on the edge of Buenos Aires where he grew up? No. They learned by dribbling, shooting and tackling without some adult hollering at them. They did it by being out there practising for every spare hour.

My earliest football memories were of watching my dad and then playing morning, noon and night on the streets in games that could be 18- or 19-a-side. If someone was lucky enough to have a ball they were king. The balls were made from plastic fibre and would cost five schillings. It was a concrete jungle on our estate but there was also a little patch of grass that we played on and called Wembley. A ball would be treasured. If it got a puncture, you would use a hot poker to mend it by moving the plastic over the split. All my mates later became dockers, but as kids we would be out playing until 9pm every night. When you got the ball, you dribbled because you didn't get it again for another ten minutes. There was no coaching. You would just try to do something special. I was lucky. My dad was a football nut. He went everywhere with me. He never missed a game. Always watching but never saying anything. Ron Greenwood, the West Ham manager, was the same. He wouldn't let the parents say anything. He never used to shout himself. Once you were on the pitch, he always knew that you had to think for yourself. He wouldn't allow the youth-team coach to shout either. Most academies now are the same. Parents are told to be quiet. They are asked to leave if there is any aggro. You have got to keep most of them at arm's length or they will drive you mad, telling you how their kid is the best player, how they are better in a different position and how, if it doesn't go to plan, it is someone else's fault.

What you see sometimes on the parks is even more frightening. I watch my grandson's team. One set of parents had a little boy who was two. He could barely walk but he was at a match along the sidelines, pushing the ball along, with his jumpsuit on. They were approached by a scout who had a Southampton jacket on. He gave them a card and said, 'Give me a ring when he is five.' The parents of the little toddler turned to me and said, 'He must see something in him. Is that normal, Harry?' I went, 'No, that's not normal. I must be honest, I think the man who has just given you that card needs help. He can't be right.' This was a two-year-old kid who had just learned to walk. How pathetic.

On another occasion, there were matches going on along rows of pitches and so I was half watching some of the other games as well. There were a few teams that, whenever the goalkeeper got the ball, the others would sprint up the pitch as far as they could and wait for a big kick over the top. They had obviously been told to do it but, even at this level, it only rarely worked. I would never interfere but, after the games had finished, one of the coaches happened to ask if I would pose for a picture with his team. 'Of course,' I said, but I also couldn't stop myself from giving the kids a quick word of advice. 'When your goalkeeper has got the ball, drop back and ask for it. Try to play football. Don't all just kick it as far as you can. Pass it. Dribble. Don't worry if you make a mistake. You might lose the ball. So what? It's not the end of the world.' This was a group of seven-year-olds but I would say exactly the same to the young players I have worked with when they were breaking into the first team of a Premier League side. I used to say the same to my own sons, Mark and Jamie, and I said the same to my nephew Frank Lampard Junior, whether it was during the family kickabouts we would have in the back garden or when he was an apprentice with me at West Ham United. I said the same to Rio Ferdinand when he was 15. 'Come out and play. Dribble. Don't kick it in the crowd. Anyone can do that. Learn to control it.'

I stood as far away as possible whenever I was watching Mark or Jamie play, and it is the same now with my grandchildren, but parents often still ask my advice. It is simple. Let them enjoy it. It's supposed to be fun. When they are coming home, don't get onto them saying, 'What were you doing? Do this. Do that.' You see people shouting and screaming at kids but, in the long run, you will drive them mad. If they don't enjoy it, they won't play. Coaches also sometimes ask me, and my advice is similar. Encourage kids to show their individuality. We are all crying out in the modern game for people with skill, individuals who can do things. If a kid tries to do something, whether it's a centre-half coming out with the ball, or a midfield player or a forward trying to dribble, don't shout at them if they lose it. Encourage them. Tell them to try again. During training with them, work on their skills. Do little skills with the ball – lots of touches on the ball. Get as many balls as you can in the group. If the kids have got a ball at home, tell them to bring it. Get them doing little drag-backs and practising step-overs.

I remember Alan Ball, who was one of the greatest players I have ever seen, tell me about his childhood. Alan lived in a row of houses and would spend his time kicking the ball against a wall. Left foot, right foot, control it, bang. A tennis ball to start with, then he gradually introduced a bigger ball. That was all he did. Master the ball. We need to encourage young kids to be comfortable in possession and confident having a dribble. How many top players now have got the ability to go and say, 'Right, I'm going to take you on,' in the way Maradona or Best did? I still remember playing against George at Manchester United and I was ten yards from the corner flag. I heard him say to Johnny Aston, 'Give us it, Johnny, give it to me. I'll score from here.' So Johnny passed him the ball and he went through four players, putting us all on our backsides.

In Euro 2016, I didn't see anyone who could beat a player. Even Cristiano Ronaldo was average. I thought it was a poor tournament. It made me think, 'Where have all the great dribblers gone?' It's a dying art. I love watching people who can do something that the average man can't.

You still get that from South America players, who tend to be the best forwards and have learned their football on the streets, but it is being coached out of them from an early age in Europe.

You can see it if you stand on the sidelines at just about any grassroots game in England. The moment a kid dribbles, all the other parents start thinking, 'Get rid of it, don't be greedy, he's too greedy.' They get the hump because they don't pass it to their kid and anyone who has a go is told they are greedy if they lose it. And guess what? He or she is discouraged from trying it again. Most coaches now are, 'Pass, pass, pass.' That's all they shout. I'd like to hear them sometimes say, 'Dribble, take him on.' There is a balance to be struck obviously. Kids need to learn how to play as a team as well, but I sense that it has gone too far in that direction. Defenders hate it when they face someone who dribbles but everyone is passing; backwards, square, sideways. They have seen Barcelona passing and think that is the way to go, but they forget one crucial point. Yes, Barcelona do pass it very well, but then they also give it to a little genius called Messi who can beat three or four people and finish it off. I don't see Messi looking to pass it so much, and he is the one who makes the difference. If you have someone who can do what he does, who can dribble and beat a player, everything on the pitch suddenly changes.

For a time during the 1970s and 1980s, coaching in this country did become very functional and it became more of a direct and long-ball game. Charles Hughes was the Football

Association's director of coaching, despite having never managed a club side, and he would preach about scoring goals from four passes or less. It was about putting the ball into a certain area and getting people attacking what he called the 'Position of Maximum Opportunity'. I think it has taken a long time to recover from that.

Another area where English clubs lagged behind was in being proactive in helping young players with issues that might be going on away from football. You hear normally only when there is a problem, but we should be taking more interest in understanding players' lives as a matter of standard practice. We all need someone to take a bit of interest in us, and I think that is a big part of being a youth manager. But how many players come in and just end up being one of a group? I don't think enough people look at the kids as individuals and really get to know how they are feeling. What problems have the kids got? Are they missing home? Are the digs OK? Are they going home and sitting with a miserable landlady? Is the food good enough? There is often no real aftercare. Maybe it is better now than it was but, over the years, it was horrendous. You often just dumped the kid in digs where the people were running it as cheaply as they could. I had been in football all my life but, even when Jamie joined Liverpool at the age of 18, I remember seeing how he needed support and encouragement. He had been signed by Kenny Dalglish and, two weeks later, he left and Graeme Souness came in. Jamie would say, 'I don't think the manager knows who I am.' Then, one day, he rang me up to say that the manager had spoken to him. He felt about ten feet tall. That's how it is with kids. A word here or there is so valuable, but sometimes we neglect that.

It made a big impression on the kids of my generation at West Ham that Ron Greenwood would always watch us if he could and, around the time when we won the FA Youth Cup in 1963, we used to get about 12,000 people at every home game. Kids appreciate seeing the manager, as do the parents, and it makes a big difference if you are competing to sign them. I tried to do the same as Ron. Every Saturday morning, me and Frank Lampard Senior would watch the West Ham kids when we were at home. I would always still go and watch Jermain Defoe play if I could when he was on loan at Bournemouth, and I know that he always noticed. I would also involve him in the first-team training whenever possible at West Ham. I remember we were once doing a finishing exercise. Jermain was 16 and he was volleying them into the top corner without a problem. I turned to the senior guys and said, 'Watch that young kid there – that's how it is done.' To this day, Jermain says that he went home and phoned all his family and friends to tell them that.

I only ever needed to look at Bobby Moore to see the difference it can make to have someone who believes in a young player. The support that Bobby got from Malcolm Allison was both technical and emotional. He has always said that he would have never ever made it as a player without Malcolm taking an interest in him. He would drop him off after training and talk to Bobby about the game. Bobby would have lots of questions and once asked him what was the single most important thing to remember. 'Know what you are going to do before you get it,' said Malcolm. It was something Bobby never forgot. Malcolm also always encouraged Bobby to drop deep, take the ball off the goalkeeper and play. He spoke up for Bobby when the other coaches were going to release him. They were, 'But he can't run, Malcolm.' Malcolm came back, 'I'm telling you now, he will be a player, he has the right attitude and wants to learn. Take him.' Bobby might have been a little tubby boy who lacked pace and was not especially good in the air, but he was always in the right position and he could play out from the back. His brain was sharper than anyone's, but who knows what would have happened without having a mentor like Malcolm. His influence underlines the power that senior players and managers have got to inspire the kids around the club. It's in everyone's interests not to waste it.

I should also stress that Bobby did also have the intelligence to listen to Malcolm. The bottom line is that, as well as ability, you do look for a certain attitude in a young player. Even the most gifted kid in the world will not automatically reach the highest levels in football. When I think back over young players, I often remember a lad at Bournemouth called Adrian Randall who was genuinely as good as any young player I have ever seen. He was a genius. He had everything technically. He was 6 feet tall and would glide over the pitch, juggling the ball on his foot and dribbling past people like they were stood still. It was poetry in motion. He could do it all. We used to play him against Tony Pulis or Sean O'Driscoll in training and he'd just tie them in knots. They could not get near him. He played with Matty Holmes, who had a very good career, but this kid was on a different planet to anybody. It was incredible. All he was lacking was the internal drive to be a player. He was a good kid but just so laid back. He was happy being with his mates out around Amesbury. I let him go in the end to Aldershot, but it remains a regret because, talent-wise, he was up with any young kid I worked with, including the lot from West Ham.

Ravel Morrison was another genius at school. Sir Alex Ferguson thinks that he was the best young player he has ever had. I could believe that from the time I spent with him at Queens Park Rangers. I liked Ravel. He was a bit wayward and easily led and distracted but not a nasty boy, and a fantastic talent. Ravel could be a world-class player, and it is not too late for him, but that desire to maximise your ability has to come from within. You can tell players a million times to go and train, to do that bit extra, but they have to that attitude of being single-minded and not caring what anybody else thinks about them. They often think that if they are out there doing extra in the afternoon, their supposed mates will think they are creeping around. That is a bad culture to have at any club. I would tell them straight: 'Your mates won't care about you when you are out of football.'

I have said it many times before but I have never seen anyone work to become a professional footballer like Frank Lampard Junior did, except maybe his dad. He had the best attitude of any player I ever saw. He would train morning, noon and night. When you have someone like that, it also rubs off on everyone else. Jermain Defoe would practise shooting every day for an hour after training, and still does now. Rio Ferdinand was another who became a better trainer. Rio would bring his little mate, Tony McFarlane, with him and they would be dead keen, asking what boots people were wearing, how they trained and what they ate. My dad saw Rio playing for the youth team against Chelsea when he was about 15 and I remember him ringing me up straight after and saying that he was the best young player he had watched in years.

Joe Cole was also something else and, at the age of 11, the best I have seen. He could dribble and beat people. He was incredible. I could stand and watch Joe play for hours. He would take on bigger people, drag it back, spin on the ball and go past two defenders. That had nothing to do with coaching. No one taught Joe that. I once said to him, 'How did you learn to dribble like that, Joe?' He just looked up at me and said, 'I used to dribble with a tennis ball to school.' I remember Joe playing against Norwich in ankle-deep mud against kids two years older and still dominating the game. Everybody got to know about him. Sir Alex Ferguson sent him a number 10 shirt and, inside, there was a message: 'This is your number when you play for Manchester United.' They took him to the Cup final on the coach. Arsenal and Chelsea were also after him. Joe's dad, George, would come to me and say that he was going to Manchester United or Liverpool to train for a week. I could have reported them as they were all breaking the rules but, if I had, he'd have probably still gone and we might have lost him, so I would just say, 'Great, George, but this is where he belongs. We want him here. He's happy here but, if he wants to have a look round, not a problem.'

Clubs can also shape the character of young players, and I do worry that it is something we have lost. Jamie Carragher called them the 'academy generation' after we were knocked out of Euro 2016 by Iceland and said that the system was creating babies rather than men. I do think young players are pampered now. There used to be no time off in the summer if you were an apprentice. You had to come in and do your work, which was painting the ground, the barriers and the bathrooms. In the season, we would train in the morning and then do our jobs, which would be cleaning up the bathrooms and getting the kit ready. Only then could we go around the back of the stand to carry on playing football all afternoon. Ernie Gregory, who was a great goalkeeper at West Ham and became reserve-team coach, once turfed us out in the afternoon when we were playing. Ron Greenwood found out and soon had a word with Ernie. The next day Ron said to us, 'If you want to stay out there until 10pm at night, I'll make sure the ground stays open. So long as you are doing something worthwhile. So long as you have got the ball and you are practising and training, you can stay as late as you like.' One of the incentives to become a professional was that you wouldn't have to do the kit or come in and paint over the summer. I am not saying that cleaning boots made you a better player but it was all part of the deal, and even to walk into the first-team dressing-room was a big thing. There was much more done to build character back then. As well as looking after the boots of a senior professional, the kids would be responsible for making sure you kept the quota of 12 balls you would be given by the Football Association at the start of each season. They had to go looking around the edges of the pitches for the balls and then scrub them as best they could so that they were decent to train with. That was how I was brought up and, even during my spell helping out at Derby in 2016, they would laugh at the sight of me rummaging around in the hedges to make sure we had not lost any balls.

Brian Clough used to make the apprentices come in and work in his garden. The club minibus would pick five or six of them up and he would rotate whose turn it was every week. OK, he probably quite appreciated the labour but, equally, it was also about getting to know the young players as people and build them as characters. Brian's wife Barbara would look after them and make them sandwiches. Another thing Cloughie would do is get the apprentices to walk his dog, Del Boy, along the banks of the River Trent. There is a funny story about how Gary Charles once let him off the lead and Del Boy was gone. He spent all afternoon looking for the dog. Can you imagine how terrified he was? I'm pretty fond of my dogs and Cloughie was the same. Gary thought he was going to have to go back and break the news that Del Boy was gone. He probably thought his career was over. Anyway, he knocked on the door, Cloughie opened it and there was Del Boy asleep on the floor. Apparently Gary just said, 'I've come to return his lead for you.' If a manager had the young players doing his garden and walking the dog now he would probably be reported to someone. Even at the age of 21, shortly after completing a British transfer record move to Tottenham, Paul Gascoigne was helping the groundsman to move pigeons off the roof at White Hart Lane. Of course, Gazza being Gazza, he fell through the roof. The young kids in the academy are not allowed to do anything beyond their football now. Except maybe drive Bentleys.

It makes a big difference if your senior players also lead by example and take an interest. Harry Kane tells a lovely story about Jermain Defoe from when he was 11 years old and had just joined Spurs. Harry was out in the streets playing with his mates when, out of the blue, a black Range Rover pulled up and Jermain got out. He then joined in with the local lads for a bit. It inspired him and was a memory that Harry has never forgotten. The great crop of young lads at Manchester United also remain in awe of Eric Cantona. They had a players' pool each year for the work they had done for the in-house media and would each get £800 every season. One year, it was suggested that they put all their money in together to make £16,000 for the first name out of a hat. David Beckham and the Neville brothers, understandably, didn't fancy it. They were young and wanted to be sure of keeping their £800, but Nicky Butt and Paul Scholes did. The winner was Cantona and, straight away, they were all 'Eric, you lucky bastard.' But what did Eric do? He cashed the cheques and shared the £16,000 between Butt and Scholes because he liked the fact that they had put their money in when they were on nothing like the same wages as the senior professionals.

As well as encouraging them to express themselves and try to build good character, it helps young players if you ignite their wider knowledge of football. Whenever we watch a match, I always point out to my grandchildren the players in their position. We talk about the game. When Manchester United were playing Bournemouth in the 2015–16 season, I said to my grandson, 'Watch Michael Carrick. Watch his head when he is waiting. He knows where everybody is so, when the ball comes to him, he hasn't got to start looking up to see. The picture keeps changing but his head keeps moving. Look at his body position. He is ready. When that ball comes he goes bang. He already knows where everyone is and where the next pass is going.'

It was similar with Teddy Sheringham at Portsmouth. I would say to the other lads, 'Watch him. Watch his volley. Watch his technique.' Teddy's body position was perfect. He took pride in everything he did. A young striker could learn more seeing him play or train than all the coaching in the world. Watching and imitating was one of the key strands in my development as a player, and it was the same for Jamie, who obviously grew up around footballers when I was playing in Seattle and then at Bournemouth. My dad would spend any spare money he had on getting us to the games. I was a winger. I saw Tom Finney. I saw the Busby Babes. In the holidays, I trained with Tottenham and, as well as meeting Bill Nicholson, would watch some of the legends at work, like Dave Mackay, Danny Blanchflower and John White. Dave and Danny would shout out to John, 'Hey, show us your tricks.' He could do anything with a football. He was a complete magician with the way he could juggle a football, and I would just be open-mouthed watching him. He was nicknamed 'the ghost' and he scored in the final when Tottenham won the European Cup Winners' Cup but he died when he was hit by lightning on a golf course at the tragically young age of 27. I also learned so much from a fella called Danny Clapton, who played for Arsenal, and Peter Brabrook, who was at Chelsea and then came to West Ham. Peter was in England's 1958 World Cup squad when he was 18 and remains a good friend to this day. They were both wingers like me, and I really benefited from watching the positions they would take up and how they would deliver the ball.

A further challenge for young players now is getting opportunities. Look at the money Chelsea and Manchester City have spent on their academies and yet where are the first-teamers? I can't see any. John Terry was the last one at Chelsea. It's very difficult. They need opportunities but they also need to be good enough, and that is obviously harder in a Premier League that is not just the best of England but the best in the world. The manager is not just going to throw them in, and there is no such thing now as a patient chairman. The chairman might say, 'Put the kids in,' but that goes out the window as soon as you start losing a few games. It's all cheap talk. There

Taxi for Redknapp? I looked into buying a cab near the end of my playing days but could not afford one, and so began coaching before starting out in management at the age of 36. My first game? A 9–0 defeat at Lincoln where the frozen pitch meant my Bournemouth team could barely stand up.

Collecting a silver salver as one of the Football League managers of the year, after leading Bournemouth to the old Division Three title in 1987. It was the first time Bournemouth had ever reached the top two divisions. I am pictured with Arthur Cox of Derby County and Graham Carr (right), Alan's dad, who was managing Northampton Town and is now head scout at Newcastle.

Relationships with chairmen can be tricky. Barry Fry (left) has told me some incredible stories about working with Stan Flashman (right) at Barnet, who would demand to see the team list on Fridays, withhold Barry's wages if he disagreed, and sometimes threaten players with physical violence.

Fortunately I got on pretty well with the chairmen of the teams I managed. Here I am with Milan Mandarić. Milan was a terrible loser and had made life difficult for managers before me but I never tip-toed around him and I think he respected that. We always made up over a drink whenever we did fall out.

Technology never played a big role when I was playing, compared to the statistics and sports science now. But, at West Ham, the presence of Ron Greenwood and Malcolm Allison meant we were ahead of our time. Here's Ron at Arsenal in 1960, trialling the first radio system to coach players by using a lightweight receiver and earpiece.

Malcolm Allison was one of the greatest coaches of all time. He was fascinated by tactics and challenged the old training methods that simply involved lots of running. Bobby Moore believes that he would have never become a top player without Malcolm's early influence.

They also didn't take physio so seriously in my day. Bill Jenkins (left), pictured here with Ron Greenwood and others from West Ham in the early 1960s, had no qualifications and no sympathy for injuries. If you were injured on a Sunday, you had to bring six lagers or a bottle of wine or he wouldn't treat you.

I worry that technology has got in the way of building spirit, which is so important for the success of a team. Coach journeys used to be great for players to bond, where you would play cards or chat – like Kenny Dalglish, Ray Clemence and Terry McDermott here in 1979. Now players mostly just put their headphones on and don't talk to anyone.

I used to listen to tapes of Bill Shankly talking about football during my drive to training when I was Tottenham manager. The special team spirit and unity he built at Liverpool also spread to the fans. It has survived all the change since and remained an incredible strength for the club to this day.

You can't underestimate the role someone like John Terry can play in a team. You need personalities who can communicate well, boss people, push the team and organise them. He is a dying breed but his value is evident in how he's remained captain at Chelsea through 11 changes of manager. His England career should never have finished so soon.

Gareth Bale is growing into a leader as well as one of the world's finest players and is probably the best I have ever managed. The Welsh Euro 2016 team demonstrated the value of team spirit – they were clearly enjoying themselves, and I'm sure that's why they got so far.

Managers and players love their superstitions, from headbutting walls to using particular toilets and travelling the same way to the ground. Here's Neil Warnock who refused to ditch his shorts because of an unbeaten run at the start of the 2010–11 season, right up until QPR's first defeat in December.

And here's France captain Laurent Blanc, who would kiss Fabien Barthez's bald head before every game at the 1998 World Cup.

A pre-game ritual can be very important – when I was managing Jordan, the players all got down to say their prayers before each match and so Kevin Bond and I joined in. We didn't know what we were doing or singing, but it felt important to be all together.

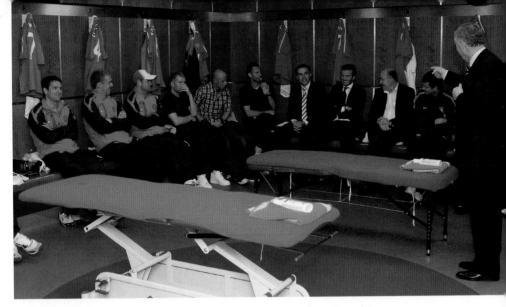

The team talk: some people think it's all about ranting and raving, but less is very often more. Sir Alex Ferguson was the master; the players still remember his talk before a game against Spurs, at a time when United were dominant. He just said, 'Lads, it's Tottenham.' That was all they needed to hear.

Full-time is often filled with emotion, and not usually the time to say too much. Here's Brian Clough, who rarely bothered with team talks, after beating Spurs 1–0 in his first game as Nottingham Forest manager in January 1975.

I've been lucky enough to know some of the greatest managers in the modern game. Arsène talks about managing as an 'addiction', and how he feels afraid of packing it in. I have always found him to be a gentleman but he has upset other managers over his attitude to the post-match handshake.

José Mourinho is very astute and organised but, like most great managers, he has an important skill: the first thing that Frank Lampard and John Terry told me about was his man-management and how he inspired such loyalty from players.

There's a daft caricature people have of Fergie frothing at the mouth, but he's much more subtle than that, and knew when to selectively bring out the hairdryer treatment. As well as being one of the greatest managers of all-time, he is also fantastic company.

are few real youth polices and most clubs are not interested in developing local kids. Of course, supporters like to see kids come through but, if their team is getting beat and stuck near the bottom, they are not going to say, 'It's OK, the kids are learning.' They will say, 'We need some experience, they won't spend any money, the manager is useless, the kids aren't good enough.' The theory of nurturing youth is wonderful, but it usually doesn't work that way, even if there is nothing like getting an outstanding crop. If kids have been there since the age of 12, they have more feeling for your club, but success still depends a lot on luck. You had the great Manchester United group in the 1990s. We had six at West Ham: Frank Lampard, Michael Carrick, Joe Cole, Glen Johnson, Jermain Defoe and Rio Ferdinand. All great players, who won just about every trophy several times over, but it hasn't happened since and probably won't again in the Premier League. For those clubs outside the very elite, it is also almost impossible to keep your younger players together for long enough before they want to leave or the owner decides to cash in on them.

A big problem is how club football beneath the first team has been downgraded. The Under-21 games became a waste of time because they lacked an edge when they were played at training grounds. They have now introduced an Under-23 league for the 2016–17 season, although you have got a problem if you are 22 and can't get in the first team. You need to get the edge back to these games by getting them out of the training grounds. There is no atmosphere and the senior players don't want to be part of it. Clubs can now only play three games at the training ground, but still only have to play a minimum of three at their stadium. The reserves would previously play at the main stadiums in the Football Combination League and you would have proper crowds, as well as a good mixture of young players and more experienced ones who had dropped down. At West Ham we also had an A team – which was effectively a third team – and it would be a great grounding to play in the Metropolitan League against senior teams like Chelmsford Town. It would give you the chance to play against men when you were 15 or 16. All the top clubs had an A team. Our coach, Jimmy Barrett, used to play with us. His dad, Big Jim, was up there with the greatest players in West Ham's history. The story was that he would go in the Boleyn Tavern on the way to the game and have a couple of pints with the fans. Then, after the game, he would be back there as well. Jimmy Jnr was a midfielder and also as hard as nails. He looked like the boxer Brian London and, every Saturday, he would have a war with someone who had been kicking us younger players.

There was one game I'll never forget. We were playing down on the Isle of Sheppey and they had this really flash geezer kicking everyone. He was a Redcoat at Butlin's. Jimmy said something and, suddenly, this geezer has gone bang and hit Jimmy right in the kisser. We all froze, wondering what was going to happen next. We were all thinking, 'He's smacked Jimmy Barrett!' Jimmy just looked at him and then went bosh with a head-butt. The guy's face exploded and he was laid out cold. He had to be carried off on a stretcher.

Jimmy was also sent off. But that's how it was every Saturday. And Jimmy was the club's youth-team coach!

You obviously wouldn't want to recreate that specific experience but I do still favour using the loan system and getting any emerging talent out in the lower leagues for real senior experience. It is what we did with Defoe, Lampard, Ferdinand and Carrick, as well as Harry Kane at Tottenham. We must also keep developing players. I come back again to that culture we should engrain from the earliest possible age at grassroots. Let's inspire a generation who want to dribble and take risks as well as pass, tackle and shoot. I think it is something that is being lost across Europe as a whole compared to other parts of the world, and that in itself presents a massive opportunity for English football.

# CHAPTER SIX

......................................................................

# DELEGATION

When I started in management at Bournemouth in 1983, I was just grateful if there was someone available to clear up the dog mess from the area of the local park in which we trained. On my first away trip as a manager, my backroom staff consisted of one man: John Kirk. We used to call him 'Captain Kirk'. He was a lovely guy who had been working in various roles at the club for the previous 20 years and became my assistant, physio, boot-man and kitman all rolled into one. By the time I was managing a club like Tottenham Hotspur or Queens Park Rangers in the Premier League 30 years later, the backroom staff at a typical away match could be around 20 or 30. The travelling squad had also grown from maybe 12 or 13, when we were allowed only one substitute, to 20 or 21. As well as the manager and his immediate coaching staff, including as many as two goalkeeping specialists, pretty much every club will also have sports scientists and doctors, a dietician and a chef, several kitmen, fitness coaches and data-analysts as well as physios and masseurs, a psychologist and a team of media staff. At Southampton in 2005, Sir Clive Woodward even wanted us to bring in a 'periphery vision' specialist, although that idea seemed to get shelved after I said in a press conference that they 'might be good for people with dodgy mince pies' but were not for me. It became a luxury, getting all the extra help, even if it did reach the stage where I had no idea who half the people were. I sometimes wondered what would happen if a punter appeared wearing a Tottenham tracksuit in the dressing-room. I doubted whether anyone would have said a word because no one would be sure which department he was with.

Delegation, then, has become an absolute necessity in football management and, as long as everyone sticks to what they should do, the advantages are clear. Most clubs now understandably want to build a support structure that is resistant to changes of manager, but you would still usually bring in a few coaches of your choice. That said, you ignore the staff outside that immediate circle at your peril. They can shape the entire culture of the club and, in everything you do, creating a positive and happy atmosphere is key.

There are examples at every club. We had two fantastic kitmen at Portsmouth – Kevin McCormack and Barry Harris – who were the soul of the place. Big Kev was ex-navy and had won the ABA super-heavyweight championship three times. I have seen him chasing rats around the disgusting dressing-rooms at Fratton Park when the toilets were blocked and the water was overflowing. Big Kev would also always have a cigarette ready for Robert Prosinečki immediately before the game, at half-time and on the final whistle. He would pamper the players. They have all got about eight pairs of boots each now and have their own particular requests. It used to drive me mad – these days kitmen have become a bit like the people who dress or do the make-up on a bloody film set. Kev's side-kick, Barry, has been doing jobs at Portsmouth for more than 60 years. He was once a mascot and would dress up as a sailor and rally the fans before games. He was the reserve team physio in the 1970s and 1980s and would do the food for the first team under Jim Smith in the 1990s. They might have been the butt of a few jokes but Kev and Barry were as much a part of the team as anyone.

Lou Macari says that the best signing he ever made at Stoke City was a guy called Neil Baldwin, who was loved by the players for the positive and fun atmosphere he created in the dressing-room. 'Nello' had learning disabilities as a kid and was a circus performer before Lou met him and made him the kitman. Nello is still there, 25 years on, at every home game and his life story was later made into a BAFTA-winning film. When I arrived at Bournemouth we had a volunteer called Ken Sullivan, who went everywhere with us. The players called him 'Nimbus' and, with his wife Audrey, he would also provide a home for young players like Jermain Defoe. Audrey and Nimbus used to keep the players out of trouble by taking them to the bingo. I also always remember beating Southampton in the Hampshire Senior Cup at the Dell (when we were hopeless but scored with our only shot of the game). As we came into the dressing-room, Nimbus was cheering and said, 'Well played, lads, well played.' I butted in, 'Shut up. What do you know? It was the biggest load of crap I have ever seen in my life. If you think that was good enough to get you in the first team, you have got to be dreaming.' I can still see Nimbus's face now. He was just stood there, open-mouthed and crestfallen, but we continued to laugh about that even decades later.

The blend of characters among those people immediately around you is also vital, and it is hard to overemphasise the complete transformation in what help is available. The manager and his assistants would do everything at a club when I was playing. And I really do mean everything. Bill Shankly, Bob Paisley and Joe Fagan are among the all-time greats, but they also helped build the dugout at Anfield. When Dunstable somehow signed George Best, it was the manager Barry Fry who was out pushing a wheelbarrow with labourers as they constructed a fence and turnstiles for his first appearance. The crowd that day rose from 400 to 4,000. When I started at West Ham in the youth team, the coaches were Ernie Gregory, Jimmy Barrett and Albert Walker, who would work all through the summer doing any maintenance and decoration on the ground. They got two weeks' holiday a year, which was the same as the people working in the factories. Nat Lofthouse was the greatest centre-forward in England and moved onto the coaching staff at Bolton Wanderers after retiring in 1960. When we were doing our coaching course at Lilleshall, some of the Bolton lads would talk about him and the jobs he would have to do. All the coaches had to clean the ground on Fridays as part of their work. That included Nat, who went to see the manager Bill Ridding one day to complain. He said, 'Bill, I'm cleaning the toilets outside and putting my arm down there and it's filthy. I'm getting all the shit on my arm.' Bill said, 'Oh, sorry about that, Nat. Leave it with me. I'm embarrassed. I'll sort that out.' Three days later Bill called Nat over: 'Nat, I've sorted it out. I've got you a rubber glove and a longer brush.' And Nat happily got on with it. Wayne Rooney would probably be Nat Lofthouse's football equivalent now.

It was similar for me when I joined Dave Webb as his assistant at Bournemouth in the old Fourth Division. The club had no money. If we wanted to stay overnight for a game up north the response was always the same: 'We can't afford it.' Dave was constantly grafting to raise some cash and would come up with different ideas and schemes. He would go to car auctions to try to make the club a bit of profit. I played in a charity match in Wimborne in Dorset and Jim Davidson was in the same team as me. He told me that he would love to come to a game, so I fixed it up. *The Jim Davidson Show* was big Saturday night TV at the time and Dave got to know he was at the game. The next thing I knew Jim Davidson was on the board of directors as well and raising funds for the club. He started coming to the games and would put on shows in the old supporters' club, which was a very basic old wooden-floored room. One week he would be picking up the *TV Times* award for 'Funniest Man on Television', the next he would be hosting a show in this dump of a room. I was never sure if the biggest attraction was Jim or the strippers, but he was great for the club. He once came on the coach with me, Dave and the players to Rochdale. We were second in the league and Torquay were top, but we won our game and Torquay were beaten by Stockport. We had gone top and it was already a raucous mood as were driving back down the M6 when the driver suddenly spotted the Torquay coach. They were heading south as well and our coach had started to overtake theirs. The players had each clocked one another when Jim suddenly got up on the seat, dropped his trousers and did a moonie out of the window. The coaches were doing virtually the same speed and so one would edge ahead and then the other. It meant that our new Bournemouth director's moonie went on for about ten minutes. The players, of course, loved it, and so did Torquay's. Jim enjoyed his football and we had some good nights with him. We would all go out with our wives in Bournemouth, although I have forgotten now which one he had back then. You had to be on your toes to make sure you didn't get the wrong name.

By the time I was at West Ham, delegation for a manager was thankfully more about sharing the coaching jobs than worrying about fixing the toilets. The game was changing rapidly. Having one or two assistants became normal, then a physio who was actually medically qualified. Next there were fitness guys who would take all the warm-ups and oversee a lot of pre-season for you. Coaching the goalkeepers also became a specialised job. Before that, the goalies would just hit balls at each other until they were needed for shooting practice or maybe a nine-a-side game.

I slowly learned the value of delegation. When you are younger, you do want to do everything yourself. I would oversee all the fitness work, take all the coaching, pick the team, do all the scouting and get sucked into worrying about every little detail of what was happening at the club. That is one of the most common mistakes that any young manager can make. You can tie yourself up in so many knots worrying about relatively unimportant issues that you lose focus on what really matters. You can also exhaust yourself and find yourself switching off some of your most important senses of all. It is amazing what you notice sometimes if you take a step back to watch and listen. Then you can often get a much clearer and more accurate view of who is doing what and how hard particular players are working. People in all walks of life and lines of business don't do enough of that. The players get fed up with hearing the same voice every day. At Queens Park Rangers I was open to bringing in Steve Black, the psychologist who had spent many years working with Jonny Wilkinson and was recommended to me by Joey Barton. I met him in Middlesbrough, found him very positive, and I think he did challenge my thinking and help us win promotion back to the Premier League in 2014.

My outlook when bringing in coaching staff was very simple. I would always try to get the best available people to come and work with me. Winning games and being successful was all that mattered. I loved it if someone could help me get an extra edge. I think maybe there is an element with some managers of worrying about their position, obsessing about who gets the credit, or only sticking with who they know. I think you have got to be insecure to behave like that but I have always had confidence in my own abilities. I was just happy to be helped by good people, whether they were bright young coaches with big aspirations or experienced managers in their own right. A quick list of some of the very different people I have had alongside me as a manager backs this up: Frank Lampard Senior, Luther Blissett, Jim Smith, Kevin Bond, Joe Jordan, Tony Adams, Avram Grant, Dave Bassett, Frank Burrows, Sir Clive Woodward, Steve Cotterill, Steve McClaren, Clive Allen, Glenn Hoddle, Tim Sherwood, Les Ferdinand, Tony Pulis and Glenn Roeder. Two of those were former England managers and one, of course, was a knight of the realm and already a World Cup winner.

I can understand why people from the outside might have viewed myself and Clive Woodward as some sort of odd couple, but the reality was that we shared an office for three months at Southampton and got on fine. I liked Clive and he had some good ideas. He would talk about players practising more and how Jonny Wilkinson would spend two hours every day honing his place-kicking. He was a big believer in encouraging players to spend time practising their free-kicks and their shots in the same way. Having seen at first-hand how people like Frank Lampard and Paolo Di Canio improved themselves with extra training, I largely agreed with where he was coming from. He would video things and felt that footballers were not so consistent in how they struck the ball, whereas Wilkinson's technique was always the same. I found it interesting. He never tried to interfere at all, but it was a very difficult time for me following the move from Portsmouth. Everybody makes mistakes and moving to Southampton at that time was probably the biggest of my career. I was living with that when suddenly the chance came to go back to Portsmouth. My decision had nothing to do with Clive. His long-term goal was to be a football manager, and I still think that there was no reason he could not have done it with the right opportunity. There's nothing that says you have to have played to be a top manager. José Mourinho never played football of any note. The same was true for Lawrie McMenemy, who was probably the greatest Southampton manager of all time. Clive was a sportsman of the highest calibre as a rugby player and manager and, while he would always have had that 'What does he know? He's a rugby man' thrown at him, you could just as well say, 'What does Mourinho know?' Clive knew about sport. He was an expert in diet, fitness and preparing players.

You take different things from different people, and I think it is important not just to have coaches who challenge your thinking but also to let them put on sessions if they have a particular idea. I didn't want someone just going, 'Yes, Harry, no, Harry.' You need people with opinions. They might say something that will spark an idea. We would be talking all the time about what sessions we might do and would often map out the week when we were travelling back from a game. There would then be a meeting at 8am, where we would finalise how that particular day would look. I would have the final say, but always felt that it was important to be flexible and open-minded. It is about having a feel for what players need at a particular moment. There would be times when you wanted to concentrate on set-pieces or patterns of play but also, if they were under a bit of pressure, I would try to get them playing by lifting the atmosphere with something fun. For example, you might just say, 'Yellow jersey for the worst player. Or £50 to charity from everyone on the losing team.' You might even just come in and feel like they were better off having a soak in the bath, a sauna and a massage. Every day you are gauging the mood, thinking about what has been happening during the past week and what lies ahead before deciding what to do.

It is all about creating the right atmosphere, and the people around you are critical in that. If one of my staff came to me and said, 'I would like to do this particular session tomorrow,' and explain why, I would almost always be, 'Yeah, no problem,' and let them take the lead. Other days I would do it myself. I liked to mix it up. You might work with the defence, or be trying to build up the confidence of the strikers by having them do some finishing. I liked to work on shape and shadowing as we got close to a game, and I loved to be out on the training pitch every day. We are all big kids, really, and being out on the training ground was the highlight of the job for me, especially when I was working with good players.

I have had some fantastic people on my staff down the years. I am delighted to see how Tony Pulis has progressed –

I had no doubts he would become a manager even when he played under me at Bournemouth and then became my assistant. He was very thorough and a real fitness fanatic. Glenn Hoddle and Steve McClaren were top managers in their own right but also excellent on the training ground, with lots of innovative ideas. Steve Cotterill and Tim Sherwood were both superb – lads who are wasted out of work. I loved getting to know Tony Adams at Portsmouth. He was such a fantastic player and, even with all the demons he had, one of the greatest captains in the history of football. Players looked up to him. Dave Bassett was another top manager and a great organiser of teams. He was different to me but innovative during the early 1980s in how he was using statisticians and analysing how goals were being scored long before anyone had even thought of Prozone. Dave was the architect of the Wimbledon team that performed such miracles in rising from the Southern League to the First Division and winning the FA Cup in the space of just ten years. He was meticulous in his planning.

I am just sorry that it was too late to get Bobby Moore involved after I became manager at West Ham United. It is one of the first things I would have done. He would have been the main man for me there. I was never one to worry about bringing people in that others might see as a threat. You sometimes hear people complain when they are sacked that someone inside took their job. I never saw it that way. It is not your job anyway if you have been sacked, and I would always rather see one of my staff get promoted. It happened when I left Bournemouth with Tony Pulis, and then with Glenn Roeder at West Ham. It was the same at Portsmouth with Tony Adams. Dave Bassett had a short go after me at Southampton, and Tim Sherwood and Chris Ramsey also got opportunities at Tottenham Hotspur and Queens Park Rangers when I had gone. I was always genuinely pleased for them and wanted to see them succeed.

You look for different things in people you bring in. Knowledge of the club is useful, and I will always say that my best signing at Portsmouth was Jim Smith. The owner, Milan Mandarić, was not a big fan of Jim and would say, 'Why do the fans sing Harry and Jim?' I would respond, 'I don't care if they sing Jim and Harry. Who's bothered?' It was great when the whole crowd were going and Fratton Park would physically shake. I knew what Jim gave me. Every club is very different and, when you get in there, you always sense a unique feel. Jim had been a successful manager at Portsmouth and was very unlucky not to reach the 1992 FA Cup final. He understood the game. He understood that it's not rocket science and, with Kevin Bond and Joe Jordan, helped me create an atmosphere that was special, one of the best I have known in football. Every day was fun. We would say things to the players that might be near the bone and take the mickey, but they would come back at us. The players could laugh at me and Jim. We hardly ever stopped laughing, and that is so important for a manager.

Maybe the greatest managerial partnership of all was between Brian Clough and Peter Taylor and, while Clough was obviously an incredible frontman and Taylor was a brilliant judge of players, I always remember what Clough said when he was asked what he most missed about his old colleague after they went their separate ways. 'He made me laugh,' Clough said. I could relate to that. Jim knew football inside out but also always made me smile. I remember him shuffling up to Teddy Sheringham when he was having a lean spell and telling Teddy all about how he got 120 goals in one season. Jim played as a wing-half for Sheffield United, Lincoln, Aldershot, Halifax, Boston and Colchester between 1959 and 1973. Teddy played for England and was one of the great strikers in Premier League history. We were all listening. '120 goals? In one season? Rubbish, Jim. How could you get 120 goals in one season?' He was adamant. 'I'm telling you, I got 120 goals in one season for Sheffield United.' It turned out that it was when he was playing with the Sheffield United Under-18s in the local league who were winning games about 30–0 every week. Teddy was cracking up.

Like most experienced managers, Jim also had that encyclopaedia of players in his head. I remember being without a striker before our first game of the season we won the Championship in 2002–03. Rory Allen, who had come from Tottenham, dropped out on the day before the opening game and we were racking our brains. Jim suddenly came up with Deon Burton. I wasn't sure. 'He'll do the job,' he said, with complete certainty. It was Friday afternoon. Derby were happy to save a few quid on his wages and we had until 5pm to get the paperwork done. The first time we saw him was in the dressing-room at 1.30pm on the Saturday before we played Nottingham Forest. After only eight minutes, Deon had scored the first of our 97 league goals that season and we won the game 2–0.

Jim was great because he also had such a rich background in football himself and could suddenly come out with these amazing stories that the players would love just as much as me. He worked under Robert Maxwell, of course, at Oxford United and was the first manager to lead them to the old First Division. It was an amazing achievement and, on the day they clinched promotion, Maxwell went onto the pitch to say a few words to the fans. He went on so long that Jim and the players almost walked off, but the best bit came when Maxwell started to introduce the team to the crowd and it became clear he did not have a clue who half of them were. He also made Jim join him with the trophy in an open-topped white Rolls-Royce that travelled in front of the team-bus for a victory parade through Oxford the next day. Jim was totally uncomfortable with it and was then left stranded in this Rolls-Royce when Maxwell suddenly hopped off halfway through to go for lunch.

The right assistant or first-team coach can also be a valuable buffer between the manager and the players. First-team coaches are usually popular. They put on enjoyable training sessions but are not picking the team, and that simple fact guarantees them a different relationship with the players to the manager. I also think a coach who is a recently retired player can sometimes communicate and relate more to the squad.

The role of captain is vital in this regard. I know that some managers, usually those from the continent, have said that the captaincy is not especially important to them, but I placed a big emphasis on my choices. The captain can be an important bridge to the other players and let you know what the mood is and if there are any problems in the dressing-room. You might sense something but not know the details, and it is invaluable to have a captain and senior players that you can approach. It could be something seemingly trivial but you need to be aware. I had one instance where the captain replied, 'Well, the lads are not happy. The club has started charging us for our dinners now.' There's always something, and you need to sort anything that is upsetting them. I found Michael Dawson to be a great captain for me at Tottenham. He was like Joe Jordan: you'd lay your life on him. If there was something that needed to be done by the players, Michael would do it or get it sorted, but he was also one of the lads. I might even ask someone like Michael his thoughts on the team selection and he would tell you what the other lads were thinking. There are not a million players around like Michael but, if you can find one, you're well on your way.

Kevin Bond is someone I have taken most places as my assistant manager. He is an excellent coach and has lots of ideas, tactically, for when you are setting up your team. He has also got a nice way about him that the players appreciate. He's got a lovely personality and a really good football brain. His dad, John Bond, was a top manager, and Kevin has spent his whole life around football. He managed Bournemouth so he also knows what it's like to come home on a Saturday when you've been beaten. That is important and why it helps to have people who have managed on you staff. That journey home is the longest of all when you have played rubbish and lost. You can find yourself looking up the coach, so pissed off with everything that you want to see if anyone is laughing or joking. You dislike the world and are waiting for someone to do something you don't like. It can be a very lonely existence as a manager and that is when you need an assistant who you can talk to and have a chat with. Suddenly you can start thinking again about next week. You might talk about the training on Monday or what changes you could make and you can begin to move on. That was definitely something I needed on that first game with Bournemouth after we had been annihilated 9–0. It was just me and Captain Kirk that day, but what was he doing on the five-hour journey home from Lincoln when I was thinking my world had come to an end? He had been rushing around doing all his jobs since about 6am and was knackered. So, with me sat there in the dark wondering if I would ever work in football again, the Captain was snoring away in the seat next door.

# CHAPTER SEVEN

# DIET, FITNESS AND PREPARATION

Combating boredom is a constant challenge for footballers, and so it did not completely surprise me to hear Ray Parlour talking about the eating competition that once took place among Arsenal players to kill time during one especially long journey. It got to the stage where players were being physically sick outside the coach because they had eaten so much, but no one could beat Steve Bould, who of course now sits next to Arsène Wenger in the Arsenal dugout on a Saturday. He apparently managed to eat nine dinners. I shudder to think what Arsène would have made of it when you consider that one of his first acts upon arriving as Arsenal manager in 1996 was to ban chocolate on the team-bus. It would prompt chants of, 'We want our Mars bars back,' but Arsène was not to be moved and his arrival did coincide with huge changes in the diet of footballers. I can't pretend I was at the forefront of this revolution. Pasta became the done thing during that period, and I was quite dismissive to begin with, pointing out that pasta did not make you pass the ball any better.

That remains true but I was not totally blind to the importance of what you consumed and, even in my very early days of management, I would keep a notebook of the weights of all the players. This became an invaluable record for me as I could look back over many years and have a good idea of what a player's weight should be either by comparing notes with their old record or knowing what someone of a similar height and build would be. One of the funniest stories was with Ian Bishop. I had signed him at Bournemouth for £20,000 from Carlisle in 1988, and he had moved to West Ham by the time I became manager there six years later. The off-field habits of some of that West Ham team were terrible. I fronted him up about it: 'You can't move, you're overweight.' He wouldn't have it: 'No I'm not. No I'm not.' So I rummaged around in the boot of my car and found my tattered old notebook. He was about two stones heavier but, fair play, he stopped arguing, lost the weight and was soon back playing at his best.

I trusted the nutritionists to get on with it once they became a normal part of a club's backroom staff, but they would look at me like I was mad when I told them stories about what used to happen. If there was one player who might have even given Steve Bould a run for his money, it was Billy Bonds. That might surprise people, given that Billy did not carry an ounce of excess weight and was so super-fit that he played on at the highest level until almost his 42nd birthday, but his capacity to consume food, especially shortly before a match, would amaze today's experts. On away games, we would typically stop at a nearby hotel before the usual 3pm kick-off and eat steak and chips followed by rice pudding. If you hadn't finished, Billy would be reaching across with his fork and getting your steak. This could be about 12.30 or 1pm, maybe later if you had been delayed. I used to pick him up before home games at Upton Park and he'd say, 'I just had a lovely steak and kidney pie.' But that would not be all. Billy might have a plate of steak and kidney pie and chips, some pears and about eight slices of bread and butter before a game and still run about non-stop for 90 minutes.

We would eat similar foods after training. There was no canteen like you have now. When I was at Derby County for a few months in 2016 we all ate at a place at the training ground called 'the Bistro'. It was like a five-star restaurant. When I played at West Ham, we would all just head for the local cafés, and there was a hierarchy about where you went, even if all the greasy food was the same. The first team would be in Cassettari's and the youth team at the Central. Cassettari's was legendary at West Ham and, on a matchday at Upton Park, you would see 40 people queuing up out of the door. Jimmy Barrett, the youth-team coach, would have a deal with John at the Central and dish out vouchers from a book. We would all have four shillings to spend each day. It was great food, although there was no sign of the steamed vegetables, yogurt, chicken, fruit, fish and protein shakes that you see piled into the players today. It would be homemade steak and kidney pie with chips and beans, or ham on the bone with egg and chips

– then a jam roly-poly pudding with custard, all washed down with two coca-colas. You would still get change from your four shillings. As well as post-match, drinking in the afternoons once training had finished was not uncommon – although that certainly accelerated once Jimmy Greaves arrived in 1970. On his first day, Jimmy said, 'Where do you go for a drink?' We said, 'We don't usually, Jim.' 'Don't worry,' he said. 'There is a lovely pub up the road. The Slater's Arms.' So we all started going there at lunchtime, until about 7pm. Jimmy's mate, Bill, owned the pub. He would get legless drunk himself and go up to bed in the afternoon and let us serve ourselves.

The culture was the same everywhere. The great Liverpool teams could drink like you would not believe, and Jimmy Gabriel as well as Denis Hollywood tell some extraordinary stories about the boys at Southampton, who Bill Shankly described as 'ale-house footballers'. They were once on a pre-season trip to Tokyo and all out drinking when Jimmy got talking to two bemused American tourists about football. He was pointing out how Southampton had just signed one of the best midfielders in the country in Brian O'Neil, and how Ron Davies had just finished top scorer in the old First Division with 37 goals. Brian and Ron were both passed out on the bar with their heads in their hands. Then one of the Americans said, 'What's that noise?' It was coming from Brian, who was peeing himself. They then had to all carry Brian back to the hotel because no taxi would take him. The twist in the story, however, was that Brian borrowed the trousers that night from his usually immaculate roommate Terry Paine.

O'Neil was an incredible character as well as a superb player. He once turned up for training at the old Dell in the middle of Southampton on his tractor because he was running late after doing a bit of work on a fence in the field next to where he lived. He also never owned a pair of football boots. Jimmy says that he would just rummage around the dressing-room and regularly go out playing in a pair that were several sizes too big. When O'Neil once got injured and was in hospital, the other players smuggled in vodka and cans of beer for him, as well as his pet dog who ran about the ward. The story that made me laugh most, though, occurred when Brian had Bobby Stokes staying at his house. Bobby, who would go on to score the winning goal in the 1976 FA Cup final, was hungry and so O'Neil had a look to see what he could find. All he had was a tin of dog food, some egg and beans. So he put it all in a saucepan, heated it up and told him it was stew. Bobby ate it all up and said that it was lovely. The dieticians often ask the players today to keep a diary of their food. Just imagine handing in that little lot on your form. Eggs, beans and Pedigree Chum.

There was still a long way to go even after I became West Ham manager in 1994. Seeing Julian Dicks eating packets of crisps and drinking diet coke would make Paolo Di Canio incredulous. He had come from a very different culture in Italy that was much more forward-thinking in terms of preparation. In his own autobiography, he summed it up like this: 'Doping in English football is restricted to lager and baked beans with sausages. After which the players take to the field belching and farting.' Paolo certainly educated us and made us rethink what we were doing, and the fact that Arsène was so quickly successful at Highbury had a huge impact. You would suddenly start hearing stories about Arsenal from the players or other managers. It would be along the lines of, 'You won't believe this. Arsenal have two guys on the coach preparing food for the players. They take their own food and they've got a microwave. One is doing the cooking and one is serving the food.' I would be, 'No. Really? Bloody hell. What's wrong with fish and chips?' I think we all eat differently now. People are more educated and health conscious. I still like what I like but, with a bit of prompting from Sandra and an ear-bending from the doctor, have stopped eating certain foods at certain times.

Unsurprisingly, given some of the refuelling habits, players would arrive for pre-season in much varying states of fitness compared with today. You rarely get the same sort of fluctuations in weight now, even if some of the older players devised special methods to try to beat the scales by positioning their toe in a certain way. The summer routine when I was a player was always the same. You would all come in and get weighed. There would not be a football in sight and you would all get on the coach and drive to Epping Forest. We would wear these white plimsolls that offered no cushioning and then, having done nothing all summer, you would start running. I can still picture it. Up the Epping High Road along a pavement that was only about a metre wide – with lorries whizzing by your ear – and then into the forest where you would run for an hour. No one ever complained. We loved being footballers. If the manager said, 'Go on a five-mile run,' you went on a five-mile run. By the finish, there would be half a mile between the first and the last player. Pre-season was the only time that you were fed lunch by the club. We had a shed where we used to change – it was an old cricket pavilion – and you would be given boiled potatoes and a bit of ham. That was all. Then you would train again in the afternoon with the footballs. Your calves would be like concrete from all the running in those plimsolls but there would be no rest. No one had ever heard of a massage. You would just keep going like that for three weeks.

The stories of players hitching a lift on the back of milk-floats during the big group runs are true. Brian Dear and Bobby Moore would jump on and pass us, usually with one of them wearing the milk cap. They would have to be careful not to give the game away. Ron Greenwood would know something was up if they finished too high up the list and so they would come back about 11th or 12th. The same thing was still happening right up to the time I returned to West Ham to work under Billy Bonds in 1992. Julian Dicks and Frank McAvennie, who left that summer, would be at the back and pull the same trick. It was harder, though, under Billy because he was so fit that he would run with the players and could keep moving from back-to-front to see how they were getting on.

Pre-season could not be more different now but, for all the advances in sports science, the players are often worse prepared for the start of the season. Every single manager will tell you that. The problems today stem from clubs going off all around the world for matches in Asia, Africa, America or Australia, all of which have got nothing to do with getting ready for the season. Indeed, if someone said, 'What is the worst thing you can do pre-season?' the answer would be, 'Get on a few aeroplanes, fly around the world, eat food you are not used to and flog the players in a different climate during a different time zone.' It's just crazy. We went to Nigeria when I was at Portsmouth. We played Manchester United, and half of their players went down with a stomach bug. Wayne Rooney missed the start of the season because of it. It's obviously all about money. The clubs are being paid maybe £1 million for each game although, with every Premier League place now worth £1.2 million, you do wonder if someone at some stage will have the brains to say, 'Is this worth it?'

It shows how the managers have lost power. None of them want it but they do not have the influence at the club to say, 'I'm sorry, we aren't going.' The deal is done by some commercial person and they are not bothered about what the manager says. The players don't want to go either. It's not like years ago when Ron Greenwood took us all to America at the end of one season and it gave everyone a massive lift. No one in the squad had been to America back then, and it felt like a different world. My mum and dad had never been on an aeroplane before they died – any holiday we had was in a little caravan on Canvey Island. The players now think nothing of a five-day trip to Florida to play golf with their mates and so have no interest in being taken to some unusual location for pre-season training.

I used to take teams down to Devon where we would stay at Woodbury Park, which was owned by Nigel Mansell. It was perfect preparation. There was a great pitch and we would do the physical work in the mornings, ball-work in the afternoons and, if they had applied themselves well, I would say to the lads, 'If you want to get a buggy and have nine holes of golf, no problem.' There would be no alcohol, and you could also fix up some good games against Exeter, Torquay and Plymouth. The furthest we would go at West Ham was Scotland. The annual highlight for us as players, that American trip aside, always used to be the match at Bata Sports, who were a local shoe company that had great facilities and a team in the Essex Business Houses League. The place would be packed. There was no stand but the pitch would be roped off, and it was about ten deep with fans. The added incentive would be getting two pairs of shoes from Bata Sports. You could go and pick whatever style you wanted – one black and one brown – and so everyone wanted to play in that game.

The philosophy of many of the old trainers when I started out was that if the players didn't have the ball during the week, they would want it more on a Saturday. Crazy, but they thought it would make a player hungrier if they spent the week doing exercise and running up and down the terraces. Yet for many players, such as Julian Dicks and Matt Le Tissier, having an interest in the ball was often what was needed to get them fit.

They weren't interested in just running. Malcolm Allison was ahead of his time on this as well as everything else. Even as a young reserve at Charlton Athletic he realised that it was a nonsense that the coach, Jimmy Trotter, had players just running around the track or the stairs in the stadium. He let him know what he thought and was promptly sent to see the manager Jimmy Seed. 'Malcolm, you insulted Mr Trotter yesterday,' said Jimmy Seed. Malcolm came back at him. 'No I didn't, I just told him the training was rubbish.' He was then transferred to West Ham, which was our gain, but not before he shook Jimmy Seed's hand and congratulated him for actually speaking to him for one of the few times in his entire six years at the club.

Many of the other old practices would amaze people now. Bill Shankly would have the Liverpool players wear big woollen jumpers to keep the perspiration in and thought it was better for them to wait until they had stopped sweating before taking a shower. It meant that they would get on the minibuses back to the stadium after training, dripping wet, sometimes in the freezing cold when it had been snowing, and have to wait maybe an hour after training to get showered.

It is obviously fantastic now to be surrounded by so much advice, and I did defer to the sports scientists in terms of the fitness work, especially during pre-season. You barely see a player asked to run more than 100 yards now in training. It is all short, sharp stuff. I did once take the Tottenham players to Epping Forest on one beautiful winter's day, but it was to be the first and last time I tried that. The sun was out and so I said, 'For a change, let's go and have a run in the forest and then have a cup of tea. There's a place there we can all sit out.' The players never stopped moaning. One of them got a calf injury and blamed it on me. He thought it was ridiculous to go for a little jog in the forest but, if you look at the game, most of your running is done without the ball. I would not always agree with the fitness guys. They will say you should only train at particular times, or that the intensity should not be too high a certain number of days before or after a match. Yet I would watch training sessions and, from all the decades I have spent around footballers, know for sure sometimes that a player had not tried in the session. I would be thinking to myself, 'I worked harder than him this morning going up and down the touchline,' but the sports scientist would check their stats and his heart monitor and come back at you – 'Yes, he worked hard' – and I would say, 'No, he was lazy. I've watched him all morning and he's hardly run.'

Some of the work can also be too prescriptive. You see young players today only being encouraged to train for a certain amount of time in case it tires them out. Then they might be put on recovery sessions, even two days after a match. As I said before, Frank Lampard would literally spend six hours a day training. Every day. When he first arrived, Tony Carr, who was West Ham's youth-team coach, would say to me, 'Harry, he can't get around the pitch, he can't run.' But then I would be in my office, late into the afternoon as it was getting dark, and see someone out there running in the distance. I used to wonder if someone had got over the fence. But it would be Frank, and he could certainly get around the pitch. At night, he would also be out running on the streets in a sweat-suit. People would tell him to stop now. They would warn that he was overtraining and that he'd risk shortening his career through injury, but someone like Frank would just ignore them. All I can say is that I saw with my own eyes how Frank approached his training, and his record is now there for everybody to see. He is 38 and still going strong. He has played more than 900 professional games in his career. He played more than 50 games a season at Chelsea eight times and set a record of 164 consecutive Premier League games. David Beckham was similar. He trained with us for a few months at Tottenham in 2011 and I loved having him around. He was always in early and always doing extra at the end, even at the age of 35.

Ledley King, of course, was at the other extreme. Juande Ramos was supposedly very scientific in his approach but, after stories that Ledley might have to retire after playing only ten games in the 2007–08 season, we got more than 20 league games out of him in three of the next four campaigns. His knee was obviously a mess and it would swell up like a balloon if he trained on it or played a game. It would then take four or five days for the swelling to come back down. It would be a juggling act as we had to decide which games we would prioritise, but there would be no long consultations with sports scientists or medics about what work he should do in the week. I just let him decide what he needed. He did not come out for training on one single day of the week until Friday. Then, on a Friday morning, he would come out, do two laps of the pitch at the training ground, and either give me a thumbs-up or a thumbs-down. If I got the thumbs-up, I used to think to myself, 'Yeah, we'll win tomorrow. Ledley is fit.' He was an amazing player; right up with the best I have ever seen. I didn't realise how good until I worked with him. I would also always listen to other players if they felt they needed a rest in the week, for one simple reason. It was not what happened between Monday and Friday that counted. Saturday was the only day we all got judged.

The other aspect of sports science that I have never quite understood is that we have all this expertise and help now in football but there are more injuries than ever. Back in the day, teams would have no doctors, no sports scientists, no masseurs and no dieticians and yet be able to complete a season with 13 or 14 players. That would be unthinkable now. I know the game is played at a higher pace and intensity, but I think that can be exaggerated. The game was also twice as physical previously. Players really did used to kick lumps out of one another. Every time the ball went up to a forward, the defender would go right through the back of him. The pitches and boots were also a world away. The grass would regularly be frozen, but they would just mark out the lines in the snow and sweep the rest away. A game would not be called off unless the snow was up around your shins and, even in a mild winter, you would be playing in mud that could be ankle deep. The pitches now are carpets. They are far better on the last day of the season than they ever were on the first day when we were playing.

I have still got a pair of my dad's old football boots and the difference is amazing. They were old brown boots with a rock-hard toecap on the end, and they used to bang in the leather studs with a nail. The pitches were so hard that the nail could push up through the sole of the boot and into the feet of the players. They would often be bleeding at the end of a match from where the nail had come through. Sir Stanley Matthews told me that he used to travel to games wearing an even heavier pair of boots so that he could make his feet feel lighter once the actual match started. We did at least have the option of long or short studs when I started playing at West Ham. We would get two pairs of boots – one with moulded studs and one with screw-ins – at the beginning of each season. If they split, you would take them to the cobbler's. If you needed a third pair, you would pay for them yourself. Gareth Bale used to get whole boxes of boots sent to him every day at Tottenham with little Wales badges on them. We could have filled an entire room with his boots, and they each weighed about the same as a pair of slippers.

I think injuries now are sometimes overblown and the players are going off for a scan over every little problem. If the players have been told that they are out for five weeks, you can be sure that they will not surprise you and be back in four. A certain amount of ignorance previously just meant that a player got on with it, even if some of the stories would make you wince. Our goalkeeper at West Ham, Lawrie Leslie, once broke his arm during a match and was just simply moved out onto the wing for the next 60 minutes. There were no substitutes and so the protocol back then was that you played on unless you had broken your leg. It was not acceptable to come off for any other reason. Bill Shankly would ignore any injured player. No matter how bad the injury, he would treat them as invisible. It was his way of stopping people being unavailable to play unless it was absolutely unavoidable.

West Ham had an even more effective method of keeping players out of the treatment room: the simple presence of the physio, Bill Jenkins, who was probably the hardest man I have ever met. He was one of the first people into the concentration camps at the end of the Second World War and had seen some horrendous sights. It made him unimpressed whenever he came across a footballer with an injury. He would punch you in the chest and say, 'What's the matter with you?' If you were injured on a Sunday, you had to bring in six lagers or a bottle of white wine otherwise he wouldn't treat you. His son, Rob, took over and he would send off one of the kids to Doug's Café down the road and the senior players would sit in the treatment room with him eating bacon and egg rolls with Daddy's sauce. Rob was based at the stadium and he would always make a call to the training ground first to make sure that Ron Greenwood was there and would not suddenly show up. The difference with most physios then was that they were just ex-players of the club with no qualifications. If anything happened on the pitch, the treatment was always the same: a wet sponge on the back of your head.

The occasional freak injury was inevitable. Ron Greenwood was once livid over a performance away at Stoke City and told us that no one could go out after the game. Some of us still sneaked out of the hotel window and went to a nightclub. We had to climb over a fence to get back into the hotel, but Bobby Moore slipped and landed on a spike. We kept him out of Ron's sight the next day and then told him that he had tripped in his garden and landed on a fence. He was out for two weeks. That was nothing, though, compared to Darren Barnard at Barnsley, who slipped in his kitchen where his pet dog had relieved himself on the floor. He suffered ankle-ligament damage and missed the next five months. Even managers have had their mishaps, and Louis van Gaal rather spectacularly hurt himself before the 2007 season. He was at a college reunion and, at the age of 56, decided he would give a live demonstration of the pole vault. He slipped and broke both his ankle and fibula. He needed six pins to put it all back together but, with the help of a wheelchair and a pain threshold that would have impressed even old Bill Jenkins, still did not miss a single match or training session at AZ Alkmaar.

Training facilities have also been utterly transformed and clubs spend tens of millions now on creating the best possible environment for their players. When we had snow one year at West Ham for six weeks back in the sixties, we simply couldn't train. In the end, they found a little sports hall out at Harlow and we would drive the 45 minutes there in the old minibus to play four-a-side matches. There was no such thing as a gymnasium at West Ham – just one wooden room where we would play head tennis – although we were still quite forward-thinking. Ron, as well as Bill Nicholson at

Tottenham, would employ a guy called Bill Watson to come in once a week. Bill was an Olympic weightlifter and would have us doing stomach exercises, quick feet on the benches and skipping. That physical side has obviously gone to a completely different level now and the players do work hard in the gym on the weights. Most of them have got a physique like Cristiano Ronaldo and just a completely different body shape. I don't know how much the upper-body muscle speeds them up, makes them play better or helps to avoid injures, but they certainly do look the part on the beach.

The importance of your facilities can also be exaggerated. Nottingham Forest prepared on the morning of their European Cup final against Hamburg in Madrid on a traffic island with two big trees for goals. After a Saturday game, Brian Clough sometimes just turned around to his players and said, 'See you Thursday.' Jürgen Klopp can also be a bit different, and before they were due to play Arsenal in the Champions League in 2014 he took his Borussia Dortmund players to Regent's Park, to the pitches that are usually used for the Camden and Regent's Sunday league. We genuinely had nowhere of our own to train when I was the manager at Bournemouth and would regularly get thrown off the grass in King's Park, next to the club's Dean Court Stadium. The park keeper would come around on his bike and we would always be pleading for extra time. It would be, 'Just give us 20 minutes, give us half an hour.' The best story was when we beat Manchester United in the FA Cup third round in 1984, when we were in the bottom half of the Third Division.

We were on the back pages of all the newspapers and on the national news. They had a cinder training pitch in King's Park and, on the Monday after what is still one of the most famous games in Bournemouth's history, the gate was unlocked. Our attitude was, 'They've opened it for us. C'mon, lads, we will go on here, have a nice eight-a-side.' It was a great game and everyone was buzzing after the weekend, until suddenly the park keeper came along and locked the gate without saying a word. We had carried on playing without knowing he had done it until the time came to pack up. It was a high fence and I remember we were all wobbling around on the top before jumping down. It really was a case of being brought back down to earth with a bang.

# CHAPTER EIGHT

........................................................

# BUILDING SPIRIT

It is amazing how much you can learn just by looking at the reaction of those on the bench when their team scores a goal. If you see all the substitutes instinctively jump to their feet and join the celebrations, you can be pretty sure that the spirit is good. See them barely move, force a smile or some applause and you soon get the sense that they are not all in it together. Football players find it hard to hide their true feelings at that moment of maximum emotion. That collective spirit is impossible for any sports scientist to quantify but is among the most important attributes in any successful team. Just look at the extraordinary achievements of Leicester City and Wales in 2016: two teams who clearly had a special spirit and consequently became more than the sum of their individual parts. Then take Belgium. I had looked through all the squads at the start of Euro 2016 and tipped them to win it. They had such strength in depth on paper, but I sensed that I had made a mistake shortly before they had even started their first match against Italy. The two teams had lined up in

Lyon and they began with the Italian national anthem. The players were all arm in arm and belting it out. The looks on the faces of Giorgio Chiellini and Gianluigi Buffon, who were together at the top of the line, were incredible. They were singing loudly and close to tears. Next came Belgium, and half of them looked like they didn't even know the words to their anthem. At that very moment I changed my mind completely and strongly fancied Italy to win the match. Their collective motivation just seemed to be on another level and they prevailed 2–0 having played some exhilarating football in what was one of the games of the tournament. It was the same when Wales beat Belgium in the quarter-finals. Man for man the bookmakers were right to make Belgium favourites. Yet it is not just about individuals and, in terms of working for one another off the ball and having that special internal togetherness, there was no contest. Wales responded when they went behind. Every time they scored, the entire bench – including the coaching staff – were all up going mad and joining the celebrations. By contrast, Belgium fell apart once they had their backs up against the wall.

One of the biggest challenges for any manager, then, is to nurture that team spirit. Your job can very easily depend on it. There are many things that you can do to create and enhance that spirit but the starting point is naturally the character of those in your dressing-room. Sir Alex Ferguson has been asked – by everyone from prime ministers and leaders of industry to top academics – for the secret to sustained success in a team, and one of his first pointers is always that you should discard any player who threatens the group's spirit. You only need one or two bad apples to poison the dressing-room. The manager gets changed in his own room in the morning and is then usually back in his office after training. You are not in there with them most of the time and it does not take much for the problems to escalate. I've been on the other side and heard it non-stop – 'This is rubbish. What's he doing? Why are we having to do this? Why have we got to go there? The facilities are shit. He's crap. The training is wrong.' There are certain people who spend their whole life moaning about everything they can find. The weak ones follow and contaminate the place. The energy sappers can very easily bring others down with them.

As I stressed earlier, you also have to consider how you delegate, as well as the staff beyond the players. I have already mentioned the brilliant kitmen at Portsmouth but let's just say you have one who is always down and moans. He spends more time in the dressing-room with the players than the manager. The atmosphere can be quickly poisoned. You don't want people like that around your club in any capacity, especially near the players. It is the same with the tea ladies or the groundsmen. It might be important for the team to train on the stadium pitch one day in the week and you don't want a groundsman whose attitude is, 'No, I don't want you on there,' because it will mean a bit more work for him. They've got to be, 'OK, great.' It is a team right the way through the club and you want people around you who can enjoy the success and feel part of it. It can make or break you. I remember at Bournemouth we had a maintenance man who was there every day complaining. As he was slagging off everyone to you, it was a certainty that he would be slagging you off once your back was turned. It was non-stop, and you knew he would eventually bring everybody down with him. In the end, people were, 'You've got to get him out. You can't have him around you.' They were right. I listened to a talk by Sir Dave Brailsford about the Team Sky cyclists and, when he spoke about what he called the 'happy ant' culture in his organisation, I realised that was exactly what we had tried to create. He explained that one of the first criteria in any staff appointment – before even their specific skill for the job – would be whether they enhanced the team spirit and contributed to a positive vibe. Team Sky apparently call it 'compassionate ruthlessness' if they let go of someone who does not fit. It sounds fancy but it's all really the same thing. As a football manager, I would call it getting rid of the trouble-makers before they get rid of you.

It is no secret that the dressing-room culture was a big problem to me in the team I inherited at Queens Park Rangers in 2012. They had brought a load of players in, supposedly big hitters, and the attitude of too many of them was that it was almost beneath them to be at QPR. There were splits in the camp and it did not help to have some of these average players getting paid way above and beyond what they would deliver. Players can accept differences in wages and teammates getting big money if they earn it, but when they look and think, 'He's not doing any better than me and his attitude is worse,' you have a problem. It is also increasingly difficult in modern football to move on players you want out. Word soon gets around and, if they are on good money but not delivering and people know you are unhappy with their attitude, who is going to take them? This was obviously another issue at QPR.

I should stress, though, that the vast majority of footballers, including those at QPR, are good lads and I have been fortunate throughout my career to have almost always inherited a sound group of characters. But you don't usually get a job if everything is right, and some changes are often necessary to improve results. The problems typically stem either from a lack of confidence or an imbalance in the squad. The latter is more easily remedied. You then try to fine-tune it and really create the conditions for the team spirit to blossom. There are times to be serious but there also needs to be some fun around the place. It changes the whole dynamic.

We had lots of that in my first job in management at Bournemouth. It was an incredible dressing-room. They were not the easiest bunch to deal with in some respects – they would get up to some mischief and keep you on your toes in terms of curfews – but that never really worried me too much if it was adding to the spirit and their attitude towards football matches and training. We would all laugh together. It was like that before we beat Manchester United in the third round of the 1984 FA Cup. On the night before the game, we all went to an Italian restaurant, La Lupa, in town for a pre-match meal. The mood was great and I had a feeling all week that we could do something. We had a glass of wine. We were relaxed. The boss of the restaurant thought that we would be rolled over and there was a lot of mickey-taking going on. This was the famous occasion he laid down a challenge to our goalkeeper Ian Leigh. He told him that he would get free pizza for life if he could keep a clean sheet. Ian was a great lad but he was a little on the tubby side; he was probably about a stone or two overweight. He wasn't the tallest either. We called him 'Nipper' and, if I am being completely honest, probably the one thing he didn't need to be doing was to be eating more pizza. Anyway, we won 2–0 and Nipper had his free pizza. For about six months, he was getting fatter by the minute, but I then bought that particular restaurant. The rules soon changed. 'Sorry, Nipper, under new management. No more pizza.' He argued, but I wasn't about to change my mind.

I remember before the game we all walked up the seafront together. That was what you did before Cup games. What was also funny after the match was that the players all wanted to go out on the town to celebrate. It was no problem with me. We were in Division Three, after all, and it was one of the great Cup upsets of recent times. Manchester United were the holders. The players were not well known enough, however, to be especially recognised, even in the town that they lived. They went to one nightclub and announced themselves as the Bournemouth team who had just beaten Manchester United. 'No you're not,' said the bouncer. 'They are already in there.' Another group of chancers had already got in for free and my players had to queue up elsewhere.

Another story that caused laughs for weeks and built spirit in a way that you could never begin to measure occurred on John Williams's birthday. The players all went out that night and they ended up at Bournemouth Pier. Someone then decided it would be a good idea to strip him. Willo is 6 feet 2 inches and a big strong guy but, between them, they got the lot off. All they left was his trainers. There was not another stitch on him, and all his mates then ran off. They disappeared home and there was no way anyone was going back. So Willo was left outside Bournemouth Pier stark naked. He lived two miles along the coast in Boscombe. Taxi? No one was going to take him in that state and he had no money on him anyway. So he walked all the way home, sprinting between lampposts and dodging in and out of the trees whenever anyone was coming. He was lucky not to get arrested. Big Willo still claims to this day that Tony Pulis spiked his drinks all night. The players were full of it, of course, the next morning and could not wait to tell me what had happened. Spirit is created through shared experiences and that can certainly include adversity but nothing, of course, beats winning.

Another Bournemouth experience that stands out was when we had back-to-back away games in 1986. First, there was a midweek fixture in York and then a Saturday afternoon in Darlington. The directors would never pay in those days for you to stay up anywhere but it seemed silly to drive the 300 miles all the way back down to Bournemouth only to turn around and make the same trip back up north later in the week. I told them, 'By the time we come back it will be

4am and we will be setting off again on Friday. I'll see if I can find a way.' We found some cheap guesthouses in York that were next to each other. Three in a room. We then hired two battered old minibuses. They were green. I can still vividly picture them in my mind. I drove one and Keith Williams, my assistant, drove the other. Old Captain Kirk, the physio, also helped out. We had a skip with the boots and kit in. There were only 13 players and they were divided between the two buses. We trained before the first game in the fields on the big driveway up to York Races. When we turned up at Darlington in the green buses, the guy on the gate tried to send us around the back of the ground. 'Supporters are that way,' he said. It took him a while to believe that the Bournemouth team had arrived and the bloke driving one of these clapped-out old buses was the manager. Anyway, we won 3–0, but what I remember most was the six-hour drive home. We all sang every minute of the way. Me included.

That might sound like another world but, with a bit of imagination, you can relax just about any dressing-room and create that spirit. I read Gareth Bale saying that Euro 2016 with Wales felt like a holiday with his mates. Don't take that the wrong way: Gareth is teetotal and works unbelievably hard on the pitch, but he loved the daily quizzes, the table-tennis and watching all the other matches in the tournament with friends he had grown up with. He also seemed to enjoy the freedom to be able to wander into the little seaside town in Brittany where they were staying for a coffee or a Nutella pancake. What was also important in that Wales team was how they had grown together since playing through the various age-groups. They had all experienced the high of qualifying, but what was a young squad had also come through the tragedy of losing their former manager Gary Speed. Many of the players, as well as the fans, mentioned Speed's legacy and memory during the tournament. That spirit and unity showed in how Wales played. Chris Coleman's man-management was also excellent, and it was clever of him to let Gareth bring his own physio from Real Madrid to France. The fact that he was so positive and happy would have rubbed off on the others. If the star man from Real Madrid feels that way, you are unlikely to get a murmur out of the rest.

It was a different time but I think there is a parallel between Wales at Euro 2016 and England 20 years earlier, which was the last time we seriously challenged at a major tournament. Jamie has told me all about the England dressing-room that summer. Terry Venables has a fantastic football brain – one of the best coaches ever – but Jamie would say that, for all the importance of Terry's tactics, Tony Adams ran the dressing-room as captain. Arsène Wenger used to say that Tony could 'smell a dressing-room' and he was vital in terms of his standards and what he inspired in others. Yes, Tony was off the rails sometimes away from football but, when it came to playing and organising, he was fantastic – a natural. I remember seeing Tony playing a match when he was 14 at West Ham's training ground and his was the only voice you could hear, bossing everybody around. England had an exceptional group of leaders when you look through that squad: Sol Campbell, Stuart Pearce, Alan Shearer, Teddy Sheringham, Gary Neville, David Seaman, Gareth Southgate and Paul Ince. They could all have been captains but Tony was special. They had fun characters as well. They would have Gazza making all the players laugh every day. He would be waking them up at 2am to play table tennis or squash. He went fishing with David Seaman one day during the tournament and fell off the jetty into the sea when he was trying to cast. It was like a mad house but it would have relaxed the players between games and stopped them worrying about all the outside expectation. It would have been the same having Gazza around at the 1990 World Cup, when we also reached the semi-final. Yes, I am sure Gazza could sometimes be a pain but don't underestimate having someone who lightens the mood and makes you smile, especially when you are under big pressure and away for a long period. In 1996 England also had a manager with a big bubbly personality in Terry Venables, who the players loved. He used to get up and sing a song sometimes. He would say that he did not want his players uptight when it was time to play. They laughed at the right times and were serious at the right times. That England team had a fantastic spirit.

You rely on good characters as well as players as a manager. They run the dressing-room and they can make or break you. You need the powerful individuals and you have got to keep them on side. If you do that, it is an easy job. If you lose them they can turn the dressing-room and, once that happens to a manager, your days are almost certainly numbered.

Lawrie McMenemy was a fantastic manager with a similar outlook who would instinctively know how to build spirit. He told me that he would sometimes come in of a morning at Southampton and find that Micky Channon, Alan Ball and Kevin Keegan would all have their racing binoculars hung up ready in the dressing-room. They wanted to get to Newbury as soon as possible after training. How did Lawrie react? He would say, 'Right, give me a good hour, then you will finish in time and you can get off.' They would come out and train like lunatics, shower and be off to the races. That's good management. Bad management would be, 'No, sorry, lads, you are here to 1pm. You can't do that, it's not on my plan. It's not in the rule-book here. It's not the thing to do.' Lawrie knew they wanted a day out and that it would do the team more good than making them listen to him and have them all moaning behind his back. Channon, Ball and Keegan were the guv'nors of the club, and you don't need to be upsetting them without a very good reason. They would have given Lawrie an intense morning of training, had a great day and, guess what?, every Saturday they would go out and run their socks off for Lawrie and play some of the most fantastic football. Yet that was all underpinned by the spirit Lawrie had created by knowing how to manage these top players.

Horse-racing was certainly something I also used to good effect many times. If I sensed that the team was struggling and feeling the pressure, it was amazing how often a season could recover momentum by taking everybody away from the training ground. A day out at the races, find a little

Italian afterwards, have some grub, a glass of wine, a laugh together and then go again the next day. Our performances would invariably take off the following Saturday. I did it with Portsmouth at Cheltenham in the season of our 'Great Escape' in 2006, when we stayed up after looking doomed, and also with Tottenham after I took over from Juande Ramos in 2008. A day at the races usually worked for my teams but, really, it was about getting time together, having fun and loosening everyone up. You have to be able to relax if you are going to play, and sometimes you need something different. It's all about doing whatever it takes to prepare for a Saturday afternoon.

That was also my attitude before the 2008 FA Cup final. We had beaten Manchester United at Old Trafford in the quarter-finals and were big favourites against Cardiff City. That could have put us under pressure so I felt that a good way to relax the lads would be an Italian restaurant down near Windsor. We also arranged for a karaoke. John Utaka, who would provide the assist for Kanu's winning goal the following afternoon, was memorable with his Bob Marley impersonation – 'No Woman, No Cry' – it was hilarious. Then came Hermann Hreidarsson, who had brought along his full white Elvis Presley outfit, including the shoes and a big gold chain. He had even had his hair done. The singing was diabolical, but he had all the moves. We laughed so much. You couldn't go after him. My friend, the entertainer Kenny Lynch, was going to sing a few songs but he just said, 'No, I can't follow that.'

I was never a manager who liked my players out boozing but I would let them have a glass of wine now and again, and we did that night before the Cup final. Brian Clough would go even further in his team building. The stories are unbelievable. When the players arrived at the hotel for their League Cup final in 1978, he simply told them to dump their bags and come to the bar. Half a dozen bottles of champagne and some sandwiches soon appeared. When John O'Hare protested that he preferred bitter, trays of ale came out. The party went on until nearly 2am. No one was allowed to leave but they won the final 3–2, with Tony Woodcock scoring what proved to be the winner. On another occasion, Cloughie made the team-bus stop on the way to a game so they could have a lunchtime pint of beer at a pub they were passing. People also think that Fergie had this iron fist and that every player at Manchester United was scared to move, but I don't think it was like that at all. The players were out socialising together at the right times and would have a day at Chester Races.

I did not like these team activities to be too organised, though, and would prefer to let the players unwind more naturally – but it has got more difficult, and you hear of many more leftfield methods that managers will try to employ. Neil Warnock once had his players stay overnight on the North Yorkshire Moors and said the experience was like something from *I'm A Celebrity ... Get Me Out of Here*. Dave Bassett would take the Wimbledon Crazy Gang to various tough army camps around England and even Europe. Dave reckons that he drew inspiration from how Dolly Parton once appeared in a film with Jane Fonda and learned everybody's lines so that she could always step in for the crew. He wanted to give the players that mindset of being instinctively willing and able to cover each other's backs. He also wanted them to learn how to feel comfortable in uncomfortable situations. He would have them in tunnels and abseiling down mountains. Eddie Howe can also be leftfield in the ways that he tries to build spirit and, when he was at Burnley, he took the players out herding sheep. The way he then took Bournemouth from League One to the Premier League was undoubtedly underpinned by the collective ethos he'd created. The entire back four of Tommy Elphick, Steve Cook, Simon Francis and Charlie Daniels came up together through the divisions at a time when they must have doubted whether they would ever have Premier League careers. I spoke with Tommy during their first season in the Premier League in 2015 and you could sense his influence on the group and also how they had all used previous knockbacks as motivation. You do find that the British lads can appreciate it a bit more if they reach the Premier League later in their careers.

Some managers get stuck in themselves. Mauricio Pochettino has walked over hot coals with his players. Martin Allen, my old player at West Ham, regularly seems to jump in rivers for the benefit of his players. Martin is mad, full stop, but the moment he takes a team I always know that he is going to do well because he has got the most important managerial ingredient of all: enthusiasm. A manager can drag even a reluctant group of players with him if he retains that enthusiasm. It becomes infectious in creating team spirit and it is the foundation, really, for the job. Bill Shankly would always say that you are nothing without enthusiasm and I think that applies to any trade or walk of life. Shankly's genius, though, was in spreading that enthusiasm beyond just the players and his staff but also into the Liverpool public. He created a unity that you felt not only out on the pitch but also among the fans on the terraces at Anfield. That spirit has survived all the change and, even against rivals with more money, remained an incredible strength of Liverpool. José Mourinho talked about how he had never before seen a club's fans score after a disputed Luis García goal took Liverpool past Chelsea in the Champions League semi-final of 2005. The spirit that ran through the whole club was also vital in how they then rallied to win the final against an AC Milan team that, on paper, should have been superior.

There has been a big change, however, during this past decade in the interactions between players. They speak to each other less, and that is a big challenge to a manager's ability to nurture spirit. It is partly down to the mix of nationalities now in the dressing-room, and an inevitable language barrier, but also technology. When we used to get on the team-coach, we would all be talking about the game. Then we might divide up into one lot playing cards and another probably still chatting about football. You would all be interacting for five hours solid. There was nothing else to do: there were no televisions to begin with and, even when they were installed on some coaches in the 1980s, you could never get a picture –

it would be fuzz all the way. Players tend to travel now in their own world with headphones on. They are playing games or listening to music. They are all in their zone, or whatever it is they call it. There's very little chat and virtually no asking each other what they have been up to. The game now is full of very, very quiet players and, believe it or not, an awful lot of them are not much interested in football beyond their own situation. It makes someone like John Terry, who is bossing people, pushing the team and organising them, still worth their weight in gold. I think that also spreads across the pitch, where you need personalities who will communicate well.

I remain convinced, though, that the unseen and immeasurable value of team spirit is often behind success. It can just flow naturally but, if not, it is the job of the manager to be creative in bringing it out. Arsène Wenger describes team spirit as 'delicate' and something everyone at the club should consciously try to improve and consider on a daily basis. In his office at the Carrington training ground, Fergie had a big black-and-white photograph from the 1930s of workers in New York eating while sitting hundreds of feet in the air during the construction of the Rockefeller Center. The picture was taken in 1932 and called *Lunch atop a Skyscraper*. In the audiotapes for his book, *Leading*, Fergie said that he would look at it and think about how those workers were prepared to trust their lives in one another. That is how you want your players to feel.

# CHAPTER NINE

## PICKING A TEAM

Sir Alex Ferguson has always said that the single most valuable quality of any manager is the ability to make a decision. As well as having good judgement, that also means being able to shut out all the outside noise and conflicting advice before simply doing what you think is right. I would take no notice of fans, phone-ins, newspapers and, more recently, Twitter when selecting a team. I did speak with my staff and I was always interested in what they had to say. It would be as you might imagine it: all sat around, notes on pieces of paper with formations and how we might play. Some weeks the team would be obvious, especially if things were going well, but there would be other times when someone would say something that made me think, 'Yeah, that does look a good balance and a better idea.' I like listening to other people, and sometimes my staff would come up with something about a player or a system that would make me review my thinking – but it has to be your decision. You have to make your own mind up. You always have lots of opinions and information, but I would ultimately usually go with my gut feeling.

Picking a team presents a never-ending series of dilemmas that a football manager is faced with as many as 50 times a year and, whatever you do, there is always one certainty: those players who are not in the team will be upset with you. Their wives will hate you, their kids will hate you and their mums and dads will not have got a good word to say to you. Players don't go around saying, 'Oh well, he's dropped me, but he's a great manager.' In that situation, their view is pretty much always that the manager doesn't know what he is doing. Different managers deal with the delicate task of delivering the news in different ways, and reactions vary greatly. They can be explosive – as Glenn Hoddle found out when Paul Gascoigne smashed up a room before the 1998 World Cup – but some are altogether sneakier. Some players will go behind your back, constantly moaning and, even worse, tell an outsider what your team is.

Danny Williams, who became manager of Sheffield Wednesday after beating Arsenal in the League Cup final with Swindon Town in 1969, had a simple way of avoiding any aggravation. Like most managers to this day, Danny would inform his players about the team on a Friday. And like many managers from his era in the 1960s and 1970s, he would do it by simply pinning a teamsheet up on the dressing-room wall, which would contain the names of the four sides. There would be a first team, reserve team, A team and youth team. There were only 13 players with each team back then, meaning pretty much everyone at the club played on a Saturday. The reserve team and the first team would rotate their matches at the stadium. There was one difference, however, with Danny. He would wait until the players were all out training. He would then come into the dressing-room and pin up the teamsheet. And then he would get into his car and drive back to Barnsley where he lived. The players would all come running in from training, go looking for the teamsheet and, of course, some would have the needle because they weren't playing in the team they expected to be in. They would go looking for Danny but, by that time, he was back at home and having a cup of tea in his living room. The next time he'd be with most of the players would be Monday morning, when the process of preparing for the next match had already begun.

Ron Greenwood at West Ham didn't quite take it that far but he was also one to avoid confrontation. We would never work on team shape during the week, and Fridays would always be a very quiet day in terms of training. It meant that the first time you would know of Ron's team would be a Friday morning. We would finish training and all be sitting around, waiting to know the teams. Ron would walk in, pin the four teams up on the board then walk straight out. No hanging about. There was no conflict, no time for anyone to say, 'Why aren't I playing?' He was gone.

I would generally tell the players what the team was going to be on the day before a game because by then you would normally be working on set-plays, shadow work and shape, but there were exceptions and things would sometimes happen outside your control. If you have doubts over players' fitness you might want to wait because there is nothing worse than picking a team, getting injuries close to the game and then having to go back to someone who has got the raving hump and saying, 'You are playing now.' We had a big problem at Tottenham before we played the Champions League quarter-final against Real Madrid in 2011 when Aaron Lennon went sick, literally a few minutes before the game. He came in from the warm-up and was not fit to play. The teamsheet had already gone in and we had to make the change as we were going onto the pitch. I did not have a like-for-like replacement, and so it meant reorganising the core of the team. Jermaine Jenas came on. Luka Modrić moved to the left and Gareth Bale to the right. Real Madrid were a very good team, but it did upset our balance and we were beaten 4–0.

The training and final preparation you might do on the day before or morning of a game can vary hugely. Some managers will prefer to be watching videos of the opposition and doing lots of tactical stuff on shape and set-plays. Others will go for something very light. I would usually work on the shape of the team and my set-plays but, equally, if you got a win the previous week after a fun nine-a-side or not even training at all, you might follow that. Under Ron at West Ham, Friday was always a day when the players were left to their own devices. Some would run around the outside of the pitch or do a few sprints. Others might just have a game of head tennis in the gym. My favourite was Johnny 'Budgie' Byrne. He was the England centre-forward and one of the best players I have

ever seen. Budgie would always arrive on a Friday with a copy
of the *Sporting Life* under his arm. He would come out of the
tunnel, walk around the pitch behind the goal and sit on the
far corner at Upton Park on the benches where the First Aid
men would be. Paddy, who was the old assistant groundsman,
would then make him a tea (in the same chipped mug every
week). Budgie would sit there, with a pen, working out the
horses for his day. He would be there for about half an hour,
studying the form, before strolling back to the dressing-room.
That was his Friday. Every week. On the Friday evening before
home games, we would all be out at West Ham Stadium dog
track. Away games, believe it or not, were often the same. We
would get to the hotel where we were staying and, if there
was a dog track nearby, we would jump in a taxi and spend the
evening there. Budgie or Alan Sealey, who was Les Sealey's
uncle, would usually organise it. They were not late nights –
we would be back at the hotel by about 10pm – but you could
not imagine that happening before an away match now.

The tradition when I first arrived as assistant manager
at Bournemouth would be that Friday was when we played
nine-a-side out on the forecourt. It was competitive and
the lads loved it. Dave Webb was the manager and the rules
were simple: no one could leave until his side were ahead. He
would then announce his team but we could all be out there
playing for two hours before we knew who he had picked for
the Saturday.

Another reason you might wait until the day of the game
to announce your team is to avoid the build-up of pressure

on a player, especially a young one. That obviously depends on their character, but one of the best examples of a managed debut was Roy Keane's at Nottingham Forest. Brian Clough never worked on team shape. He wanted to keep everyone on their toes, and so it was not unusual for him to even wait until an hour or two before kick-off before revealing the starting XI. Forest were playing Liverpool early in the 1990–91 season and his first-team squad had already travelled up on the Friday afternoon before the game. Roy had played on the Thursday for the reserves and was nursing a bit of a hangover when he was told to call around to Cloughie's house on the Friday night to be taken up to Anfield to help with the kit. Keane rang the bell, Cloughie opened the door and immediately made the youngster drink a pint of milk. They got to Anfield and, as expected, Roy began helping out with the kit. He was getting the boots out and hanging up the shirts. There was 60 minutes before kick-off when Cloughie suddenly told him to try on the number seven shirt. Roy did so, but still had no idea what was going on until Cloughie just turned to him and said, 'Irishman, you look that good you're playing.' The rest of the team did not even know who he was. His advice to Keane was simple: 'Get the ball, pass to someone else in your team.' Keane was brilliant that day, even though Forest lost, and he pretty much stuck to Cloughie's advice for the rest of a wonderful career.

You wouldn't want players to be happy about being left out but you do expect them to respect the decision and get on with it. Most do and, unless it was a very exceptional circumstance, I would not tell the players individually. It just made it even worse for them if other players saw them being called into the manager's office and could guess that they were not in the team. Instead, I would usually just gather them as a group on a Friday morning and say that, if anyone was especially upset and wanted an explanation, then we could have a chat on the Monday morning. I would start by telling the group that it had been difficult to pick the team. That was always true. I would say, 'Some of you will be disappointed, I understand that, and it's not easy for me either. I wish you could all play; but this is the team. Anyone who is upset, come and see me on Monday morning. We're in it together. Let's all stick together now and get a result.' It was as simple as that but, of course, you are still going to get players who complain.

John Moncur used to sit on the bench behind me at West Ham and would be in my ear half the game: 'C'mon, get me on. I've got kids at home. I'm not earning good money like the rest of them. I'm on peanuts. Put me on. I need my appearance money, my wages are crap.' Eventually I would say, 'Get your gear on, then,' and would stick him on. He would always seem to get booked straight away. Even worse, I remember picking a team for West Ham against Newcastle United in 2000 and I had made Paulo Wanchope a substitute. We had signed him from Derby County for £3.5 million and, although he'd scored in the previous match, we had lost 7–1 at Manchester United. I went with Paolo Di Canio and Freddie Kanouté and so Wanchope took a massive strop before the game. He would not be a substitute. He wouldn't get changed.

We ended up begging him for about 40 minutes to sit on the bench. It felt like I was talking to a three-year-old. Paolo Di Canio got involved as well. I can still see him now, with his hands waving around, saying, 'C'mon, Paulo, we need you, we are a team, we fight together, we help each other. Be with the boys, please.' He did eventually get changed. We were losing 1–0 and so I brought him on after 53 minutes. He scored two goals and we won the game but what I also remember, as he came running past the dugout when he scored, was him sticking his fist up towards me. Up yours. You had to laugh, and it all worked out well in the end as he also scored both goals in a 2–1 win over Derby three days later.

A similar problem occurred with José Bosingwa at Queens Park Rangers. We were in the middle of a relegation battle and due to play an important London derby against Fulham. Bosingwa would not sit on the bench. He had been playing for Chelsea and Portugal and thought he shouldn't be a substitute. I thought his attitude was disgraceful. I fined him two weeks' wages, and that was when I discovered that he was earning more than my old players at Tottenham, who had just finished in the top four. I did not pick him again for more than two months, and he left the following summer.

Something else that happens an awful lot – and I have to say that it is far more common with the foreign lads – is that first-team players are very reluctant to play for the reserves or be one of the overage players in what are now Under-21 or Under-23 games. They are not used to it and, even if they might have been injured and out for several months, it can be very difficult to get them playing in those sort of games. I would estimate that 75 per cent of the foreign players will not want to play for the reserves. It can be a nightmare, even though you are only trying to get a game out of them for their fitness. They think that they have trained every day and they don't need it. I am the first to recognise the limitations of reserve football nowadays, but the refuseniks are still wrong. It has become a common source of confrontation between players and managers. Players will also increasingly complain to their agent, although, as I mentioned, it has become rare to hear direct from an agent about your team selection. If they want a moan, they will usually go straight to the chief executive or chairman. If anyone did come to me, my response would be simple: 'What it's got to do with you? What do you know?' They almost certainly did then go to the chairman or chief executive but at least they stopped bothering me.

Another relatively new issue these days concerns how team information is instantly spread. Mobile phones, social media and the way players are in touch with each other so much more easily has made a huge difference for the manager. You now get to know the opposition team every week. Somebody who has been left out will ring one of his mates at your club, talk to them and give them their team. It got to the stage where I was thinking, 'I am finding out every week, so someone else is probably doing the same with our team.' I sometimes waited until Saturday before announcing my team to the players for that reason. Even then, the players have got a good idea of the team from training during the week. Mostly, I did not care and was more worried about what we were doing, but a leak can make a big difference. In that game against Nottingham Forest, on the first day of the season at Fratton Park in 2002 (when Deon Burton scored on his debut), we felt sure that they would play a certain way. Then Nigel Quashie came in and told me that they were playing 4–5–1 with one central striker. He had spent two seasons at Nottingham Forest and still knew plenty of the lads there and one of them had spoken to him. It was really useful information because I was going to play with three centre-halves and we would have ended up with three against one at the back which would have left us outnumbered in midfield. We won the game 2–0 and, although it was only one match, it provided a springboard for the season and we ended up winning the Championship.

Just about every week since then, for the rest of my career, we always seemed to know the opposition team. It is terrible, really. That player who has been gossiping has let their team down, and sometimes I even got to know who it was. I felt like telling the opposition manager after the game and, although I never did, it would certainly put me off signing such a player in the future. I am not saying that our generation would have been much better when we were playing. The biggest difference then was simply that we didn't have mobile phones. We weren't ringing each other up, texting each other, tweeting or whatever it is they do. You just didn't have that contact with people.

Technology has also completely changed the process of picking a team for many managers. The amount of available statistical information is extraordinary, and sometimes it can help. You can also very easily confuse yourself. Usually the right decision is staring you in the face, and you must also think about getting a balance to your team in other less obvious and tangible ways. Bill Shankly would say that, 'A football team is like a piano. You need eight men to carry it and three who can play the damn thing.' Similarly, Lawrie McMenemy used to talk about how he always sought a blend of what he called 'road sweepers and lead violinists'. You can't just have the same type of personality or player running through your side, even in different positions. You have to look at your team as a whole and ask yourself questions: Is there enough pace? Enough height? Enough experience? Enough bottle? Plenty of organisers? Enough leaders? Lots of flair and imagination?

Pace is vital. It can come from different areas of the pitch – just look at what Héctor Bellerín gives Arsenal from full-back, or Jamie Vardy at Leicester City as striker – but you must have that outlet in your team. If not, opponents can simply play a high line in the knowledge that they can recover even if somebody gets behind them. It is similar with height. If you have not got several tall players and cannot deal with set-plays, then that will soon be exploited and you will have little chance. You ideally want four or five big lads in your team who are especially strong in the air.

I always liked to have people in my team with opinions. When you have got good leaders in the dressing-room, you suddenly have very few problems on the pitch. It is important then to look after them, listen to them and treat them well. I have been lucky over the years to have plenty of these characters. You knew what you were going to get with a Stuart Pearce or a Jimmy Case. They were great for me at West Ham and Bournemouth but I had to smile when Matt Le Tissier told a story about when the two of them played against each other. Jimmy was quiet, but a great guy, a fantastic character and he could really play. He won three European Cups at Liverpool and, in an era of very tough players, was one of the hardest of all. You really did not mess with him. I remember a game at Brentford when their left-back kicked one of our Bournemouth players. It was one of our young kids. Jimmy just sort of looked at him, didn't say anything, but he waited and waited. Suddenly the ball went between the two of them and Jimmy absolutely cut him in half. His match was finished and he knew it. He started mouthing off at Jimmy: 'You dirty bastard,' and all the rest. Jimmy was getting on for 40 at the time and simply stood over him, put his hand down his jockstrap and pulled out his hearing aid. He then held it out and said, 'Sorry, mate, you better speak into there.' Andy Gray said Jimmy was the hardest player he ever encountered in his career and tells a story about how, after coming off worse in a tackle with Case, Jimmy simply smiled and waved him off the pitch.

Pearce, though, was one of the few players who was arguably just as tough. He certainly terrified people. When Jimmy was at Southampton, before we signed him at Bournemouth, he also used to look after the younger players and help them through. The likes of Le Tissier, Alan Shearer and the Wallace brothers still look up to Jimmy but, in one game, a few of them were on the receiving end against Pearce. He wouldn't have gone near Jimmy but, even so, the younger players were hoping that he would get involved. They turned to Jimmy, as if to say, 'Are you not going to do anything about it?' and Jimmy just simply shook his head. 'Sorry, boys, not today.' Players like Pearce and Case have an aura that affects the whole team.

Graeme Souness was similar. He would never ever go into the players' bar after a game at Liverpool. He always wanted to keep a distance between himself and any opponent. The two teams would all be chatting after the game but he had that mystique about him and never wanted to lower his guard or get close to the opposition. Never. Only one person has ever scared Graeme, and that is his wife Karen. Roy Keane was another whose mere presence could change the culture of a club and ensure certain standards from the other players. I loved the story of Dwight Yorke's first day of training and how Keane smashed the ball straight at him. When it bounced off him, Keane simply said, 'Cantona would have controlled that.' In a different way, Bobby Moore gave us something at West Ham just by being there around the dressing-room. He was our leader. Everybody naturally followed him. If he had a key-ring hanging off his belt, suddenly everyone had one.

Putting a team together is still all about a blend, though, and, as well as a couple of hard nuts, I love people who can really play and create in my teams. When I had Paolo Di Canio at West Ham I knew at any second, even if we were losing, he could get the ball and turn the game for us. It's a lovely feeling to be in the dugout knowing, even if your team is under the cosh, that you could score at any time because you always feel you've got a chance. If you've got no one who is likely to create, as it was in my third season at West Ham before Paul Kitson and John Hartson arrived, you really are in trouble. I always wanted to have a Di Canio, a Paul Merson or a Gareth Bale who, whether it was the first or last minute of the game, could do something incredible and suddenly get the ball, beat two or three players, bend one in the top corner and just change a game on his own. You never give up then.

I also had Robert Prosinečki at Portsmouth and I remember another coach saying that he was a lazy player. Utter rubbish. It was incredible to watch him in midfield. He was a genius – one of the best footballers I have seen in my life. His influence kept Portsmouth up in 2001–02. People would say, 'Can he do it at Barnsley?' Well, he went to Barnsley one night and delivered one of the best performances I have ever witnessed. He got a standing ovation from 14,000 supporters on both sides when I took him off with a few minutes to go. He was that good. People with class can play anywhere in any era and they are also usually tough. That is what people forget sometimes. Lionel Messi is like that now; Diego Maradona was so before him. They get hit and still keep wanting the ball. One of the most amazing sights I ever saw was when George Best rode Ron Harris's tackles for Manchester United against

Chelsea. Ron came in and could have snapped him in half but George played like he was on skis. How he didn't break his leg I'll never know. George just rode the tackle in ankle-deep mud, drew the keeper and rolled it in the corner. Magic. If you are lucky enough as a manager to have a great player, or someone who can produce something a bit different, show them your confidence by giving them the freedom to play. They will almost always repay you.

One of the biggest frustrations as an England fan was how we struggled to find a system that would get the best out of all those fantastic central midfielders we had in the early part of this century. Of course you do sometimes have to leave players out to get a balance, but I always felt there was no reason on earth why Frank Lampard and Steven Gerrard could not play together if someone just picked the right team around them. They could both run all day, they could both tackle, shoot and head it. There was nothing that they could not do. All they needed was someone to sit in the middle, just behind them and let them get on with it. Paul Scholes would have been my choice. He could have sat in there easily, got it off the back four and dictated the play. If he had played in that holding role for England, he would have had 120 caps, 120 touches a game and, on a bad day, given the ball away once. With those three in the midfield, you could then have played a flat back four or three at the back with wing-backs, as we had such great centre-halves back then as well.

That is not to say you can always get all your best players onto the pitch and, if it comes to a choice between sacrificing your balance or playing someone out of position, I would always prefer to leave a player out and keep the team balanced. The best example I can think of to illustrate that came during the 1966 World Cup. I played with Geoff Hurst and Jimmy Greaves at West Ham United, and Sir Alf Ramsey was right: he couldn't get them both in; it was one or the other. Roger Hunt worked his socks off and would create the space for his partner. Did Alf get it right ultimately? I could never say we wouldn't have won it if Jimmy had played. I am his biggest fan. He was a genius – the greatest goalscorer I have ever seen – but Geoff got a hat-trick. However you looked at it, Alf made the right call. He was brave. It was one of the toughest decisions that a manager has ever made and one that was made on his gut feeling. It's a simple game, really, and, when picking a team and trying to get the blend of personality and position, you can give me all the data in the world, but I am still happiest to let my eyes and instinct be the judge.

# CHAPTER TEN

.................................................

# MATCHDAY ROUTINES

Managers are all a bit loopy sometimes. I've stood on the touchline clutching a plastic angel in my hand. My wife, Sandra, gave it to me during Southampton's relegation scrap in 2005 in the hope that it would bring us good luck. Bryan Robson, who was managing West Bromwich Albion in the same battle for survival, was no different. He went around carrying a mini-Buddha charm in his pocket that his children had bought him during a holiday in Tenerife. I had that angel in my hand or pocket during the entire run-in to that season. I have always believed in fate but now I do feel like it was written somewhere that we would go down. That team should never have been relegated. We were good enough but, even with the angel, everything that could go wrong did: losing or drawing games that we had dominated from winning positions; players getting sent off at critical moments; injuries at the wrong time; big decisions going against us; and West Brom, with Robbo and his Buddha, pulling off one of *the* Great Escapes. The game against Everton was among the most freakish of my career. We dominated and had played fantastic but were only 2–1 ahead. The match was deep into injury-time when Peter Crouch only needed to keep it in the corner to see out a win, but he gave away a goalkick. They booted it up-field, Duncan Ferguson flicked it on and Marcus Bent produced a worldie of a finish to volley it in. That was the last kick of the game. Bloody hell. We could never quite get the result that would give us momentum and some breathing space. It really was like it was not meant to be. I think the angel ended up in about Row Z of St Mary's on the final day of the season but it still reminds me of how much a matchday can be influenced by habit and silly superstitions.

Changes in technology, sports science and just basic knowledge mean those matchday routines have evolved enormously since my playing days but it is funny now to look back. If you were playing at home, you would simply report to the ground whenever you wanted before about 2pm. The manager might start worrying if you were not there by then, but that was pretty much it. No one went onto the pitch, you did not see the crowd, and we had no facilities anywhere else. We were just sat in what might be a very cold and cramped dressing-room. Warm-ups did not exist in British football in the 1960s and there would be no teamsheet up on the dressing-room wall. You would just have a look at the paper or the programme, have a cuppa and slowly get ready. The manager might have a little word at about 2.30pm but, at most, he would simply sit you down and say, 'OK, lads, let's get ready, let's play our football.' While that was going on, a band would be outside entertaining the fans. The players were not allowed out on the pitch but there would be a 30-piece band stamping their feet. By the end of September, there would not be a blade of grass left in the 30-yard area where you ran out. I saw Sir Trevor Brooking at West Ham's first game at the Olympic Stadium in 2016 and we were looking at the magnificent playing surface and reminiscing about how the band would be out there even in the rain or snow ruining all the grass in our day.

I can still vividly picture Jimmy Greaves and Bobby Moore before games. They were two of the greatest footballers of all time and they would each stick to a very quirky but definite routine. Jimmy would always keep his suit on until 2.45pm. No hurry. Then he would hang his suit up and get changed into his kit, kick his legs out a couple of times, go into the toilet, have a quick fag and then, when the bell went at 2.55pm, he would be off – probably to go out and score a hat-trick. Bobby was different. He would also always arrive early and look pristine. Letters from fans would be left out for us in piles. The biggest pile was always for Bobby, then Budgie Byrne, and there would be a third pile for the rest of us – about half of which would be letters asking if we could get Bobby's autograph. Before a match, Bobby would always wait by the door for the others to get ready with his shorts still in his hand. He would never put his shorts on until everyone else was lined up and about to go. It was his superstition. He would just stand there in his jockstrap waiting, although Martin Peters did once call his bluff. He took his own shorts off after Bobby had put his on. Cool as you like, Bob just took his off again until Martin could not leave it any longer. Then, when the final call came, on went his shorts and out he would go with the ball under his arm by his hip. No other player has ever led a team out with such class. Bobby would go straight to the centre circle on his own, still holding the ball. There would only be two other balls between the other ten players but, by now, it was three minutes to three and Bobby was doing the coin toss. You might have touched the ball twice, done a few little sprints, but there was no stretching, no warm-up and you were off. That was how it was. Every Saturday. We did not know what a stretching exercise was.

We didn't know any different, but things did change during the 1970s as English football became more familiar with the European game. Tottenham were one of the first to adapt after they played Grasshoppers of Zurich in 1973 and were offered the chance to warm up on some grass adjacent to the pitch. That was normal on the continent. Manager Bill Nicholson could see that it was a good idea, even if some of the Spurs players still point-blank refused because it was a change from what they knew.

You get between a player and his pre-match routine at your peril. It is impossible for me to be critical because I have tried just about everything but, when you take a step back, some of them are pretty barmy. Tommy Elphick, the former Bournemouth captain, walks straight into the post with his head and shakes it before every match – after once doing that by accident and his team winning the subsequent game. At the

1998 World Cup, we all became accustomed to the sight of Laurent Blanc kissing Fabien Barthez's bald head before every France game. Tony Gale used to drive the West Ham kitman mad by demanding a fresh pair of socks for every match.

There would also be some bizarre sights in and around the dressing-room. The late John McGrath at Southampton would always nut the wall three times, while the great Liverpool teams of the 1970s would have an unmarked bottle on the table before the players went out. What was in it? Brandy. Part of it was habit but, according to Jimmy Case, it really did get the blood circulating and warm you up. Rio Ferdinand was another creature of pre-match habit. He was a brilliant and dedicated defender who was also a very deep thinker about the game. Before he went to sleep, he would visualise who he was playing against and think about their strengths and weaknesses. He would think about his first tackle, his first header and what he would do. It would be the same when he woke up. In the dressing-room, he would always strap his left ankle even if he didn't need to and then he liked to play two-touch football. With Manchester United, he would always find an area with Paul Scholes where they could hit the ball to one another and, even when you might have other lads sat quietly, there would be balls flying all about the place. If Rio was not the captain for a game, he would like to go out onto the pitch behind the goalkeeper in third and, if anyone tried to take that position, it would be elbows out to stop them.

Even during my brief time at Derby County in 2016, there were similar superstitions. Two of the players would always run into the toilet at half-time and after the game. You'd be thinking, 'What's the matter with them?' It has always been very common to get players who want to change or park their car in a special spot. Some, such as John Terry, would even insist on a particular toilet. I heard that Carlos Tevez and Sergio Agüero once clashed at Manchester City over where they got changed. Tevez had a particular space but, when he missed several months of games, Agüero started sitting there. A confrontation when Tevez returned would have been difficult to avoid.

A very different sort of routine became established at Portsmouth. We had quite a few religious players in the squad and they would go to what they called their prayer room shortly before kick-off at Fratton Park. I say 'prayer room' but it was actually Kev the kitman's room. The tumble dryers would be going and it would get quite smelly and hot, but players and even some staff would cram in there. Linvoy Primus organised it and it grew and grew: Kanu, Sean Davis, Benjani and Lomana LuaLua were among those who would join in. Before one game, they literally had 17 of them in there, like sardines in the kitroom. I was very happy for them to do it. Results were good and it seemed to get them into a positive frame of mind. What I do remember, though, is going into the home dressing-room just before we were due to play Manchester United. There were only three players left in there with me and Joe Jordan. I was handed the Manchester United teamsheet and turned to Joe, 'Where has everybody gone?' He said, 'They are all in Kev's kitroom saying their prayers.' I looked over the teamsheet again: 'Scholes, Ferdinand, Ronaldo, Rooney, Giggs. I think I better join them.'

There were also incidents at West Ham that still make me smile. Martin Allen was one who always liked to wear the same clothes if he thought they had brought him luck the previous week. For away games, the dress-code would be the team tracksuit, while at home it would be a lounge suit. We were playing at Stamford Bridge in the 1994–95 season and I gave Martin permission to make his own way to the ground because he lived in west London and it made more sense for him to go straight there. So he got his claret and blue team tracksuit on at home but could not find his trainers. We were waiting for him to turn up and all he could find in his house were a pair of shoes, wellington boots or some garish pink Converse boots. There was no car park at Stamford Bridge and he was already late, so he ended up running in through all the crowds along the King's Road in his West Ham team tracksuit and these horrible pink Converse boots. You can imagine the stick he got. Anyway, we won the game and Martin scored with a diving header. I decided not to mention it, thinking that it would just be a one-off and things would be back to normal the following week. But what happened? We were playing at Upton Park and in walked Martin with his grey suit on, his tie and these supposedly lucky pink Converse boots. The rest of the dressing-room fell apart laughing, but this time I did tell Martin what I thought and we didn't see those boots again.

Those last few minutes before kick-off are quite a personal time. Some players want to shout and holler. Others are very quiet. Some are very relaxed and all friends with the opposition;

high-fives and swapping shirts at half-time which did not always go down well. Others could barely bring themselves to look at an opponent. Rio would ignore opponents even if he was quite close to them, which would always confuse someone like Jermain Defoe who had known him for years. Gary Neville was the same. He apparently even did it when his brother, Phil, tried to say hello when he had left Manchester United and was playing against him for Everton.

Music is also a big feature of a dressing-room. Neil Ruddock loved Elvis. I would pretty much let the players get on with it although there is a great story about Wimbledon in the Crazy Gang days when they tried to take a liberty before a match against Brian Clough's Nottingham Forest at the City Ground. The Wimbledon lot would play loud music. They would make their arrival known – it seemed like a way of showing that they would not be intimidated on somebody else's patch. Anyway, it got to the stage where it sounded like a nightclub down the corridor from the home dressing-room. The walls were shaking. Cloughie asked Alan Hill, who was on his coaching staff, what was happening, and he told him that they had something called a ghetto-blaster on. Cloughie sent Alan off to ask them to turn it down. Vinnie Jones opened the door in his pants and nodded at the request. The music was turned down but, just a few minutes later, it was back on again at full blast. Cloughie dispatched Alan a second time and, on this occasion, he advised him to say, 'Please.' Exactly the same thing happened. Vinnie answered the door, the music went down for a little while and then it was on full volume again. At this point Cloughie lost his patience. He left the home dressing-room himself, opened the door of the away dressing-room and marched in without a word. Even Vinnie Jones was probably in awe when he saw the great Brian Clough, complete with his tracksuit bottoms and green sweat-shirt, walk straight past him, pick up the ghetto-blaster and drop it onto the tiled floor. 'Now play your music,' he said, before returning back to the Forest players. Apparently none of the Wimbledon lads moved a muscle until Cloughie had gone. They also lost the game.

John Beck was also up to everything and would do things like leave the heating off in your dressing-room in the winter but then turn it up in the summer. He would have his teams taking cold showers before a match and favoured a direct style of football to the extent that he would supposedly incentivise long passes with bonuses. John played under me at Bournemouth, and the irony was that he was a really high-quality passer of the ball. His management style was the exact opposite of how he played, but he was successful doing that and he got some outstanding results. His Cambridge United team was also one of the most difficult I have ever played against.

As well as the angel, I have had plenty of other daft superstitions going on at different stages of my career. For a long time, I would drive the same way to the Bournemouth ground and park in exactly the same spot. It did not matter if there was a problem on the roads and the traffic was terrible. I would still go the same way. I would never change a winning suit and so, at Bournemouth, I had one run of 26 games sporting exactly the same blazer, shoes, shirt, socks and tie combination. I had bulldog cufflinks that I would always wear but, once we lost a few games, they went in the bin. When we reached the play-off final with QPR in 2014, it had poured with rain in the semi-final against Wigan Athletic. My suit was ruined but, even though we all had special new suits for the final at Wembley, I still wore the old one. And what do you know? We were outplayed for most of the game but the lucky suit paid off and fate smiled on us when Bobby Zamora scored the winner with just about our only attack in added-time. That is not as bad, though, as Neil Warnock in 2010. It is obviously sometimes quite hot at the start of the season and he was wearing shorts. QPR did not lose. So he kept wearing shorts, through some freezing-cold weather, right up until their first defeat in December.

Many other managers are the same. Don Revie at Leeds United was probably the most famous and took it to real extremes. His lucky blue suit became so worn that the players would joke that you could see his pants through it when he took his coat off. He would always walk from the team hotel to a particular set of traffic lights and back before every game, but it went much further than that. There was this theory that Elland Road was affected by some gypsy curse that he began to blame for any bad luck. So Don then took up the offer from a gypsy from Lancashire to come to the ground to remove the curse. She went into Elland Road and stood in the middle of the pitch, scratched the grass and threw some seeds down before doing the same at each corner flag. She then went for a cup of tea in Don's office and promised that Leeds's fortunes would change. That was in 1971 and more trophies did soon follow. Before that, his fear of birds had made him banish the owls from the club's badge.

Sir Alex Ferguson also once told me that I should consider dropping Gareth Bale for Tottenham when he went 24 Premier League matches without being on the winning side. I'm still not sure whether he was joking but I do know that he was also very superstitious. In the end, I simply stuck Gareth on with six minutes to go when we were already 4–0 up against Burnley. We couldn't muck it up from there and it made sure that bizarre run came to an end.

More general matchday routines evolved greatly, and they obviously differed depending on whether you were playing at home or away. They would also be heavily influenced by the previous result. If you were on a good run at home, for example, and had been having the pre-match meal at the stadium, you would stick with the same routine. It would be the same with your training patterns. Some clubs now have their players get together at a hotel on the night before home games but I always preferred having the players sleep at their own places so that they had more time with their families. I thought that by staying away, you also risked making it feel like an away game. Every club was a bit different. At Portsmouth, they would always stay in a hotel on the night before a game but I changed that when I became manager and told them simply to report to the ground by 1.30pm. I just felt that sitting in a hotel, maybe getting uptight on the night before the game, was not what they needed. I read that Pep Guardiola did the same when he arrived at Manchester City in 2016.

At Tottenham, we also used to meet at the stadium. Players would arrive at around 11.30am to 12 noon so that they could eat there as well. We had a room at White Hart Lane with televisions on, newspapers available and all the right pre-match foods and drinks. You would then make your way to the dressing-room at around 2pm and the players would soon be out doing their full warm-up. The managers rarely get involved in that now. I could often be sat in my office 15 minutes before the game with the other manager, especially someone like Fergie, and we might be watching the 2.45pm race from Newmarket while the players were going through their preparations. People might think at that time you are frantically going over all your set-plays and last-minute issues but, by then, your work is largely done. It would be the same at Old Trafford. Fergie was old school as well in that sense. There was nothing plush about his office. No great luxuries or trinkets showing off his achievements – just a desk, a few chairs and a telly. Usually he'd had a bet, I'd had a bet, there would be a few furlongs to go and, as soon as it finished, we would be out of the door with our final instructions.

The players now tend to have their families at home games, and it is a nice atmosphere for them afterwards, with all the kids together, especially if you have won. The players usually go home with their families about an hour after the game. They go out socialising much less than in my day but, if they do, it is mostly somewhere out of sight, up the West End or to private parties. It was very different in the era when I was playing at West Ham. The players had all grown up together and come through the youth team together. We were all from the same area of east London and it would be rare back then to have someone in the team from Birmingham or Manchester let alone continental Europe, Africa or South America. We would play on a Saturday and, by 5.30pm, we would all meet in the Black Lion in Plaistow or the Baker's Arms. The Motown music would be going and the landlady would have the most fantastic food out on the bar. There would be big plates of chips, roast beef sandwiches, jellied eels and king prawns – all the old East End grub. Our mates would be there, as well as fans that we knew, and we would have a drink. It would be lager, not champagne, like some of the players drink now. The wives would come down later on for some food. Everyone would be all dressed up and the atmosphere really would be amazing.

Travel for away games is an element of preparation that has been transformed too. In the early days at West Ham, we did not have a coach and so would meet at the ground to go by minibus to Euston or King's Cross and then take the train with the fans to wherever we were playing. Martin Peters had a little blue Anglia and he would see me walking and stop to give me a lift and save me the three-mile walk. The minibus was painted in claret and blue but was about eight years old. You would have Bobby Moore and Geoff Hurst in there and we'd all be sitting with two skips down the middle of the seats. One had the kit in and the other had the boots. That's all we took and we'd all be hanging onto these skips. When we went around a bend too fast they used to fall all over you. Team-coaches rather than the train then became the norm. You might make some huge journeys by coach on the morning of the game if money was tight. I can remember with Bournemouth setting off at 7am for a 3pm kick-off at somewhere like Bury. Mostly, though, the rule of thumb was that you would travel up by coach on the morning of the game if the journey was less than four hours. If it was more than four hours, then you would go the night before. You could end up stuck on a coach for seven or eight hours if you were going to Newcastle on a Friday afternoon. Even if you had driven up on matchday, you would usually book a hotel for a pre-match meal and aim to arrive close to where you were playing by about 12 noon before heading to the ground about 90 minutes before the game. If you could not afford to do that, there might just be sandwiches passed around the coach. Delays were not uncommon and sometimes you would cut it very fine. Nottingham Forest once got stuck on the motorway for a game at Tottenham because of roadworks. Brian Clough's solution? He simply got out, moved the traffic cones and directed the bus up the empty lane. They were stopped by the police but, instead of getting in trouble, Cloughie simply persuaded them to give the team-bus an escort all the way to White Hart Lane.

Coming back from an away game, footballers would always eat fish and chips. Heading back south, we would often stop in the same place in Walsall. Whatever the score, we would order them as soon as we got on the coach. It would be, 'Twelve fish and chips, six chicken and chips, brown sauce and ketchup.' We'd get there a few hours later and it was all ready. That was the staple post-match diet.

Journeys did not always go to plan, especially one year when we did a deal with a supporter who had bought a coach specifically for the Bournemouth team. We would always pick up the chairman, Dickie Walker, in the New Forest on the way to a game, but this bus was an old banger and would often break down. On one occasion we were stuck on the M1 but, as luck would have it, the Aston Villa team-bus drove past. They stopped and gave us a lift. The biggest nightmare was a midweek game against Preston. It was 10.30pm in the middle of winter. The coach would not start and so we all got out. Me, the players and a few staff were all running along behind giving it a push. It got going but then, 30 yards later, it stopped again. We all got out again and gave it another push, but the same thing happened. Eventually we got it going but, as it would not go above five miles an hour, we had to find out where the local bus station in Preston was. We then waited two hours while they tried to raise a mechanic to see if he could fix it. It was no good but what they did do was offer us the use of a big red double-decker bus. So we all got on that and were spread out all the way back to Bournemouth on this massive bus. It was 7am by the time we arrived home.

The experience of travelling by coach was also very different. It was just rows of seats to begin with, and you would all have to wait for the service station stop to go to the toilet. A big change was when we had tables on the coaches and then suddenly a bit of music. John Bond was managing Bournemouth when I first went there as a player in 1972 and he did everything right. Our coach was better then than West Ham's and John would pick the music on the big eight-track cassette recorder. It was always Neil Diamond. The tables were handy for those who liked to gamble. Not everyone would play but you would have a couple of card schools going on – usually three-card brag – and that could get a bit heated. People would regularly lose their wages. A lot of players back then would go betting in the afternoon and end up in trouble. They were from working-class backgrounds and a game of cards or a bet was a big part of dressing-room culture – until the influx of foreign players and managers. I was 16 when I made my very first senior away trip for West Ham and I ended up playing three-card brag with some of the players. I was winning on the cards on that first away trip when the coach got to Mile End, two minutes from my house, where I was getting off. Tony Scott, a first-team player, had done his money, got the hump, and I remember him saying, 'Where are you going?' I said, 'I'm getting off.' He said, 'No you ain't. We don't finish until Upton Park.' He wouldn't let me off. He was ready to physically stop me. So I sat on and played until we got to Upton Park. I won another few hands off him and he was even more annoyed by the time we got back. My pockets were full of his money but I did then have to walk the three miles back home.

Now, of course, teams fly far more often and the train has made a comeback. It is a relatively new change and I can remember even when I was managing West Ham in the Premier League we would take the coach to Sunderland or Newcastle. Paolo Di Canio hated it. 'This is crazy,' he would say. 'This has taken us nearly seven hours and tomorrow we play a big game? How can this be right?' He had a point. No one had really thought about it and Paolo challenged our thinking. More common now is going by plane, even for relatively short trips. In the 2015–16 season, for example, Tottenham Hotspur made the journey down to Bournemouth by plane, and Arsenal did the same when they went to Norwich City. The only exception is that the train is sometimes used in and out of London as that can be easier than going through Heathrow or Gatwick if a team is staying centrally. It makes sense. You hire a first-class compartment and the journey time from Manchester to London is two hours. It can easily take that long to get into London on a busy afternoon from Heathrow or Gatwick. Everything possible is now done for the benefit of the players and there can be separate transport for the unbelievable quantities of kit you take. It is like an army going away for a year.

# CHAPTER ELEVEN

................................................

# TEAM-TALKS

The team-talk: a part of the manager's job that holds enormous fascination to fans and around which a million myths and legends have been spawned. Part of that is because it is one aspect of our work that is basically unseen and, through various films and fly-on-the-wall documentaries, a distorted picture has emerged. A load of noise, swear words and abuse might make for good television and entertain people's imagination but, in the longer term, is of limited practical use to a football team. It will also eventually end with you losing the respect of the players. There are, of course, moments when something needs to be said but, in 40 years of coaching and working with footballers, I struggle to remember the times when shouting and hollering, telling players that they are useless or worse, has ended up with a positive response.

A team-talk certainly can be vital. Finding the right words, the best tone and the ideal moment to get your message across to the players can be transformative but it must also be backed up by the substance of your decision-making. Most of the work is done through the week. Most of the players already know what to do by matchday and, while there would still almost always be a group team-talk, players often respond best to a series of brief and quiet individual conversations rather than some grand speech.

There are basically two types of team-talk: the ones you deliver before the matches, and those during the week. The mid-week ones are where you have really thought about what you might say. There is less emotion. Then there is what happens at half-time and sometimes even full-time on a matchday. What you say to the players here has been directly shaped by what has just happened on the pitch and so is governed far more by instinct. This has the potential to be more explosive but still rarely goes that way, and is generally more tactical and concerned with what is happening during the game. If you are playing at home, you would usually have a team meeting on a Friday morning, when you would look at a video of the opposition and talk through tactical pointers. For away matches this would normally be done at the hotel on the Friday evening. You would then often go for a walk on the morning of the game after breakfast and have another meeting and a chat at the hotel at about 11.30am before you had lunch and went to the ground. It can vary but this might be when you would deliver your main messages, and it would be less tactical and more about building confidence in the players.

Some managers can find it intimidating to address a group of players and, to begin with, that part of the job is a completely new experience. The dressing-room is a harsh and unforgiving place. One slip will be remembered and players make quick judgements about you. No matter how much football knowledge you have got and no matter what clever ideas and tactics you might possess, if you struggle with talking to a group, find it difficult to hold their attention and cannot get your message across, then you have gone into the wrong profession.

I was 36 when I got my first managerial job at Bournemouth and I cannot say that the team-talk was something I ever found scary. I think it just comes down to your personality. I would always have a clear idea in my mind of what I wanted to say. I would think about it beforehand but I have never written it out or stood in front of a mirror rehearsing. To impact on a footballer, it has to come from the heart, be authentic and not seem scripted. Every week is different, but you always want to get a clear message over about how you will play and what you need to do to win the game. Above all, you have to find the words to make the players feel good about themselves and put them in the right frame of mind to play. That means being relaxed, confident and concentrated. You have to understand your audience. Maybe some people like listening to very detailed speeches, but I can promise you that does not apply to 99 per cent of professional footballers. Most of them are bright lads. You rarely get to their level without applying yourself and being able to absorb information but, equally, the manager cannot go on and on. A player's attention span is short and there is no need to be talking for 20 minutes when you will probably have lost them after 10. After that, their brain switches off. They are thinking about something else. You want them to know their role in the team and be mentally ready to go out and play a game of football, not sit and take some complicated academic exam. You want them up, focused on what matters but not cluttered in their thinking because you have over-elaborated something to make yourself feel clever. You must also keep things fresh and varied.

Occasionally you might use something from outside. I told the Bournemouth players before we caused that FA Cup upset against Manchester United in 1984 that all their players were so confident that they were in the directors' bar watching the racing only 20 minutes before kick-off. There's also that old adage about finding something disparaging that had been said about your team: 'Pin it up in the dressing-room and the team-talk is done.' I have seen that work, but no more than once or (a maximum of) twice a season. After that it becomes boring.

You mix it up and many managers also like to try something unexpected. Players do like that. A lot of their life is routine and, when something a bit different happens, it can really lift them. You have to be able to carry it off, though. Brian Clough certainly could. About 15 minutes before the kick-off to one game, I have been told that Cloughie once suddenly started singing 'Fly Me to the Moon' to his Nottingham Forest players. There was stunned silence and, when he had finished, he simply turned to them and said, 'I am a good singer but you are good footballers.

That's why you play for me. Now go out there, in front of your grandmas, your grandads, wives and girlfriends and your kids – go out there and make them feel proud.' They won, needless to say, but a totally left-field approach does not always get the reaction you want. Phil Brown is a clever manager and, although his decision to chastise his players out on the pitch at half-time during Hull City's 5–1 defeat against Manchester City in 2008 did stem the second-half goals, it was followed by only one league win for the rest of the season. Louis van Gaal can also be a bit different. He apparently wanted to show that he had the balls to drop any of his star players at Bayern Munich and so, in front of a squad that included the likes of Bastian Schweinsteiger, Philipp Lahm and Arjen Robben, he dropped his trousers. He later claimed that it was about delivering a message to do with team spirit, although I am not sure if the players got it. They lost the game 3–2.

Less is very often more. Roy Keane raves about Sir Alex Ferguson's pre-match team-talk for a game against Tottenham which, I hasten to add, was some years before I became their manager. It was just three words: 'Lads, it's Tottenham.' At a time when United were so good and had been so dominant against Spurs, that was all his players needed. Barry Fry says that Matt Busby never bothered with anything long-winded either. It was usually just along the lines of, 'Go and express yourself. We are better than them.' I have spoken to players who were managed by Cloughie and it was actually quite rare for him to even bother with a team-talk. He certainly never worried about the opposition. He would send the substitute off to get him a whisky. Peter Taylor, his assistant, might just tell some jokes and, if Cloughie said anything, it would usually only last a minute and be along the lines of pointing at the ball and saying, 'That's your best friend for the next couple of hours. Treat it like your wife or girlfriend – caress it, love it.' Apparently he would often sit in the dressing-room simply throwing a squash ball about the place while everyone was getting ready. He would also skim his flat-cap across the room and try to land it on a peg. The nearest player would have to pass it back to him if he missed. This would go on until the referee was knocking at the door, asking them if they were ready, but Cloughie would ignore him until he had landed his cap on the peg. Only then would they go out and play. It was a way of simply relaxing his players.

I learned at Bournemouth that the actual pre-match presence of a manager can be limited when I once stayed behind to watch the youth team in the morning before driving up after the first-team coach had left to play Crystal Palace. I had a nightmare journey. There was a train crash that day and the roads were even worse than normal. It was horrendous. I arrived finally at Selhurst Park just as the match was starting. The players had not seen me. What happened? They were fantastic. They totally dominated Palace, who were top of the league at the time, and went in 3–0 ahead at half-time. I finally said my piece and we got battered in the second half. We just hung on for a 3–2 win. It made me wonder if I should have just stayed with the youth team, or at least not bother with a team-talk the following week.

Sir Alex Ferguson was an absolute master of measuring his message. Clubs pay thousands now for the help of sports psychologists but, really, I find it hard to believe that there has been anyone much better than him, or Cloughie. Alex certainly could resort to a more explosive approach, although more often than not he would be calm, measured, but also quite unpredictable. For example, he might suddenly tell his players about a childhood experience, or about the characters at the dockyards in Glasgow where he grew up; an ex-teammate, a certain player or, perhaps, even just someone he might have met who was not necessarily famous but he found inspiring. He would often just mention how amazing it was for them all to be sat in a dressing-room together; players from all corners of the world. Sometimes his message would be nothing to do with football and it could work across sports. It was just a way of giving them some perspective about life. That can go a long way to easing pressure.

When Fergie helped out with the Ryder Cup team of 2014, one of the European team's sayings became, 'Remember the geese.' That stemmed from the time he told them about how he used to stop training sometimes and point to a flock of geese in the sky. He loved how they would be organised in a perfect V shape, each selflessly taking their turn at the front into the wind. He would say that if the geese can behave like such a team for their 4,000-mile journey, a squad of footballers can do the same across a 38-game season. Once he had delivered his message, I am told he would sit with his cup of tea and read the programme. He would often then invite the opposition manager into his office. The message was that he believed in these players. He was totally relaxed. The daft caricature people might have of Fergie frothing at the mouth and over-hyping his players before a game was total nonsense. Why would you want to create any unnecessary panic, fear or uncertainty in a quality group of players?

I know that Eddie Howe at Bournemouth is also incredibly detailed and thoughtful about his communication with the players and the messages that he gives. He really thinks carefully about every word he uses, how it will come across and make a player feel. There was one instance when his Bournemouth team had gone quite a few games without a win and he was trying to think of something different to freshen things up and get a reaction. So, with 15 minutes to go before kick-off, instead of the usual team-talk, he simply put an angry red face up on the whiteboard. It was one of those things you see on a mobile phone. I think they are called emojis. Eddie apparently still does that sometimes. Nothing too complicated. An image often works better than words and, again, it is simply all about putting your players in the optimum frame of mind.

Videos are used more and more these days. Chris Coleman did not bother with a team-talk in the moments before Wales played their first group match against Slovakia at Euro 2016. It was their first international tournament for 58 years and, instead, he simply played messages from the players' families telling them how proud the whole country was. The squad had already been away for several weeks and it was just what they needed at that moment.

Once you are at the stadium, the players will do their warm-up in the hour before the game and then you will usually have a few final minutes with them before kick-off. You might have a last message for a minute or two, or just go around individually before they walk onto the pitch. Everybody needs something different and, again, it is a case of building confidence in your team. It is usually simple and along the lines of, 'I look around this dressing-room, it gives me confidence seeing the players we have got. I wouldn't want to swap you lot for them or any other team. If we play as we can, we will win the game today.'

It is important to tell people what they are good at and play to their strengths. That is the message I would almost always give them. I'd simply say to Luka Modrić, 'Run the game, Luka, they won't get near you.' He would feel ten feet tall. I would tell Big John Williams at Bournemouth that strikers might win you games but defenders like him got you promotions. It was the same with building up someone like Kanu. Before the FA Cup final in 2008 when he scored Portsmouth's winner, my last words to him were simply, 'King, you are the best, they can't touch you.' It was similar with Rafael van der Vaart. He has since said that he especially appreciated playing under me because there were 'no long and boring' talks about tactics and I made him feel like he was back on the streets of Heemskerk in the trailer park where he grew up and learned how to play football. Good. It might sound simple but that is exactly how I wanted my team-talk to make a van der Vaart, a Kanu, a Modrić, a Paul Merson or a Gareth Bale to feel.

Half-time is different again, and more influenced by the emotion of a game, but is also the moment when clear and calm thinking can make the biggest difference. The first thing to say is that there is not much time. The players have a wash, they might get changed, some of them will have gone for treatment and some of them will start talking among themselves about what has happened. If you have good leaders, who are talking sense and saying something that needs to be said, let them get on with it. By the time everyone has got themselves sorted and is back in with you, there is usually only about seven or eight minutes, sometimes less.

You talk about the game. You basically try to keep going what has gone well or put right what has gone wrong. If you want to change the system or make a substitution, it is not a time to shout but to explain what you are doing and why. I would usually have a quick chat with the coaching staff – to discuss any changes we might make – before addressing the players. Good judgement rather than ranting and raving makes the biggest difference at half-time. One of the best examples here was Rafael Benítez when Liverpool were 3–0 down against AC Milan in the Champions League final and performed a miracle to win on penalties. He was planning to substitute Djimi Traoré, who I subsequently had at Portsmouth, and play Djibril Cissé down the right but was then told that Steve Finnan had a groin injury. He weighed it all up and very quickly decided that Didi Hamann should instead replace Finnan and he would switch to 3–5–2. He wanted to find a way to out-number Andrea Pirlo in the middle, and it worked brilliantly because that also gave Steven Gerrard more space to inspire the comeback. Even so – and this applies just as much to myself when I have made a good decision at half-time – I do always find it funny when we get all the praise. If the manager was that clever, he would probably have done it in the first place.

Half-time is also about judging the mood of your players and the approach from the majority of managers has changed a lot in my time. There have been managers who would throw cups of tea at the wall and start shouting and screaming, effing and blinding, at players. Some managers thought that is what you had to do, that it was all about having rows and throwing things, but those days are finished. You do not get anywhere like that now.

It is an approach that especially did not work with the first wave of foreign players. They just weren't brought up that way and were not used to having people criticise them in front of the group. They did not handle it well. Players of my generation were brought up differently and were used to getting a rucking off the manager at times. Today, rollockings are used sparingly and very often saved for when you are winning if you sense an air of complacency in the players. I know this was the case with Alex Ferguson. The hairdryer would only come out once or twice a season and it would have much more impact that way. Jock Stein always told Fergie that there was nothing wrong with losing your temper if it was for the right reasons. Fergie would sometimes premeditate it but the spark was usually either if he wanted to keep somebody's feet on the ground or if they had defied him or confronted him in some way. That was explosively evident when Aberdeen played Argeş Piteşti in Romania in 1981. It was the second leg and they were ahead in the tie but struggling. He shouted at Gordon Strachan, who turned around and let it be known that he thought Fergie's tactics were the problem. Fergie came in at half-time and there was this big tea urn in the dressing-room that he went to smash but it nearly broke his arm. That just made him madder, and so he booted the tray of tea everywhere and it ended up all over the walls, dropping down the backs of players. Former Manchester United players also love the story about Peter Barnes, who hid in the bath after being substituted and actually held his breath under the water in order to avoid Alex following a match in the 1986–87 season.

Another manager whose rage resulted in something comedic was Dundee United's Jim McLean. He once kicked a washing basket on the floor and it got stuck on his foot so, while he was still ranting and raving, the fitness coach was down on his hands and knees trying to free it up. Brian Clough kept it simple when Nottingham Forest were playing QPR in an FA Cup replay in 1978. He booted the door clean off its hinges and, said, 'You fucking bastards, you've dragged me back from Majorca to get you through against this shit from London.' That was it. They won 3–1 and he flew back to Majorca the next day.

All managers are different. I was brought up with Ron Greenwood, and he didn't shout and scream at anybody. He was always very constructive; he would talk about the game and analyse what had gone on – it was usually more about calming things down and getting the players to focus. David Seaman has told me about Arsène Wenger's approach and how it was so different to what they had known under George Graham. Arsène would come in at half-time and usually wait ten minutes before saying a word. He wanted his players to refuel, get themselves physically and mentally ready and calm down completely before he started speaking. He would then deliver his pointers just before they went back out, but the talk would literally last just a few minutes. That is different to most managers.

One advantage of the less is more approach is that when you do have something to say, it carries more impact. Against Liverpool in December 2009, Arsenal were losing 1–0 at half-time and Cesc Fàbregas said after the match that he had never seen Arsène so angry. It was reported – and not denied by Arsène when it was put to him – that he had told the players they were not fit to wear the Arsenal shirt. They went on to win the match 2–1. José Mourinho really believes that his team-talks are vital for him but did not say a single word to his players at half-time of a match against Fulham in 2014. He was so annoyed with the performance that he came in and just gave them the silent treatment. That would probably have shocked them more than anything he could have said and they went out and won the game 3–1. When they'd beaten Manchester City 1–0 earlier that same year, he also let the masseur Billy McCulloch, who was a bit of a cult figure among the players, deliver the team-talk. It would have been a way of relaxing the players for what was such a pressurised game.

Full-time is also often filled with emotion and, although it is not usually the time for much talking, words can be exchanged. Full-time saw the moment for one of my angriest outbursts. I was at West Ham and we were beating Southampton when, in the last few seconds of the match, Don Hutchison let their full-back run past him. They went down the line, crossed the ball and missed an open goal. I came in and started having a row with Hutch, and he was sort of having a bit of a go back, which was winding me up more. John Moncur suddenly got up to get a sandwich. He hadn't even played. I turned to him and said, 'What do you think this is? A holiday camp?' He was answering back as well, 'I haven't even played, what are you starting on me for?' The sandwiches were sitting on the edge of the table. The tray was just hanging over the edge and, with that, I booted it. They all went up in the air and landed on Don Hutchison's head. He had watercress and egg in his hair. It was all dripping down his face but he didn't flinch, he just sat there, still not accepting that he was wrong and still arguing with me.

Whenever I see John Moncur he always reminds me about another incident when he scored but then gave a penalty away for an equaliser. He came in and I started rucking him, giving him grief for conceding the penalty, but he was, 'Harry, why couldn't you let me enjoy it? It was the first goal I had scored in nine months.'

By far the biggest danger is going on too much at the players after a game and saying things in the heat of the moment that, a few minutes later, you wish you had not. There have been some pretty explosive incidents that have gone down in football legend. Mark Dennis was a very fiery character at Southampton and was once punched by his manager, Chris Nicholl, after a defeat. Apparently Chris immediately went to confess to a director that he had hit Denno but was simply met with the response, 'Well, it's about time someone did.' The flying-boot incident with Fergie and David Beckham also happened straight after a match and, again, flared up because Alex felt that Beckham had failed to track a player.

Fergie, though, would say that he had become a 'pussycat' by the later years of his career, and that one of his greatest qualities was to instinctively adapt to the changing personalities of players and find new ways to motivate them. Indeed, ahead of his final year at Manchester United, he brilliantly used the pain of losing the Premier League title with the final kick of the 2011–12 season to Manchester City. In the dressing-room straight after the match, he came in and told the players about how, when they lost the title on the last day of the season to Leeds United in 1992, the young players came out and Liverpool fans were asking the players for their autographs and then tearing them up. He told them to remember this day and told them never to forget the Sunderland fans cheering. He knew how to positively use the emotion of a defeat and, that following season, United never really looked like faltering in winning Fergie's 13th Premier League title.

Chris Coleman did something similar when Wales lost their Euro 2016 semi-final against Portugal. The players spent two hours together in the dressing-room reflecting on what had happened with the staff. They resolved to use what had been such an unforgettable experience as a springboard for more success. It was the perfect moment to have that conversation and should stand them in good stead going forward.

Usually, though, you have to wait until the Monday to talk again as a group about the match. You can then look back at the game, go over it and have a much clearer picture of what has happened. That was my style, and you can't really go against your nature. Jim Smith, who assisted me at Portsmouth and Southampton, did used to say, 'I never see you get really upset with the players, Harry.' If Jim had his way, he would have shouted and screamed a bit more. It was not something he would do all the time – and Jim was successful doing it his way – but he could occasionally go into one. You do also need to remember as much as possible what it is like to be a player. They are often emotional after games as well and, by and large, they do really care. I am also well aware that, for all my preaching here about calmness, I reacted terribly after a row with Ron Greenwood during my penultimate season at West Ham. He had taken me off against Newcastle United and brought on Trevor Brooking. I felt that I was being singled out and that I had been one of the better players. I walked as slowly as I could from the far side of the pitch to the tunnel. I was sitting in the medical room after the game when Ron came in and made it clear that he was not at all happy. I lost it. 'It's always fucking me,' I said and, as he was walking out and the door closed, I threw a bottle of beer against the door. Even now, 46 years later, I get embarrassed thinking about it. It's crazy and, after you do it, you do think, 'I was wrong and I shouldn't have reacted like that.'

When you become a manager, you then realise even more just how much defeats hurts. The job, though, is always to respond and find the right message the following week. The next team-talk is usually only a few days away. You have to keep it fresh and, whatever else has gone right or wrong, the aim once again is to reset the players and try to create that frame of mind at 3pm on a Saturday where they feel relaxed, confident and concentrated.

# CHAPTER TWELVE

# TACTICS

It was Len Shackleton's *Clown Prince of Soccer* autobiography that famously included a chapter titled 'The Average Director's Knowledge of Football' followed by an empty page. I know that there might be some readers who will see a section on 'Tactics' in a book by me, and wonder if they might find something similar. It is true that I sometimes sound off when I hear people bang on and on about tactics but, equally, I think most players and people who have worked with me would accept that I know how to set up a team and react to what is happening during a match.

One of Milan Mandarić's favourite stories is of a half-time encounter he had in the Crystal Palace boardroom with their chairman Simon Jordan in 2002. It was during what was only the third match of my first full season at Portsmouth. Palace were 2–0 up but it could have been 4–0 or 5–0. Simon saw Milan. 'We'll see how clever your manager is now,' he said, smiling. Unbeknown to him, I was completely overhauling our system as he spoke. We went to three central defenders and won the game 3–2 after two rare goals by Jason Crowe, who we had pushed forward to wing-back. Milan then saw Simon at full-time and, Milan being Milan, could not resist. 'You see, Simon,' he said, 'my manager is very clever.'

Paul Merson had also just joined us and always seemed to remember that game. 'I went to Portsmouth and I didn't know Harry really, but people would tell you that he's a bit of a motivator,' he said. 'But he came in at half-time when we were getting slaughtered and went, "Right, you off, you off, you two on. Three at the back." He changed everything.' Merson had worked with some top managers and his opinion was that I was tactically the best, but I know that there are plenty of others who just think, 'Harry's a wheeler-dealer, Harry's a motivator,' or whatever. That's football. People like to pigeon-hole you and I am well aware of being characterised as someone whose strengths lie far away from the nuances of diamonds, sweepers, wing-backs, tiki-taka or the 'gegenpress'. Yet it is not that I don't understand these methods or even that I can't see their benefits. It is just that it gets a little irritating to hear people excitedly give something a new name and talk like previous generations had never thought of things like passing the ball and pressing an opponent. It goes around in circles and, when someone is successful playing one way, everyone jumps on the bandwagon.

Don't get me wrong, I love talking and thinking about systems, formations and tactics. I must have spent thousands of hours doing just that with some of the biggest brains in the history of the game – but maybe that is what also makes me skeptical about the attempt to intellectualise things and present so much of what we see today as new. I was lucky, of course, to grow up at West Ham with two of the best coaches there have ever been, in Ron Greenwood and Malcolm Allison. Both men were implementing things you still see on the training grounds today. Malcolm would be fascinated by tactics and talk at great length about Herbert Chapman's old W–M formation at Arsenal and why England's heavy defeats against Hungary in 1953 and 1954 prompted this huge change in how we saw football.

Ron was more of a teacher than a manager and his influence on the 1966 World Cup win was huge. He transformed Geoff Hurst from a very average midfielder into a world-class striker by teaching him how to get across defenders and make near-post runs. It was the same with Martin Peters and, as wingers, we were taught to deliver the ball into spaces before they got there so that they could time their runs. Ron also invented the idea of full-backs overlapping with midfielders in the way that is so common throughout football today. It was something we just did naturally at West Ham and I remember that the coaches at Lilleshall were taken aback when they first saw a group of kids turn up one summer doing what Ron had taught them. Ron was well spoken and educated – very different to the average football guy at that time – and he was too nice, in a way, to be a manager. Players did get away with murder in some of their off-field habits but he really taught us about football. We all had to take our preliminary coaching badge when we were still teenagers and all the people that worked with him – the likes of John Lyall, John Bond and me – took so much of what we picked up into our management careers.

Malcolm was also hugely innovative and he taught Bobby Moore about defensive positioning and dropping off to collect the ball when the striker was expecting him to compete for the first header. He would then be encouraged to make an angle and clip the ball into his own striker's chest. Three of England's four goals in the 1966 World Cup final came pretty much directly off the West Ham training ground.

I was never wedded to a set philosophy or formation for the simple reason that I believed that the most effective system was dependent on what players you had in your squad. I was then flexible and knowledgeable enough tactically to organise the team accordingly. It was never a question of thinking, 'This is how I play. I only want people who can fit into this system.' It was much more about thinking, 'Is he a good player?' and shaping the formation to what I had. It was important, then, to understand what the players were most comfortable with, and I liked to involve my captain and senior players in discussions about how we would set up. I have had captains come to me and say, 'The lads are not happy playing three at the back. I know you want to play that way, gaffer, but we're struggling with it. We feel happier playing in a different way.' Or they might ask why they can't play two up front and tell you that they need someone else who can hold it up if they play balls from the back. You obviously don't always do what the players want but, equally, you need to know how they are feeling, and you have a problem if you try to force them into a system that they are really not happy with. It's no good saying, 'No, I want to play this way. This is it, you're going to play that way, like it or not, because I want to do it' if they're not comfortable. You're not trying to create something just for you. It is about making the team successful and, as much as you might think it's the best way to play, you've got to change if you really don't have any agreement from those players who you are asking to carry it out.

I had two very good little wingers at Bournemouth, so we basically went 4–2–4 and played our way into what is now the Championship in 1987 for the first time in the club's history. A lot of people thought we could not get away with it, but in Mark O'Connor and Richard Cooke we had two superb footballers and we surprised people by playing them whether we were home or away. Mark has been everywhere on the coaching staff since with Tony Pulis, who played in central midfield for us alongside Sean O'Driscoll. They were two fantastic ball winners who would cover every blade of grass, but then later I went to playing Shaun Brooks and Ian Bishop in the centre, who were great passers and rarely ever lost possession. They were real silky-smooth footballers, so the style evolved partly around playing how I wanted to but also who I had at my disposal.

I have mentioned the importance already of adding Trevor Aylott as a striker to the team and, again, that was about understanding what was needed to make our system work. I remember him arriving on the Thursday before the 1986–87 season had started and spending the entire Friday hitting balls to him. We had not won a single pre-season game. We got smashed by Crystal Palace and lost even to non-league teams like Bath City and Weymouth. There was no pattern to our football but, with Trevor, we just worked on dropping balls up to him and then playing from there. The ball stuck to Trevor. That's all we did: use our good wingers, get it out wide, and then deploy Carl Richards and David Puckett, who were our other strikers, to run off Trevor. I have generally always been quite instinctive in my use of substitutes but, at Bournemouth, we also worked on a change to our formation that would make us more difficult to score against if we got ahead. I had a midfield player from Liverpool called Bobby Savage, who was very quick and could also play at the back, and I would just drop him in to play three in defence if we got ahead during games. It almost always worked.

If I really felt that I had got two fantastic strikers in my squad, I would always try to get them into my team, whether by playing 4–4–2 or a diamond with one in behind. If you have only one top striker you have to find a system with one striker. If you have good wingers, as I did at Bournemouth, you find a system that makes the most of them. That was also the case at Tottenham, where we mostly played Aaron Lennon and Gareth Bale wide and then one up front with Rafael van der Vaart in behind as the number 10. That meant we could get Rafa between the lines. If I didn't have Rafa available, I could play Peter Crouch and Jermain Defoe up front together. They worked well off each other in a similar way to Paul Kitson and

John Hartson at West Ham, and neither of those two could play in any other positions.

I would always rather change the system than put people in positions where they were not comfortable, and so we were quite flexible tactically at Tottenham. To begin with, Luka Modrić also played off the left but I brought him inside against Chelsea, even though some of my staff argued against it because they felt that he was not physically imposing enough to play in that area of the pitch. Arsène Wenger was put off signing him for Arsenal for that same reason, but we played him alongside Tom Huddlestone against a tough Chelsea midfield that included Frank Lampard, Michael Ballack and John Obi Mikel. We won 2–1 and Luka still ran the game.

Having good players obviously gives you options in your systems and tactics. It was a bit different if you were Sir Alex Ferguson and could turn around to your bench and see Ole Gunnar Solskjaer, Teddy Sheringham or David Beckham. I had some of that luxury at Tottenham. Against Young Boys in the qualifying round of the 2010 Champions League, we were in real danger of losing the tie before half-time, but it was easy to ask Gareth Bale to drop back to left-back and then take off Benoît Assou-Ekotto so that we could add another holding midfielder in Huddlestone. I then moved Niko Kranjčar to the left, knowing that he would cut inside to give us more presence in central midfield and also leave space for Bale to overlap from deeper. We came back in that tie from 3–0 down to eventually go through 6–3 on aggregate.

Rafa could also play off the right as well as through the middle, and that gave me the choice in some matches of bringing on another out-and-out striker in Defoe and moving him out wide. That made the difference when we beat Arsenal 3–2 in 2010 because we were able to narrow the focus of our attacks and stop them playing through us in midfield.

It is often quite simple. People asked what my instructions were to Roman Pavlyuchenko, via a Russian-speaking interpreter, when he came on and won us a game against Liverpool shortly after I became Tottenham manager in 2008. My reply drew plenty of laughter. 'I told him to tell Pav to fucking run around a bit,' I said. The games I am probably asked most often about are those involving Gareth Bale against Inter Milan in 2010. We were 4–0 down at half-time with only ten men. I found a side room at the San Siro with my assistants Joe Jordan and Tim Sherwood where it was suggested we take Gareth off, rest him for the weekend and thicken up the midfield. I felt he was our best attacking player and refused to change him. He went on to score a hat-trick and destroyed Maicon, the Brazilian right-back, in the second half. We lost 4–3 but it felt like a win when we travelled home, and we just carried on where we had left off in the home game. My tactical message? I said to the other players, 'Give it to Gareth and keep giving the ball to him.' That was it. Anyone could see that Maicon was scared stiff and, sure enough, Gareth murdered him again and we won the game 3–1. Inter didn't have a plan to stop him. They just let him play and Maicon, who was supposed to be the best right-back in the world at the time, took a real dip in his career after that match. The Inter manager that night was Rafael Benítez. I really don't mention that to rub it in. He has had a great career and I have had plenty of bad days, but it just makes me laugh when certain managers, including Rafa, are made out to be tactical geniuses who can supposedly see things that the rest of us can't. Those games against Inter also marked the arrival of Gareth as a world-class attacking player. He could also have been the best left-back or left-winger in the world but, as he developed, I eventually wanted to set him free. I know Tottenham fans would sing, 'Gareth Bale, he plays on the left,' but what was maybe not appreciated was how much easier it is tactically to contain someone if they are stuck out on the touchline and you know where they are going to be. Opponents could just park a player on him, whereas if he was roaming free they would have to decide whether to do a proper man-to-man job on him that would be very difficult to execute and could also open up big spaces elsewhere.

I would rarely ask players to do a specific man-marking job on an opponent, but you might set up in a specific way if you needed to counter an opponent who was especially influential. I remember once doing that at Portsmouth with Richard Hughes. He was not starting regularly for us but I used him as an extra midfielder at Anfield against Liverpool in the hope of stopping Steven Gerrard from playing. It worked and Stevie was complaining to our players about Hughsie being 'a rash' and how hard he found it to find space during the match, which we drew 0–0.

Maybe the most famous man-to-man marking job was Vinnie Jones on Paul Gascoigne back in 1988. I see Gazza from time to time as he lives near me in Bournemouth, and the story behind one of football's most famous photographs is one he loves telling. The match was at Plough Lane and Vinnie actually marched straight up to him in the tunnel before the game. 'It's you and me, fat boy,' he said. 'I cannot play football and neither will you today.' When Newcastle had played Wimbledon previously Vinnie had been suspended, but his teammates had all told him about this 20-year-old kid, Gazza, who was just on a different planet to anyone they had seen before. Vinnie knew all the tricks. He would pick up opponents by the hairs under their arms and he would think nothing of treading on someone's toes. It was a time when there were fewer cameras at football grounds and players could get away with a lot more.

Bobby Gould was the Wimbledon manager and had told Vinnie that he wanted a man-to-man job done on Gazza but, when they practised it in training during the week with one of the reserves, Vinnie got the needle. He got sick of chasing someone round in circles and stormed back into the dressing-room. Don Howe, who was Bobby's assistant, had to talk him around, and Vinnie duly followed Gazza everywhere that afternoon. He did a great job for his team in nullifying Newcastle's biggest threat in what was eventually a 0–0 draw. Yet what Vinnie did not know was that the photographer, Monte Fresco, had heard him trying to intimidate Gazza before the game. It prompted him to just put the camera on the two of them for the entire 90 minutes. Vinnie now says that he was only 12 when he was first taught to grab an opponent in the crutch if they got too close to him, but he would still have never imagined that a photographer would capture the moment so perfectly when he squeezed Gazza. The next day, Vinnie went down his local and someone said that he should take a look at the front and back-page of the *News of the World*. And there it was. One of the most amazing football photographs you are ever likely to see. They both saw the funny side and, after the match, Gazza sent some roses for Vinnie to the Wimbledon dressing-room. Charmer that he is, Vinnie responded by sending Gazza back a used toilet brush.

Credit also to Bobby Gould and Don Howe. They had been clever enough to set up their team in a way that got the best outcome. That is all you can ever do as a manager. The make-up of my squad persuaded me to play three at the back several times during my career. At Portsmouth, it was simply because I had good attacking full-backs like Matty Taylor, who were not so great defensively, and someone like Steve Stone, who could also do that wing-back job for me on the right. I had some very good centre-backs around that time – people like Arjan de Zeeuw, Hayden Foxe, Linvoy Primus and later Dejan Stefanović – and so it seemed obvious to play with a defensive three. I then brought in Paul Merson and, with the extra midfielder, could play him spare so he had no defensive responsibilities. I would just ask him to get on the ball and make us play when we had possession. He didn't have to worry about anything. You didn't ask Merson to track

back; you didn't ask him to do something that he couldn't do
or that he didn't want to do. It was the same with the freedom
that Alan Ball gave Matt Le Tissier at Southampton. You slot
players in where you can maximise them. We did the same with
Eyal Berkovic for a period at West Ham when I also played
three at the back. My instructions for Eyal were the same as
for Merse or Bale: 'Go wherever you want to go. Just get on
the ball and play.' Eyal was a fantastic footballer and, with
him, that system also worked. Above all, you have to know
and understand the strengths of your players. I wanted to play
in an entertaining way that would excite crowds. That is why
I would always want to sign a Di Canio, Kanu, Merson, van
der Vaart or Berkovic, but you can't be dogmatic or idealistic
about it. Once you have a player like that, your job is then to
find a winning system that best utilises them, and there are
many ways to do that.

So I do know that formations and tactics are important.
And I also know that, on occasion, they can make the
difference. There has been a massive increase in the specific
preparation you do about the opposition, and usually two
meetings a week will be spent talking about what they
do and how they play. My wider issue, however, when I
hear people go on about tactics, is that 90 per cent of the
difference still comes back to the quality of your players
and how you man-manage them. In my experience, just
about every manager knows about different systems but the
really great ones also know how to handle people. I have
not met too many tactical geniuses, and there are dangers

to excessively drilling the players. It can risk boredom and resentment on the training pitch. Players will soon be muttering on a freezing cold morning, 'What the fuck are we doing out here?' You can also inhibit players and make them frightened to play if you have filled their heads with tactical stuff. I felt that happened with lots of teams at Euro 2016. So many teams were playing on the counter-attack as if they had worried themselves to death about what the opponent could do and had forgotten about their own strengths. It was like watching two boxers when they are both frightened to throw a punch.

It's easy in hindsight but I felt we probably should have had a different balance at Derby County in the Championship play-off semi-final in 2016. I was helping Darren Wassall, who is a great young coach, and we obviously had access to every possible statistic before the match – how many goals Hull concede from corners; how many crosses they put in ... the list goes on and on. Before the first leg, we studied videos of how Hull were going to play and worked hard on that with the players. We lost 3–0. We took a more laid-back approach before the second leg. We didn't look at any stuff about them and just had a chat with the players. The message was simple: 'Lads, we have had a bad first game. We have got to go again and our pride is at stake.' We then went out and played fantastically and almost turned it around. More than ever, I think managers can paralyse players with too much information. You can also drive yourself mad worrying about what an opponent might do when the key is being relaxed to go out and perform yourself. I try to look at it the other way. What about making them change their style? If they are playing with wing-backs, let's make sure that we get the ball wide and our full-backs are spare. If we are playing with an extra man in midfield rather than behind the striker, let's play from the back, play through him and dominate the first 15 to 20 minutes. Let's make them question how they play because they are getting overrun by us. My message would almost always be to seize the initiative and make them worry about us.

I think my outlook about tactics and systems is supported if you study most of the greatest club teams and managers in Britain. It is something I did as a young coach and what struck me was how the same answer kept coming back. I haven't seen so many great coaches in my time in football but I have come across some great managers. I got hold of tape recordings of Bill Shankly and I would listen to him talking about football when I was driving to work. The tapes were riveting but there was nothing highly tactical in there. He would not be worried about the opposition or who played for them. It was all about instilling confidence, spirit and unity in the players, the fans and even the wider Liverpool community. There was no, 'We've got to watch this, we've got to do that, they're going to play this way.' That didn't happen. He would just do things like watching the opposition get off the coach and walk in at Anfield, and then speak to his players: 'They just got off the coach, they look like a bunch of pansies, they're scared out of their life – you can see the fear on their faces coming to play against you boys at Anfield.' That was how Shankly would talk to his players.

When my son Jamie joined Liverpool under Kenny Dalglish in 1991, I was straight on the phone to him: 'Jamie, what do you do in training?' I was the manager of Bournemouth and was looking for the secrets of Liverpool's success, the mythical 'boot-room'. But Jamie would say, 'Nine-a-side, Dad.' I would be, 'What, every day?' 'Yeah,' he'd reply. 'Every day it's the same. We come in, have a jog around the pitch. Two laps while Ronnie Moran sets up the pitch and then a nine-a-side. But a fantastic nine-a-side. Everybody buzzing. Everybody passing and moving. Everybody wanting to win. Half-an-hour each way. Then finished.' I asked, 'Do you do any team play?' Jamie said, 'No. Everybody knows what they are doing. We just go out on a Saturday and play at that intensity.'

Foreign managers and scouts used to go and watch Liverpool's training during the 1970s and 1980s and could not believe the simplicity of it. They became convinced that they must be coming back in the afternoon because they were hiding secrets. But they weren't. Liverpool were just a special club and their values were old fashioned but so effective. It was common-sense football from people who knew the game inside out. They would sit and talk sense about football. There were no videos or Prozone and certainly no obsessing about the opposition. The magic formula involved great players and sticking to the basics, and that was why they could look within for so long when changing manager.

Liverpool would also have these little traditions that contributed to a unique atmosphere. Every Friday, they would bring chocolate biscuits in and all have a cup of tea while they talked about football. I sometimes play golf now with Graeme Souness and, when we are driving back, we often get talking about Liverpool. There was clearly a time when they barely needed the manager because the players themselves would maintain the standards and dig out anyone who stepped out of line. Graeme told me about the European Cup final of 1984 and how, for once, Liverpool had done a bit of homework on the opposition. They had decided that Sammy Lee should do a man-to-man marking job on Roma's playmaker. But the players didn't know who he was. Sammy just walked out the dressing-room and Joe Fagan said, 'Sammy, you are doing a man-to-man job on their playmaker. You'll find him. The one who keeps getting the ball.' Liverpool went out and won the European Cup.

It was no more tactical with another of the greatest British teams – Nottingham Forest under Brian Clough. I know because, when I was at West Ham United and signed Stuart Pearce in 1999, one of the first things I did was sit him down and ask him about it. 'Tell me all about Brian Clough. What did you used to do in training?' I said. Stuart looked bemused. 'We might have a walk up the River Trent,' he replied. 'Or play a five-a-side. Have a cup of tea and a biscuit.' 'But what about drills? What about tactics?' He was, 'We didn't have any. A free-kick? Shoot. An indirect free-kick? Pass and then shoot. If we've got the ball, they can't hurt us.' When he took over at Leeds, one of the backroom staff offered Clough the big dossiers they had on opponents that had been drawn up under Don Revie. He put them in the bin and said simply that what counted was what his players did. Clough never spoke about the opposition. Yet what he did do was inspire a team of virtual cast-offs to become double European champions. It was just about understanding the game and getting the very best out of the players. John Robertson was little, fat, smoked and ate all the wrong food but Clough woke him up, got him playing, and what a winger he was. He turned him into one of the best in the world.

The key to Leicester City's miracle in 2015–16 also lay in how Claudio Ranieri arrived and was actually clever enough not to tinker with anything. He did not get all tactical with formations but largely left the team as it was when they finished with seven wins in nine games the previous season. That in itself was brave but great common-sense management. It was also a testament to Nigel Pearson's work the previous season and how the club had recruited players so effectively. Robert Huth was a brilliant and influential signing in their defence. He brought with him the experience of winning a Premier League title at Chelsea 11 years earlier. They also scouted players effectively. It was not luck or formations; just a very good team of players, even if nobody quite realised how good until about halfway through that extraordinary 2015–16 season.

Even now, when I look at other really top teams of the modern era, I am not convinced that it is so very different.

The Spanish lads say that Vicente del Bosque was not some great tactician but that the players loved him and wanted to do well for him. Sir Alex Ferguson was not a big coach or tactician particularly. He was a great manager. He understood people, could set up a team and inspired his players. He played 4–4–2 with wingers early in his time at Old Trafford and then adapted with an extra man in midfield, but there was nothing especially different about Manchester United tactically. They were always very well prepared but, first and foremost, they went out and imposed their game. It has been similar with Arsène Wenger at Arsenal during the last 20 years. It has not been rocket science: he has had great players, and he encourages them to express themselves and not worry excessively about what the team against them might be doing. Arsène will be the first to say that he had a great back four when he first arrived at Highbury, as well as David Seaman in goal, and every year he added one or two to it. But his starting point was Tony Adams, Martin Keown, Lee Dixon, Nigel Winterburn and Steve Bould. He then only had to tinker with it.

Manchester United were the same once Fergie had rebuilt the side and they won their first Premier League title. What's hard is when you are starting out with a rubbish team and need to change nine or ten players. Pep Guardiola has this reputation as a tactician, but I spoke to Thierry Henry about him and the first thing that he said was that he just has a lovely way about him with the players. They want to work for him and, let's be honest, he has inherited a few decent teams so far in his career. Josè Mourinho has a fantastic CV but, again, the first thing that Frank Lampard and John Terry will tell you is how the players loved him and he inspired such loyalty with his management. If you actually went and watched him work, you would not see anything that other people are not doing. Josè will know that himself to an extent, and I thought it was interesting in one interview when he said that he was not worried about his former assistants or friends having access to some of his coaching plans and dossiers. He then pointed to his brain and said, 'They can't put a data-stick in here.'

So much of management is about instinct or feel, and you can't plan for every eventuality. You can also be as tactically astute as you like but you have no chance if that bond with the players gets broken or seriously strained. There is no right way for managing a successful football team. You do what it takes, and so I still can't help but smile when I think back to Brian Clough and the simplicity of his instructions to the players at the start of every season: 'Goalkeeper: stop the ball from going between the white posts. Centre-halves: head the ball away from our goal. Full-backs: defend. Midfield players: pass the ball. Wide players: take on the defenders and cross the ball. Strikers: put the ball in the goal. And get your bloody hair cut.' The players would have remembered and responded to that more than any complicated tactical presentation about their opponents.

# CHAPTER THIRTEEN

# THE DUGOUT

People often ask me what it is like down in that dugout. How does it feel? What thoughts go through your mind? Well, I can let you into a secret. Whatever a manager might say in public, and whatever they might tell their players, we all have moments when our true emotions are no different to the supporter who might be watching their team from behind the sofa. So, yes, there were days when I would take a team to Old Trafford or Highbury and be stood on the touchline thinking, 'I hope we don't get murdered today. I really hope they don't get an early goal.' I would look at my watch and think, 'Yes, 15 minutes gone. They haven't scored.' It would be the same at 30 minutes, at half-time – or even after an hour, if we got that far. There were occasionally days when I really felt we could take it to them but, if you were managing Portsmouth against Arsenal's 'Invincible' side or much of that treble-winning Manchester United team, you realistically knew they were in a different class. Within the confined space of the dugout, and all the adrenalin flying around, that moment in

215

the seconds before kick-off really is a feeling like no other. It is what you have built up to all week and, however well or badly things have gone in your preparations, you know that pretty much anything can happen in the next 90 minutes. That area of about 25 square metres is where you take the decisions that can make or break your career, and so you do see people's entire personality change.

You would only have had to witness me and Kenny Dalglish at the Soccer Aid charity match in 2008 to realise what a dugout and the sight of a football match can do to two grown men. I was managing England, Kenny was managing the Rest of the World. We had known each other since 1966, going back to when I would give him lifts to the West Ham United training ground in my old Austin 1100 when he was on a two-week trial. Soccer Aid is about raising money for Unicef UK but, with 20 minutes to go, the score was 3–3 and at least one of us had an eye on the result. Alan Shearer and Paolo Di Canio had each scored two goals apiece earlier in the match but I had a problem. I had put Gareth Gates on at half-time but he was already knackered and I had used up all my substitutes. I was not sure of the rules but I figured that no one much would mind if I brought Craig David back on after he had already been substituted at half-time. Kenny was straight on to me: 'What's your game?' he said. And so we ended up having a row in front of thousands of people at Wembley over the substitution of a singer in a charity match. It was so silly, although I am happy to add that we did eventually get Craig David onto the pitch to help nick a winner. Yet if that is what

I love hearing stories about Brian Clough. His genius was in understanding how to get players relaxed and in the right frame of mind to perform for him. He never cluttered minds with complicated information about the opposition. Here he is launching the *Football Fortunes* computer game in 1986, in which gamers could put themselves in the position of team manager. He quipped, 'I'm going to programme mine to pick our team, run the club, take my dog for a walk and attend board meetings.'

The 'Ron Manager' character on *The Fast Show* was based on a great old character called Alec Stock, who was one of my early mentors at Bournemouth. A lot of people like to let you think that there is some kind of complex formula but I learnt from Alec that it ultimately boils down to knowing a good player and how they can fit into your team.

The team behind any manager is hugely important. They need to understand how low you can get but also challenge your thinking. I surrounded myself during my career with many people who were also fantastic managers in their own right. Joe Jordan and Kevin Bond are the sort of people you could lay your life on.

Knowledge of the club was useful and I will always say that my best signing at Portsmouth was Jim Smith. Jim had already been a successful manager there. He understood the game, and helped me create an atmosphere that was special. We hardly ever stopped laughing. I loved it when Fratton Park would shake to the 'Harry and Jim' chant.

When Arsène first started in the Premier League I remember him being described as the 'chess professor', because he seemed so relaxed. Well, Arsenal were winning at the time. As soon as they started losing, he joined the touchline nutters. Here he's having quite an argument with the ref in a match against Porto in 2010.

There are a huge number of funny stories about what happens on the touchline. This is one of my favourites, when Big Ron accidently ended up in the wrong dugout before his first home game in charge of Nottingham Forest in 1999. He must have wished he really was managing that Arsenal team.

It is vital for managers to know when to give encouragement and when to get angry. Paulo Di Canio was a time-bomb and you knew that his shorts and boots could come off if you started hollering at him. He sometimes got special treatment at West Ham but the other fellas accepted it and I loved managing him.

Throughout 13 years of playing under Ron Greenwood, Bobby Moore would say to me that Ron had never once said, 'Well done.' We all love a pat on the back and you get far more from people by telling them what they are good at. This photo is from when they won the FA Cup together in 1964.

Managers will try just about anything to get a reaction, and you never know how a more left-field approach will work. Phil Brown is a clever manager and, although his decision to chastise the Hull City players on the pitch at half-time of Hull City's 5–1 defeat against Manchester City in 2008 stemmed the goals, it was followed by only one more league win that season.

We had a difficult situation with Luka Modrić in the summer of 2011 when Chelsea were trying to buy him, but he was never a minute's problem to me. People did not think he had the physicality to play in central midfield but I would just tell him to go and run the game. More often than not, he did.

Dealing with the media has become a much bigger part of the job. The best interview I ever saw was Don Revie and Brian Clough going at it on live television a few hours after Clough had been sacked by Leeds United. They hated each other. Can you imagine something like that now? The PR people would never allow it.

I've always been quite relaxed about my dealings with the media. Here's one of my signature interviews through my car window on transfer-deadline day. I would stop because I knew they had a job to do and had been waiting in the freezing cold for hours.

I've never had a strategy with the media, and don't plan what to say before a press conference. I try to be honest as much as I can. I don't think many fans are fooled when you see some manager talking rubbish about taking lots of positives from a heavy defeat.

Dealing with supporters is a totally different ballgame to when I was a player, when fans from opposing teams could stand alongside each other on the terraces, no problem. I felt the full force of ugly club rivalry when I left Portsmouth for the first time and it was probably my biggest mistake. Portsmouth people really are fanatical about their team but some of the sickening abuse you now hear around football is one of the worst things about the modern game.

Celebrating promotion to the Premier League with West Ham in 1993 next to Billy Bonds and Steve Potts. Peter Butler (right) was a fantastic influence on what was initially a difficult group. Winning is the best feeling but the satisfaction is fleeting and you are always thinking about the next challenge.

Being a manager is the best job in the world but the lows were horrible. No one feels the loss as badly and sleepless nights were part of my life for more than 30 years. You can see the weight of the world on my shoulders here after we lost to Chelsea in the 2012 FA Cup semi-final but I have still loved nearly every minute of my lifetime in football.

it can be like down in the dugout during a fun game, you can imagine how it can get if your livelihood hinges on the result. Gordon Strachan, the Scotland manager, put it like this in his autobiography: 'You look across at the other manager and think, "Daft bugger." Then you realise you are behaving the same way. One minute you are saying to yourself, "You need to calm down," and the next minute you are going off your head again.'

No dugout has the same feeling. There are those right on top of the pitch, like Fratton Park, and those which are set back, a bit like Old Trafford, where you actually go up a few stairs before taking your seat. There are those where you come straight out of the tunnel and you are immediately in there, but also others where you walk all the way along the touchline in front of the fans. At Craven Cottage you walk across the entire width of the pitch at the same end as the away fans. At some grounds there are supporters very close to the dugout – I know some managers have been unhappy at the Emirates, where it can get a bit abusive. Being the manager of Tottenham Hotspur obviously does not make you the most popular man in the stadium on a Saturday afternoon either. Arsène Wenger got involved in the design and actually deliberately positioned the dugouts far apart to reduce the potential for conflict between managers. When the difficulty of making his voice heard to either the fourth official or opposition bench was noted by Neil Warnock, Arsène simply said, 'Don't worry, I'm sure you'll find a way.'

At Southampton they consciously made the home dugout larger than the away one in the hope that it could produce some sort of psychological advantage. There are grounds that you go to where you get nothing but grief from the home fans, and you know even before you have started that you are going to get slaughtered. Going back to Southampton, for me, is one. I also always had a bad time with the abuse at Villa Park, although I have no idea what I ever did wrong to upset Villa fans. I had a 50p chucked at me there for no reason, which happened to catch the linesman just above the eye and split it open. Half an inch lower and it could have taken his eye out. It turned out that the culprit was the director of a company who was watching the match with his son. A fan at Millwall also once chucked a ball hard enough into the face of my assistant, Joe Jordan, to break his glasses. Of other grounds, I always found Liverpool and Everton to have particularly knowledgeable fans who weren't nasty. To be stood there at Anfield, hearing the crowd sing 'You'll Never Walk Alone', remains one of the greatest sights and sounds in football, even for an opposition manager. I would always try to savour it – Liverpool was one club I would have loved to manage. I really felt that there was nowhere in the world with an atmosphere quite like it.

You are at varying heights in relation to the action depending on the ground. It's particularly low and hard to see what's going on at Elland Road as the dugout is beneath pitch level but, generally, the managers have actually got just about the worst view at virtually every stadium. You miss that broader picture when you are so close to the pitch, and you do definitely get a better view from the directors' box. Managers like to be able to see the pattern of the match, but few will actually watch even part of the game away from the touchline. One obvious problem from higher up is the physical distance from your players while issuing instructions and communicating substitutions. That can be overcome with technology but the biggest issue I had was that I found it difficult to be sitting up there in the directors' box hearing all the stupid things that a lot of the idiots around me would be saying. You would hear people criticising a player even if he was doing exactly what you might want. They would also be voicing opinions on your selections, your tactics, your substitutes and anything else they could think of. Eventually, I would get the hump listening to their nonsense and react by saying something that I shouldn't have. The rubbish they would talk might also distract me from following the game itself so, in the end, I found it better off to be on the touchline. It might not exactly be the calmest place but I could concentrate better and you do feel more in touch with your team.

Steve Coppell was one who would often watch from the directors' box in the first-half and would leave just before half-time to be in the dressing-room ready for his players. There is a story, though, that was told in the book *Tales from the Dugout*, that illustrates one potential drawback of this approach. Steve's Reading team were losing 1–0 against Preston before equalising in the few seconds while he was making his way down the stairs from the main stand to the dugout. Steve had not seen the goal and so apparently gave a half-time talk as if they were losing. It was not actually until one of his assistants questioned his touchline tactics deep into the second-half – when he was instructing players to push forward – that they all realised he still thought that they were losing.

Everyone has their own style. Louis van Gaal very rarely got off his bench to say anything. You'd look at him and think he might as well be sat upstairs, but that's just how it is: some managers don't really get involved, they prefer to intervene only sparingly and believe that has most impact. People like Tony Pulis, Gary Megson, Neil Warnock and Martin O'Neill, by contrast, are kicking just about every ball from the edge of the touchline. Bill Shankly was one who would be adamant that he could transmit his thoughts to the players just by appearing on the side of the pitch. You do feel like you're contributing something if you are down there, whether you are looking to make a substitution, getting them to push up or changing how you're playing. You think you are involved in the game and, in your head at least, you are out there with them.

The reality once the match starts, of course, is that the players are concentrating on their game and probably hear very little of what you are saying. You can shout and scream as much you like, but it definitely goes over their heads if you do it too much. I have heard former Aberdeen and Manchester United players say that they would wave to acknowledge

Fergie when he was shouting at them just to quieten him down, even though they did not really have a clue what he was saying. The only player you can shout at, really, is the poor full-back or winger on your side. They always cop it the most off a frustrated manager.

I have calmed down a lot over the years but the pressure and intensity of a match can get to anyone. If you don't believe me, think back to the first few years of Arsène Wenger in the Premier League. I remember reading an article about him in which he was described as 'the chess professor'. On and on, the writer went: 'Look at all those other idiots jumping around, shouting and screaming. Then there is Wenger. The master. He is calmly surveying the pitch. He never takes his eyes off the game for a second. He just sits still and studies every move.' Arsenal were winning every week at the time, with Henry, Bergkamp, Pirès and Vieira in the team. I reckon I could have sat there with a cigar going if I'd had that lot. Anyway, once Arsenal started to lose a few games, Arsène turned into one of the biggest nutters of us all. Bottles were getting thrown down, bottles were kicked, and a fair few shoving matches took place on the touchline. I have always found Arsène to be a nice man and he can be very humorous, although he is not someone you are likely to get to know well. It is no big secret that a few of the other managers don't like him. It might seem like a small thing, but a lot of it comes down to when he shakes hands at the end. He holds his hand out and he is gone. You would never get a cuddle and a few words from Arsène. He is always straight off down the tunnel. He did not shake hands at all with Clive Allen, who was part of my coaching staff at Tottenham, after we beat them in 2011, and Clive was pretty angry as they went into the tunnel. There's no warmth at the end of a game with Arsène, but I don't think you can judge him on that. It is a pretty exceptional moment and, from the times I have gone into his office for a drink, you can see that he's a very decent guy.

It was inevitable as well that the dynamic would change when more managers from different cultures arrived in the dugout. The British managers would all know each other much better – because you were from a much smaller pool of former players, but also because of the time you'd have spent together each year on the managerial courses at Lilleshall. The courses took place at the end of the season, and so it was a time to relax, laugh, share ideas, maybe do a transfer deal and also talk about some of the problems you might have at your club. The hour or so after a match also used to be less pressured. You would be in the opposition manager's office for a glass of wine or a cup of tea and bit of scampi and chips.

The foreign managers generally are less into this tradition, and it has got more difficult with the scale of post-match media demands – and then also the travel arrangements, which often mean dashing off to an airport by a certain time. It was quite common years ago for an away manager to spend a good half an hour in an opponent's office. You especially did not feel like hurrying back to the players on the coach if the team had lost. My attitude was sometimes, 'They've been crap all day, they kept me sitting out watching that, they can sit there waiting for us now.' It's changed now. You don't really get to know other managers like you used to – today it generally is not much more than saying, 'Hello. Goodbye,' and a handshake.

Joe Jordan, who was with me at Portsmouth, Tottenham and Queens Park Rangers, is another who is completely different once he gets on that touchline, and he would row just about every week with someone. The best known incident was when he squared up to Gennaro Gattuso when we beat AC Milan in the last 16 of the Champions League in 2011. Joe was the scariest centre-forward in his day. He would take his teeth out and have those great fangs but even against Milan, just a few months shy of his 60th birthday, he was ready to go. Joe was getting ready to knock Gattuso out. He had taken his glasses off at the end of the game and I had to step between them. Graeme Souness, who was commentating that night for Sky Sports, goes back a long way with him in the Scotland team and said that he would have loved to see Gattuso 'have five minutes in a room with Joe'. The irony is that Joe is the quietest man in the world from Monday to Friday; an absolute gentleman. I have also heard that Gattuso is a good guy and that he has been among those who have tried over recent years to help Gazza, who he played with at Rangers. Joe would worry about the other bench shouting and saying something to the fourth official. He would get the hump but nothing was ever planned, and I took the view that it was up to him how he'd fight his own battles.

Any rowing on the touchline really wasn't something that bothered me. I think it is a nonsense when I see other managers shouting at each other. It became a bit like wrestling and you wonder with some people if it as much for the crowd as anyone else. When I first started out with Bournemouth I did have a little period when I was up before the FA quite regularly, but it was mostly for stupid and sarcastic stuff. Really daft things like, 'Did your mum buy you that referee's kit for Christmas?' which the referee would not like and report me for. I always used to hope that Barry Bright from the Kent FA would be on the disciplinary committee that heard my case as he was a lovely fellow – always as good as gold with me – who I think realised that I did not mean much harm. Being fined a fortnight's wages certainly concentrated my mind. I didn't have any money at the time and would be thinking, 'This is ridiculous, I'm working two weeks and going home with nothing just for the sake of saying something to the referee that won't change anything.'

Well, that is very much my mentality now: you can't change a decision. The game is over, so what difference can it make? I know there are some managers who try to exert pressure on referees and their assistants – you even hear of the home dugout being positioned to make it easier – but I never felt it made any difference. I don't think you can influence the linesmen. They're going to make their own decisions. With referees, some of them are mad keen football supporters and so I think some managers might wonder if human nature could take over if their team is in a relegation battle and there is a slight edge to a decision, but I don't know. You trust that they're honest guys and they make what they consider to be the right decisions. We had one in 2011 at Tottenham when we were competing with Chelsea to finish fourth, and a winning goal was given for them that subsequent replays showed was a few millimetres short of the line. I could have gone off on one at the assistant referee, Mike Cairns, but it's the hardest job in the world, and I was sickened to subsequently learn that someone had sent him a threatening message. The best thing that has happened now is bringing in the new technology that can answer the goalline question immediately – even if I'll never know how it has taken so long.

In the old days managers could holler at the referee in the knowledge that the ref probably could not hear you anyway. Now everything can be reported by the fourth official although, in practice, they just cop all the abuse on behalf of the referee. It's ridiculous, really. They are like human sponges soaking it all up. They are not making the decisions and yet take all the grief even when they probably know too that the referee has made a ricket. I was only ever really interested in the game and what we were doing once it started, and have never found any benefit in arguing with officials. It was the same with other managers, although I did feel like sticking my foot out and tripping him up when my old mate Barry Fry ran down the touchline to celebrate when Southend United once beat West Ham.

There are plenty of comedy moments in and around the dugout. Mick Halsall, who was Barry's old assistant at Peterborough, once got so animated shouting at the players that his false teeth came flying out of his mouth. Paul Merson tells a story of Gordon McQueen being handed a teamsheet when he was working at Middlesbrough. He suddenly shouted, 'Yes, get in there,' at the top of his voice before a match against Aston Villa. When the rest of the staff asked why he was so excited, he simply said, 'I've got Ian Taylor in my fantasy team.'

Television means that just about everything is captured now and you don't always know you are doing something. You see Arsène Wenger so absorbed in what he is doing that he can barely do up a zip, or Sir Alex Ferguson jumping out of his seat at a burst balloon next to him. Substitutions can very easily become confused. Sir Bobby Robson could get people's names wrong and, for England, he once sent Gary Stevens down the touchline to warm up before actually bringing Trevor Steven on. I made a substitution in the quarter-final of the League Cup in 1999–2000 that cost us badly. We beat Aston Villa at home but I put on Manny Omoyinmi in the last few minutes without realising that he had already played for Gillingham during a loan spell that season in the same competition. The mistake was obviously including him in the squad in the first place but, to this day, I still don't know why I stuck him on when I did. I looked around and I just wanted to waste a minute of injury time. He could run, and I put him out on the wing and just thought he might run the ball down to the corner. I think he touched the ball once and, even then, it was to one of theirs. We still had to replay the game and got beat 3–1.

I always found that it was difficult to really plan substitutes. There might be certain things you do defensively to see a game out, or do the obvious by bringing on another striker if you are losing. You might also know that a particular player can only last 60 minutes and plan for that but, in the main, I would judge the situation as I saw it and not have any preconceived idea in my mind.

Big Ron Atkinson was a brilliant, larger than life character who produced one of the funniest dugout mistakes when, after being appointed manager of Nottingham Forest in 1999, he arrived pretty much direct from a holiday in Barbados for his first game at the City Ground. He was lapping up the attention as he took his place on the touchline, only to notice about ten seconds later that he was in the wrong dugout, flanked by a bemused group of Arsenal substitutes. He looked down the line to see Dennis Bergkamp, Emmanuel Petit and Nicolas Anelka before coming out with a classic: 'How are we bottom of the league with this lot?'

Ron was always renowned for how long he took getting changed and he would even lock his staff out of their changing area after training while he got himself ready. The story of a sunbed in his office at the Manchester United training ground was true, and apparently the players once saw inside the little briefcase he carried with him. They expected to see notes about the game and maybe information about the opposition. What did they find? A bottle of after-shave and a can of hairspray. As you might imagine, Ron was certainly one manager who could be relied upon to invite you in for a drink after the game, and he'd have his office full up with all his pals. He loved champagne. He once invited me into his office and looked horrified to find that there was an empty fridge. He got straight on the phone to his secretary and she came down with six bottles of pink champagne. He looked at it, winked at me and said, 'Do they make it any other colour?' Win or lose, he would hold court, have a laugh and then he would be out on a Saturday night and have people around for karaoke back at his place. He liked to sing and would have loved getting up and doing his Frank Sinatra on *Stars in Their Eyes*. His five-a-sides were also legendary and, even when he was getting on for 60 while managing Coventry City, he would join in, pretending to be Maradona or Pelé.

Another image I have of Ron is of him rowing with Neil Warnock on the touchline and then stepping back into a bucket of ice-cold water. It reminds me of a story that Jimmy Gabriel would tell about Ted Bates, the old Southampton manager. Ted would get totally engrossed in a game and was just the same at a pre-season match at the old Victoria Ground against a Stoke City side that included Sir Stanley Matthews. They were in a little dugout with an iron roof and all the supporters were banging on the roof and making a real racket. Ted might have been totally focussed on the football but the old trainer, Jimmy Gallagher, got involved and kept telling the mouthy fans to keep the noise down. Jimmy then went on to treat someone and, on the way back, he gave a little spray of his sponge to one of the loudmouths that had been smacking the dugout. Next thing he knows, the guy is down there screaming at him. 'You sprayed my wife,' he said. With that, he picked up the bucket. Jimmy saw what was coming and ducked. So too did Denis Hollywood, who was also sat on the bench, but

Ted, who had not taken his eyes off the game amid all this commotion, copped the lot. He was drenched.

Just about anything can also happen out on the pitch, especially when you have Paolo Di Canio in your team. One of the games I am asked about most often is West Ham against Bradford City in 2000. We were losing 4–2 and Paolo did have three pretty blatant penalty appeals turned down. He came marching over to the touchline asking to be subbed: 'I don't play.' He was sat in front of the dugout with his arms and legs crossed saying that he would not finish the match. I was, 'Paolo, get up, we are losing, get up quick.' Next thing, the Bradford players were dribbling around him sat there and Dean Saunders had missed a really good chance to make it 5–2. The fans came to my rescue. Paolo would always respond whenever they started singing, 'Paolo Di Canio', which they did, and he suddenly jumped up and beat about four players. Paul Kitson then won a penalty and it ended up with Paolo and Frank Lampard doing a tug of war over the ball for the penalty. It was like something you would see on a school playground. Frank was supposed to be the penalty-taker but Paolo knew that he would score because he had such confidence in his own ability. Even so, it took some balls to do that because no one would have forgotten if he had missed. It was a nightmare for me. You are helpless, 50 yards away on the touchline, but still worrying about how it looks and just thinking, 'Please sort it out.' Neither of them wanted to back down but Paolo eventually snatched it and smashed his penalty in. Joe Cole then scored to make it 4–4 before

Paolo delivered some more magic and laid it off for Frank Lampard to score the winner with a few minutes left. It was one of the great Premier League games, but is still most often remembered for Paolo's antics.

Very serious moments can also suddenly occur in front of you that can change people's careers or even lives. No one who was at White Hart Lane on 17 March 2012 will ever forget Fabrice Muamba collapsing in the match against Bolton. It was eerie how silence just fell over the stadium when he was being treated. When he came off, we all thought he had died. The doctors thought he was gone as well. It was just lucky that it happened to him inside a stadium where they had so much expertise, including one of the top heart specialists in the country who persuaded stewards to let him run onto the pitch from the crowd to help.

Another potentially career-changing moment was when Ben Thatcher forearm-smashed Pedro Mendes to the floor in 2006 when Manchester City were playing Portsmouth. It was one of the most reckless and dangerous challenges that I have ever seen in football. I really do like Ben a lot – and I know that he regretted terribly what happened – but what he did that night was a real liberty. I remember calling Stuart Pearce, who was the manager of Manchester City, after the game. Stuart had gone on TV and said, 'His momentum carried him into Pedro.' Stuart had been my player at West Ham and, when I spoke to him, I said, 'Stuart, look, you are respected by everyone. You epitomise everything about English football but people are listening to you there and they think, "What are you talking about?" You know what's happened. The man in the pub knows what's happened. The people will lose respect for you for coming out with what you are saying. Everybody is watching it on TV. Everybody knows what Ben Thatcher has done and you're trying to make out it was his momentum that carried him into Pedro and that it was an accident. You know it wasn't. Come out and tell the truth.' He went, 'I hear what you're saying, Harry,' and about an hour later he made another statement, saying that he'd looked at the video again and realised that it was a horrendous challenge.

There are times when the dugout is the best place in the world, but there are inevitably also moments when you are almost willing it to swallow you up. You are constantly trying to make a difference but ultimately, of course, it usually comes down to the quality of your players. I remember Howard Wilkinson telling me about one of his first games as manager of Sheffield Wednesday. They were getting beat by six at West Ham and Howard was thinking, 'Oh my God. What do I do?' A message went along the dugout to Jimmy Sirrel. He had been a successful manager for several decades and was something of a mentor to Howard. He was a wily old Scot in the Bill Shankly mould. He duly whispered something that went back down the line to Howard, who was hoping for something tactical along the lines of, 'Change it up to 4–4–2 straightaway.' Not quite. What was Jimmy's carefully considered advice? 'Tell the driver to get the coach warmed up. Get the fish and chips ordered for the journey home and let's get out of here as quickly as we can.'

# CHAPTER FOURTEEN

# ARM AROUND THE SHOULDER

I'm getting on for 70 now. I started out in management in 1983 and, do you know what? I still love it when a chairman gives me a pat on the back and praises the team or a decision I have made. Sir Alex Ferguson would say that the two most important words that a manager can ever use to his players are simply, 'Well done.' I could not agree more. No matter what line of business or walk of life you are in, you will get more out of people by making them feel good about themselves and telling them what they can do rather than worrying about what they can't. Yes, of course, there are times when you need to go the other way but, in the main, you motivate people by encouraging them and making them feel confident. If a player senses that you like him, that you believe in him and will stick up for him, you have already given him a reason not to let you down. Give people expectations to live up to, not live down to, and make them aware of their qualities. They almost always respond positively.

I think it would always have been in my nature to see the best in players, but probably the single most influential conversation I have taken into management was with Bobby Moore. It is something I have said many times but it is worth repeating for its importance in shaping my outlook. It was how, throughout 13 years of playing under Ron Greenwood, Bobby would regularly say to me that Ron has never once said, 'Well done.' Having Malcolm Allison telling him how good he was might have made up for it in his early years but even Bobby Moore, England's World Cup-winning captain, still wanted that in the latter part of his career. Yes, with some players you have to withhold praise and use it sparingly, but that is not the case with most of them. Confidence is everything, really. I still love listening to John Robertson talk about Brian Clough and what it meant to him when he would get him that little trademark sign with his thumb and index finger to show that he had done what he wanted. Or when, in among calling him a scruffy git, Cloughie would suddenly chuck in a comparison to Picasso. It made John grow in self-belief and want to please him even more. Bobby did think that Ron was fantastic in most others ways but a bit more encouragement would have made him an even better player, and it was a weakness in his man-management that always stuck with me.

It also goes much deeper than simply saying 'well done' and constantly building someone up. You have to take time for a chat and get to know your players as people so that you gain an understanding of what makes them tick and how they are likely to react to certain situations. Your basic starting point in just about every decision is the same: 'What will give us the best chance of this person playing well when we need him on a Saturday?' Within reason, and provided that it will not seriously undermine you in the eyes of other players, you simply work back from there.

Unless you have been a manager, you would struggle to believe the range of problems that can arrive across your desk on a daily basis. The vast majority have nothing much to do with football: problems with their wife, problems with gambling, problems with booze, problems with someone else in the dressing-room; not getting paid enough, someone else getting too much; schools, families. You are responsible for about 50 people and you cop it all. You do also get issues from totally out of left-field but you can rarely just say, 'That's not my problem.' Your approach can influence what happens on the pitch and, if you can help them in any shape or form with their lives, that's what you are there to do.

I've had someone have an argument with his girlfriend and then the girlfriend's dad come down to the training ground because they are not happy with the way your player has treated his daughter. I remember managing Bobby Savage at Bournemouth and his wife suddenly arriving at training. 'They've cut the leccy! We've got no leccy!' She was a real Scouser and it took me a while to work out that she was talking about the electricity. Even then, my first reaction was, 'What am I supposed to do? Come round and fix it?' I think we ended up getting someone from the ground, probably the maintenance man, to talk to the electricity board and see what the problem was and get the bill paid or whatever it needed.

I also still smile to this day when I think about Carl Richards, an absolute gem of a fella who came to Bournemouth for me from Enfield in 1986. I will never forget taking him up to the Royal Victoria Hospital to see the kids who suffered from disabilities and how gentle and caring he was with them. Carl was special but probably also the most naïve footballer I have ever met. I can still see him arriving at Bournemouth on his first day with his wife and little baby. He was 26 and one of the first things he said to me was, 'Where do I live? Do I rent somewhere?'

I said, 'No, you need to buy somewhere. Get yourself on the housing ladder.' He looked confused.

'How do you do it? How do you buy a house? Where do you go to get one?'

'You know those shops with pictures of houses in the window? Go there. Go up the Cooper Dean roundabout, turn left and head down there.'

I told the story of how I eventually saved Carl two grand on the price of his house in my autobiography in 2013 – then Carl basically got us promoted the following year, in 1987, into what is now the Championship for the first time in Bournemouth's history. I remember when we played Birmingham at home he absolutely ran them ragged.

Their chairman came over and said, 'He is a player, your centre-forward.'

I said, 'Yeah, he is good.'

'Would you sell him?'

'We wouldn't want to.'

They offered £75,000, which we refused, but they came back with £85,000 and we sold him. We were skint, always struggling, and it was a good deal for the club, but Carl liked it at Bournemouth and I almost had to push him out the door. I did not hear from Carl for years but then, out of the blue when I was managing West Ham and sat in my office at Chadwell Heath one day, the phone went.

'Harry. Carl.'

He had got my number from someone. 'Carl, how are you doing? Lovely to hear from you.'

'I'm all right but I've been watching your team on television.'

'Yeah, yeah, we're playing OK.'

'I think I can do a job for you.'

'Doing what?'

'Striker.'

'We're in the Premier League, Carl. Who are you playing for?'

'Cray Wanderers.'

'How old are you?'

'34.'

I said, 'Look, Carl, if I can ever help you out in any way, let me know but it is a bit of a step up. I'm sorry.'

I've never heard from Carl since but I would really love to see him again. It is nice when players you have previously managed want to come back to you. It shows that they think you can get the best out of them, and I am proud to think of the people who liked playing in my teams. Peter Crouch, Jermain Defoe and Niko Kranjčar were all players I had at three different clubs and, as well as being excellent professionals, they were people who thrived on being confident.

I first saw Crouchie in Tottenham's youth team when he was 16. He was unorthodox and the fact that he was ungainly put some people off, but you could see straight away that he had a good touch. He was a very skilful player with a lovely technique; he could hold it up, score goals and, with the correct delivery, was obviously unplayable in the air. Crouchie was also low maintenance but, after Portsmouth had sold him to Aston Villa for £5 million, he went through a spell when he did not play a huge amount and was a bit low on confidence by the time I took over at Southampton. I would tell him every day that he could be a world-beater, and so did Jamie, who was also playing in that team. I think he started to believe us.

The right words at the right moment can transform a player. Matt Le Tissier has never forgotten Alan Ball's first training session at Southampton. He simply gathered the squad and said, 'Whether you like it or not, he's the best player at this club by a million miles. His goals will keep us up. He can't run and tackle. Do that part for him and give him the ball.' Bally was proved right and Le Tissier, who actually thrived on responsibility, rewarded him with the best football of his career.

Kevin Keegan says something similar about the impact on him of Bill Shankly. He was 20 when he arrived at Liverpool from Scunthorpe in 1971 and Shankly simply told him, 'Son, you'll play for England.' Coming from Shankly, Kevin believed that it must be true. I know that Frank Lampard also felt a huge confidence boost when José Mourinho suddenly turned to him one day at Chelsea, literally as they were both in the shower, and said, 'You're the best player in the world.'

You also need flexibility in how you treat players. They are individuals. If they are experienced and trustworthy people, I would not think twice before making an exception, letting them change their routine. David James, for example, came to me before a game against Everton at Goodison Park in 2007. He had a family wedding on the Friday but was up front about it, explaining why it was important to him to be at the wedding. I knew that he would not be lying and that he would not be drinking, so it was a simple decision. Yes, going to the wedding involved a drive of about seven hours and meant that he arrived late at the team hotel on the night before the game, and he might be a little bit tired. Yet Jamo was 37 by then and knew his own body. He always had his own routines anyway and the possibility of a slight physical drop was far outweighed by the potential benefit of him being in a good frame of mind. I would have a happy player, someone who would be doubly determined to justify the faith I had shown and who, in the future, would be more likely to be there for me and the team. I think it took me about two seconds to say, 'Jamo, you go if you want but don't let any goals in on Saturday.' It was a bit tongue in cheek. You can't guarantee a clean sheet but, equally, he needed to understand that I would expect him to meet his usual high standard. David subsequently said that no other manager would have considered letting a player attend a wedding before a game but, in the circumstances, I saw it as a simple decision. Players remember if you do something for them and you hope that they will pay you back. There were plenty of players who would have received a straight 'no' to a similar request but people are not all the same and, to me, that means your man-management must also be adaptable.

Sir Bobby Robson told me a story about handling the Brazilian legend Romário at PSV Eindhoven that underlines the importance of flexibility. They once finished a training routine and Romário was furious about something another player had done and stormed off straight to the changing-rooms. They were getting ready to do nine-a-side and Bobby was giving the bibs out among the 18 players when he realised he was one short. He looked up to see Romário walking back towards the changing-rooms. He shouted, 'Romário, Romário,' but the Brazilian turned to Bobby Robson and gave him a brush off with his hand and continued walking away. It was a disrespectful gesture but, as Bobby told me the story, he explained his subsequent thought process. 'What do I do?' he said. 'Chase after him and have a row? Do I take him in my office and have a big bust up with him? Suddenly, there's a bad atmosphere around the place for the next week. Or do I say, "Fuck it," and pretend it never happened?' It was a Friday and they were playing the next day. Romário was volatile but he was Bobby's best player and, if they were going to win the game, he would probably win it for them. Bobby took all of this into account and so he went the other way. He decided, 'Fuck it,' and let it go. That's not weakness. That is good management and underlined by how Romário scored 30 goals in 29 games under Bobby as PSV won the Dutch league during that 1990–91 season.

You have to read your players and sometimes rely on instinct when confronted with an unexpected situation. Lee Sharpe tells a great story about the day at Crystal Palace in 1995 when Eric Cantona jumped into the crowd and delivered that kung-fu kick to an abusive fan. They had been useless even before the incident and Lee told me that Fergie had gone mad at half-time and was digging out all the players. They weren't any better in the second half and the game finished 1–1, but obviously everyone was now talking about the Cantona incident. As they were coming off the pitch, some of the United lads were thinking, 'Thank God for that. It gets us off the hook. He'll be too busy slaughtering Eric. There will be murders in the dressing-room.' One of the experienced players said to Lee Sharpe, 'Take your time getting in, let Fergie get in first and he'll be dealing with Eric.' So they all hung back and went off the pitch very slowly. Yet when they walked into the dressing-room, Fergie was there and straight away he started on everybody individually. They were all sat there thinking, 'Eric has just jumped into the crowd, beat someone up and got sent off and he has not said anything to him.' Finally, after he had finished slaughtering everyone else, he did turn to Cantona. 'Eric, son, you shouldn't be doing things like that.' That was it. Fergie knew Eric was a time-bomb and could throw a wobbler. He knew that one big bust-up could be the end of Eric at Manchester United.

The subsequent suspension also really hurt Eric as he loved playing so much and, after being banned even from friendly matches behind closed doors, he was planning to go back to France. Fergie made a trip to Paris to see him and ended up on the back of a motorbike looking to find the restaurant where they would have dinner. He spent most of the evening talking football and reassuring him that it would all turn out right. Eric changed his mind, won another two Premier League titles at United and, to this day, Fergie regards it as one of the best things he has done.

Yet even if you looked back before he arrived at Manchester United, it was obvious that Cantona was never someone who would respond simply to a sergeant-major approach. There was a story about his time at Auxerre in France back in the 1980s when he would disappear after matches because he had fallen for a woman down south in Aix-en-Provence. It was a near six-hour drive and Eric would make the journey in his old Renault 5 after every game. This worried the manager Guy Roux, who certainly must have learned how to handle players during 44 years as Auxerre manager. He was concerned that Eric might have an accident and so, one day, he called him in: 'Go on loan to Martigues and, when you come back, I want you married.' The woman from Provence became Eric's wife and Roux's man-management was something he always appreciated. Yes, Eric was high maintenance and you might have to make exceptions for him but, in the long run, he was worth it. Not just because of what he could give you on the pitch but for the example he would set the younger players. The Class of '92 group all still talk about how they became inspired by Eric's dedication to training.

Paolo Di Canio was very similar for West Ham United and, if Fergie had got his way in 2001, he could have been a great signing for Manchester United. Paolo says he was so surprised when Fergie called him on Christmas Day that he initially told him to 'fuck off', thinking that someone was winding him up. People said I was walking a tightrope without a safety net by taking him after his 11-match ban for pushing over referee Paul Alcock, but I saw him as an unbelievable bargain at just £1.5 million. I was also confident that I could bring out the best in him. I didn't shout and scream at Paolo because he was a time-bomb too. At Chadwell Heath I always used to put him on the same team as Nigel Winterburn, Stuart Pearce, Stevie Lomas and anyone who might boot him in a training match because, if someone did, it would all kick off. You always had to keep him on the wining team and keep him happy. He was like a kid in the playground wanting to do everything, from corners and throw-ins to free-kicks and penalties. Every day was a test trying to make sure he didn't blow up. You knew that if you started hollering at him the shirt and boots could come off. I still loved managing him because he had such high standards. Some of the things he did on the pitch made you gasp, and it was a privilege even to see him train. The other players accepted him being treated a little bit different because they saw how he trained and knew he could win games for us on a Saturday. I am sure it was the same with Cantona. Fergie knew that Eric was aggravation and he picked his targets. Managers do. They know some players are also easier to leave out than others. One might take it but someone else would be, 'Fucking this and that.' If it's an even toss-up, some managers will think, 'Maybe he's a little bit easier and it's not such aggravation to leave him out.' It can happen.

Paul Gascoigne was one who would have been difficult to leave out because he had so much energy and such a pure love of simply playing football. You could always see that almost child-like desire to be involved, to get on the ball, even in the later years of his career. Jamie has told me how Gazza would struggle to sleep before games, especially if he didn't know whether he was playing or not, but, in Bobby and then Terry Venables, he had England managers who clearly knew how to handle him. The players did not know the team before the Scotland game at Euro '96 and Gazza, naturally, was worrying much more than most about whether he would be playing. Terry was not planning to announce the team to the players until the day of the game but, eventually, knew he had to make an exception for Gazza at about 10.30pm. He told him, 'You're playing, now get to sleep.'

Terry would also try to keep Gazza's emotions level and his feet on the ground by realising that the last thing he needed when he had played well was too much praise. Equally, excessive criticism would also be counter-productive when he had struggled. Gazza, though, eventually worked out that Terry would tell him he was crap when he had played well and that he was brilliant when he was crap. Terry also knew Gazza well by then after managing him during four seasons at Tottenham, but it was still not always easy. The fact that Gazza still remembers and tells people the story about the day he told Terry to 'fuck off' in front of the team during a post-match row speaks volumes for how astutely he handled the situation. Terry, who would never swear in front of his players, quietly summoned Gazza to his office. Gazza soon realised what he had done and was terrified. He tried to think of something and so went to the players' lounge on the way and brought two pints of lager as a peace offering. Terry apparently looked at him, realised that he was petrified, and just said, 'I could fine you and I probably should for bringing beer not wine.' He then told him to go.

Paul Merson was another player who could be highly strung and high maintenance, but in a very different way. If we were playing one-touch in training, he'd want to play two-touch. He was always moaning but, like Cantona, Di Canio or Gazza, was also a match-winner. We had a perfect system at Portsmouth to give him the freedom to play, and he loved it. We were top of the league and we were flying when he famously came to me during two weeks off in January after losing in the FA Cup to Manchester United.

The story has been told plenty of times by both of us, but what people do not know is that I did actually think about disciplining him yet couldn't bring myself to fine him. I knew that he'd lost all his money gambling anyway. Merse had claimed that he was struggling with his addictions and needed some time away to go to Tony Adams's rehabilitation clinic. 'Sure, no problem,' I'd said. At the same time, Sandra and I had gone to Barbados for a few days and one of the guests at the house we were staying in had only bumped into Merse down on the beach. They told me exactly where he really was. The good thing was that I'd had time to think about it by the time I next saw him. At first I was annoyed, but my next thought was, 'Hang on, I need him Saturday. What am I going to fine him for? Do I want to take money out of his pocket when he hasn't got any? He's my best player. He is scoring goals, making goals and he is my captain.' We could either have had a row, which would have ended in a ruck and me doing my nut, or I could do nothing. Things were going great and we were top of the league. Did I need to upset that? So Merse bounced back into training looking all tanned and told me he that he was feeling great. I thought, 'I bet you fucking do,' but simply said, 'Merse, as long as you feel better, get yourself ready. We have a big game on Saturday.' It was not until a few years later, long after he had joined Walsall, that he found out I knew about his little trip to Barbados.

There were a few others at Portsmouth for whom exceptions would sometimes be made but, as with Merson, the only outcome I sought was success for the team. Nwankwo Kanu was such an easy-going lad: laid-back, never a bad word about anyone and a very special character who sometimes did need different treatment. He had incredible skill and he had already pretty much done it all in his career at Ajax, Inter Milan and then Arsenal. He was treated like a god back home in Nigeria. We played Manchester United once in Nigeria – an exhibition game – and there were thousands waiting at the airport. Not for us. Not for Manchester United. But for the man they simply called 'King'. It was the same at the hotel. There would be fans waiting night and day to catch a glimpse of the King. They loved him. He was into his thirties by the time he joined us but still well capable of winning a game on his own. He barely trained and, rather than use the one flight of stairs we had up to the canteen, he would always wait for the rickety old lift so as not to put any extra strain on his legs. We would basically just save him up for the game on a Saturday. That was his weekly exercise. Monday was usually a bit of a warm-down day and Kanu, who knew his body pretty well, had clearly decided that he could afford to miss it. He would ring me on a Sunday night at about 11pm every week to say that he had an upset tummy. It was a bit of a drive for him to Portsmouth and, in the end, I told him just to come in later in the week. If having Mondays off was going to make Kanu more focused and motivated for me on a Saturday then, really, it was a no-brainer. People thought he was finished but Kanu was still playing at Portsmouth six years after I signed him.

Emmanuel Adebayor was a player with a reputation for sometimes being difficult but I really never found him to be any trouble at all at Spurs. He was like a lot of players: from a distance, you might look at him and think, 'He's very confident.' But there can be a lot of bravado. Ade needed reassurance and wanted to know that you really wanted him. He was never any problem for me and could make me smile.

We used to have a 'Worst Player on a Friday' competition at Tottenham and the loser would pay a £50 fine to the local kids' hospice up the road. Once, he was late paying his. Sébastien Bassong was, 'C'mon, Ade, you earn £200,000 a week and you haven't paid £50 to the charity for being the worst player last week.' Ade turned around and, as quick as a flash, said, 'Don't insult me. I earn 225.' Everybody fell about laughing and I think he paid it in the end. I would also add that most of his money at that time was coming from Manchester City.

Ian Wright, for all he had achieved in the game with Crystal Palace and Arsenal, was another who still thrived on a bit of encouragement when he came to West Ham late in his career. I think he was 35 but he still reminds me of the voicemail I left him when the deal was agreed. I sang 'I'm Forever Blowing Bubbles' down the phone and told him how delighted I was that he would be joining us. He said that it gave him a real buzz, and he was a fantastic character to work with.

It's not just about adapting to those players with the loudest personalities. A quieter player may not require such obvious man-management but you ignore them at your peril. We had a difficult situation at Tottenham in the summer of 2011 with Luka Modrić, and I was caught in the crossfire. Luka had an offer to go to Chelsea that would almost treble his wages but the club did not accept it. Daniel Levy, the Tottenham chairman, turned it down. Luka came to me and said, 'The manager for Chelsea is ringing me every day.' André Villas-Boas. The ironic thing was that he ended up as

Tottenham manager and must have been grateful to still have Luka after I left the following year. I could have got on to him and challenged him about it. What happened was a liberty, really. I could certainly have had a row with Chelsea, but it happens in football. I decided to be sympathetic to Luka. I said I could understand where he was coming from. Luka didn't sulk and he didn't throw his toys out of the pram. He played well and was not a minute's aggravation. I was lucky because Luka wouldn't know how to go off the rails or what it was to cause a problem. It was not in his nature, but he also knew I was on his side. I felt that if we were going to turn the offer down, he should at least get a new contract. I thought, 'If he's worth £45 million, then pay him what he is worth.' You have other players worth tuppence ha'penny, doing nothing for their money, earning twice as much. He got on with it and got a great move to Real Madrid the following summer.

I also got a focused Luka for another season and it was a privilege to have worked with him. He liked a pat on the back as much as anyone and, after games, I would say to him, 'Fantastic, Luka, I'd have paid to watch you play today.' Unlike with one or two others I have managed down the years, I really meant it too.

# CHAPTER FIFTEEN

. . . . . . . . . . . . . . . . . . . . . . . . . . . . . . . . . . . . . . . . . . . . . . . . . . . . . .

# BOOT UP THE ARSE

As much as I might have liked, there was no way you could just persist with an arm around the shoulder and a 'well done' with every player. A pat on the back can probably only really work if the player knows that you are also capable of delivering a boot up the arse. It does not have to happen often but, if they come to think that it is not in you at all, human nature dictates that liberties might eventually be taken. In the main, I think people outside of football get carried away with slagging players off because they have got big cars or whatever. So what? In more than 30 years managing, you are going to get a few problems but they are mostly great lads and 99 per cent stay just the same as they have always been. They are boys who always wanted to be footballers – and what a way it is to make a living. They come in during the morning and train with their mates. They get well paid for it, have everything done for them and are usually back home again straight after lunch. I would remind players constantly how lucky they were and how these were the best days of their lives. I wanted them to appreciate what they had. A bit of perspective can often work wonders on the mindset of a footballer and consequently give the manager fewer problems.

I had a very famous player once complain to me before a Sunday match against Manchester United at Old Trafford because I had not selected him in the team or on the bench. Fair enough, but what really riled me was when he then added, 'Why have you dragged me up here this weekend?' I told him what I thought. 'What do you mean? Why have I dragged you up here? You get £30,000 a week. You train. You came up last night and you stayed in a fantastic hotel. You are at Old Trafford today. OK, you are not a substitute but you are part of my squad. That's why you get paid.' My little rant did not end there.

'Think how you would feel in five years' time, when you are retired, if somebody said to you, "I want you to go to Manchester on Saturday night. You can fly up with your mates. We are going to put you in the best hotel. Nice dinner, and next day you can go to Old Trafford to watch the Manchester United game. Oh, and I'm going to give you £30,000 spending money." What would you think then, when you are out of football, and you are earning a few hundred quid a week? You wouldn't believe your luck. And you are moaning to me about coming up here. Get in the real world and, in five years' time, remember what I'm saying. There aren't any other £30,000-a-week jobs out there, unless you become a clever big businessman who makes a fortune – about one in 10,000 players will do that.'

Lecture over. But I still stand by every word of it today. The players can lose track and it does them good sometimes to be reminded that they are living the dream and should enjoy what is a unique time in their lives.

There are, though, several options open to a manager for genuine disciplinary issues. You can get cross and speak to the player – a sharp telling off in the heat of the moment is very often the end of it. Or you might speak to them at more length one-to-one. You try to be constructive and hope that will resolve whatever issue there is. If you have strong characters in the dressing-room, they can sort out other players for you fairly quickly if they think that they have stepped out of line. That was more of an option in the past, however, simply because you don't have many people in the dressing-room with the personality to do that now. A John Terry figure at Chelsea is a dying breed, but his value is evident in how he has remained captain through 11 changes of managers over the most successful 12 years in the club's history.

It also does not have to be the captain or star player setting an example. At West Ham, after the club had been relegated in 1992, we signed Peter Butler from Southend and he was grounded and had a very positive influence on the group's attitude. You often find that with lads from the lower leagues. Having had more exposure to life outside of a top football club, they really respect the opportunity that they are getting and are utterly determined not to waste it.

All teams have a load of guidelines for players about what is and isn't acceptable. You set some rules down at the start of the season, although some managers obviously go into far more detail with this than others. I heard that Louis van Gaal was big on discipline to the extent that, if someone did not put their used towel in the laundry basket the guilty player would have to take it home and wash it himself. Van Gaal also liked his players in the club suit, jacket buttoned up, with matching tie and shoes. Fabio Capello made plenty of headlines for all his rules with England. He would call the players by their surnames as well as ban room-service, flip-flops, mobile phones and shorts around the public areas of the team hotel. It did not seem to do much good.

Having seen Paolo Di Canio as a player and how furious he would get listening to Neil Ruddock talking about what he had got up to the night before training, it was no surprise to hear about the standards he would expect as a manager. At Sunderland he wanted the players to arrive an hour early for training. He told them that he would throw their mobile phones in the North Sea if they brought them inside the training ground. Certain foods, like ketchup and mayonnaise, were soon out. Paolo always felt that they were bad for your body system and removing them from your diet would ensure fewer injuries and a better performance.

I was never one to go crazy with rules. Yes, if the players were not out on the pitch for training at 10am there was a fine. The same if you were late for the bus for an away game. No mobile phones in the medical rooms. It was that type of stuff, and I would leave my assistant Kevin Bond to enforce them. I was much more worried about winning a football match on a Saturday.

If I did discipline a player with a fine for a more serious incident, I would always much rather see the money go to charity. There was the well-known issue with John Hartson and Eyal Berkovic at West Ham United where John obviously had to be fined the maximum two weeks' wages, but the good thing to come out of it was that the money went to Leukaemia Busters. The cameras were there that day and John kicking Eyal in the face was probably the worst thing I have ever seen between teammates on the training ground. Eyal could not eat properly for two days. Even so, I do maintain to this day that it was totally out of character for John. He wasn't usually a bully in any way. He had a heart as big as his body, but something happened that morning. He just lost his rag and totally blew up. It shows that you never really know what is going on in people's minds. Looking back, I think John was low with himself at that time. He had a serious problem with gambling – something he has addressed later in his life – and, while his actions in those few seconds were inexcusable, it was not an accurate reflection of his whole personality.

I didn't enjoy fining people but, whenever I see Neil Ruddock, we can now laugh about one of the exceptions I made. It was at the end of the 1999–2000 season. Razor was injured. He missed the last game and I had said that anyone who was injured needed to continue coming in for treatment until they were passed fit by the medical people. I did not want people going off on holiday until we had done what we could for their injuries. Anyway, the following week came, and there was no sign of Razor. He did not turn up but clearly had not forgotten completely because a message arrived at the club that he was supposedly ill. I did not think much more about it until the papers dropped and there was a big story that weekend. It was reported that Razor had been in a fight with Mike Newell at Gleneagles golf club, said to have happened in the restaurant there. One report quoted eyewitness staff saying that potato wedges and dips had gone all over the place and food was smeared across the windows. The scuffle itself with Mike Newell was something that I would probably have let go. I wasn't there and didn't really know exactly what had happened, although Razor later admitted to an incident that he called 'handbags at ten paces'.

The issue I had was that he was supposed to be ill, or having treatment, and not playing golf at Gleneagles before going out drinking. So I fined him. He had got caught – it was a fortnight's wages. I thought that would be straight forward enough but he appealed and we all ended up having to go to a Football Association tribunal. I was there for West Ham with Peter Barnes, the secretary, to explain the reasons behind the fine. Razor himself turned up with some Australian barrister, who looked like a film star and was the cleverest boy I have ever met. Within minutes, he had got us completely tied up in knots. It was embarrassing. The barrister was so sharp that we didn't have a chance. He started off with the letter that you were supposed to send within a certain timeframe to notify a player that disciplinary action was being taken.

'Did you post the letter, Mr Redknapp?'

'No, I didn't post the letter.'

'So who did post the letter?'

'Someone in the office. I'm not sure who it was, but it was sent from the office.'

'How did you know it got posted on time? Who posted the letter? Can you prove that it was sent on time?'

It went on like this. Question after question about the process we had followed. Razor just sat there, letting his barrister do all the talking. By the end, Peter and I were pretty much, 'Leave us alone. Let us go home. Give him his money back.' Inevitably, we lost. Razor had won the case. He was all smiles and the club was forced to reimburse a fortnight's wages. I think it was £20,000 that he had been fined.

Anyway, the barrister then got up at the end and turned to Dave Richards, who was chairman of the Premier League and on the FA's board. He said, 'OK, thank you, Mr Richards. I'm afraid I don't come cheap. This is the bill for my work.' He handed his bill to Dave Richards. It was £30,000. Dave Richards said, 'But it's not a court of law, we don't cover costs.' Razor's face was a picture. It meant that he had to pay, and his barrister was going to be charging him more than the fine. He would be walking out with a £30,000 bill instead of the original £20,000 payment. As we got up to go, he turned to me and said, 'I can't believe it.'

I just said, 'Unlucky, Razor.'

There were bigger disciplinary issues to be dealt with at West Ham when I first arrived. I think the players and some of the staff expected it to be laid back and a laugh a minute under me but that is not my style either, and there were issues that I felt needed addressing. At my first game back at the club, we lost to Newcastle United but it was still lagers out and players all joking on the bus. Stronger stuff was sometimes also being handed around. I remember Tony Gale saying that I was a miserable bastard when I came in, and he was right. I soon banned alcohol on the team-bus and in the players' bar at West Ham. It was one of the best things I did. Some of the players were coming out very drunk at 6.30pm on a Saturday. I'd seen kids waiting to speak with them or get their autographs and catching the players worse for wear. It wasn't on. If they wanted a lager or a glass of wine after the game no one would be complaining; getting on the booze with their mates – and a lot of it was people outside the club having freebies – was a liberty. With us near the bottom of the league at Christmas in my first season in 1994–95, I still had to talk Dale Gordon out of hiring an open-top bus for the players' party to take them from the training ground to the West End of London with a jazz band playing. I couldn't believe what I was hearing. They ended up taking a few minibuses but a Dutch player called Jeroen Boere set light to the seats. I received the bill for that as well as damage to the Dormy Hotel in Dorset where we had stayed after a friendly a few months later. Action had to be taken but we got there in the end and did turn the culture around. I never understood this need for mid-season parties at football clubs, and my attitude towards them did have me down as a bit of a Christmas Scrooge. Alcohol is one of the worst things when you are looking to recover from playing and Christmas is the time when you have the most games and a particularly high risk of injuries. It does not take a genius to work out, then, that it is just about the worst time of the year for footballers to be going out drinking.

Every club has had aggravation with Christmas parties at some time or another. Lads go out. There are photographers waiting to take pictures of it late at night. You don't need it. They should look after themselves during the season and, if they must have a drink, there is usually about six weeks off in the summer when they can have all the parties they want. I have got no time for it. It might be all right for their mate, who is cleaning windows, if that is the way he wants to live, but footballers should be dedicated to their profession and set a good example to young kids. It really winds me up. At Tottenham, after Ledley King and a few other players were photographed out drinking, we put in place a complete alcohol and nightclub ban.

People like Di Canio and Gianfranco Zola did also have a major influence on our football culture. They would just have a glass of wine with dinner but didn't drink the 10 or 15 pints of beer which some of the British boys could put away. Paolo's own fitness trainer would come in and work with him on a Sunday. It is similar now with Gareth Bale. I would say to the players, 'Do you really think Paolo Maldini or Ryan Giggs, who played on at the highest level into their forties, were going out and getting drunk on a Saturday night and falling over?' I can't imagine that. The issue for me was whether the players were getting the best from their ability.

Julian Dicks, for example, was just a natural. He had a brilliant left foot and no one could beat him for pace. He was just unlucky that Stuart Pearce was around because, in any other era, he would have had 50 or 60 England caps. I don't think he was that bothered about it and could be disruptive. If he didn't like something at training he might just boot the ball over the railway line. He was like a throwback to the old pros in that he would not warm up, he would not stretch and was basically a law unto himself. But he was a class player and would always be there for you on a Saturday. Razor was like that as well, no matter how he lived during the week. He could pass the ball and was a very good player. The frustration is that he could have been even better.

I think that Adel Taarabt is another who might very well look back on his career one day and think, 'What could have been?' He has the ability to be one of the best players in the Premier League, but I found him impossible, really, at Queens Park Rangers. I tried. Everybody has tried. I don't think he played a game for Benfica in the season after he was sold there in 2015. What was the problem with him? He just didn't seem committed enough. I think he felt being at the casino was the life he wanted. I think he wanted the money and everything that goes with being a professional footballer without all the hard work. But you can't do it. You have got to be focused to play in today's football. It's a short life, a great career, but you have to dedicate yourself. You can't burn the candle at both ends. He would turn up for training but, with the way he lived his life away from football, I had concerns he wasn't fit enough. I know I upset him with the public comment about his weight in 2014 but, overall, I still think that I let him off lightly. I didn't tell the truth about him a lot of the time.

Patrick Collins, who seemed to hate me – and anyone without a posh accent, like Sam Allardyce or Terry Venables – wrote a column in the *Mail on Sunday* in which he slaughtered me. He then backed Taarabt. But how can you do that? Here's a boy who is a professional footballer and I get a report that he has been in a casino at 5am on the Friday night before a big game. I pulled him in and he went, 'No, no, I wasn't in there until 5am. I was there Thursday until about 5am but not on Friday.' He carried on, 'But you don't understand me. I go home, go to sleep, go to a casino at night until 5am.' I said, 'You're right, I don't understand. Don't you realise you are a fucking footballer not a croupier?'

If you want to be the ally of a man who is taking about 70 grand a week and doesn't fully dedicate himself to the job, that's up to you, but maybe take a look at the rest of his career as well. There's always someone who will stick up for a player, even when it is actually the last thing they need. It was not as if I was some sort of massive disciplinarian or was never willing to try in my career with someone who might be a difficult character. I regularly held back or supported Taarabt when I was asked questions. I truly wished that Adel could have answered me with his performances on the pitch – and also that he can still have a great career – but how many league games has he started since then?

An admission, of course, is needed here. Yes, as players, our generation would get down the pub after matches. Ron Greenwood, the manager, would also sometimes say, 'You are not going out,' and we would defy him and sneak out. We would find a way. You would plan how to get back in without being seen. Every team did it, but times have changed completely. It would not be possible to play in the Premier League with some of the lifestyles that were common-place back then.

Bobby Moore and Jimmy Greaves, for example, were staying at the Lancaster Gate Hotel before an England fixture with Portugal and Sir Alf Ramsey, who liked a gin and tonic himself, had said that they could not go out. They did and they were caught, with Alf just leaving their passports on their beds before they were due to travel to Lisbon for the match. It was enough to seriously frighten them and they did stay with the squad for a 4–3 win. I would be lying if I claimed that managers always approach every situation the same. They are pragmatists. Bobby and Jim were vital to Alf. Would we have treated less important players the same? I am not so sure. Whatever a manager or a club might say, their better players usually do also get more leeway in a disciplinary situation, especially if the breach is more serious. When it is not such an important player who has broken the rules, it is easy. He's gone. If he is a top player, worth £20 million, you won't find many clubs willing to sack him. It is not right but, in football, that is usually how it works.

There are managers who might also get after a player for something fairly innocuous or humorous, just to keep everyone on their toes. Fergie once fined John Hewitt at Aberdeen for overtaking him on a public road in his car after training. He blasted him but, as John came out of his office looking terrified, Fergie apparently just simply winked at the other players. Another favourite of mine is told by Trevor Francis. Cloughie once presented Kenny Burns with a typed-up notification of a £50 fine at half-time of a match for an earlier tackle he did not like.

Cloughie certainly did not always get it right, though, and my old assistant Joe Jordan has told me all about his incredible 44-day stint at Leeds United. Joe says that, yes, he really did walk into this Leeds dressing-room full of great characters and fantastic footballers with the opening line, 'You lot, you can throw all your medals in the dustbin, you got them by cheating.' It is unbelievable when you go through that team and the players he was dealing with. There was Johnny Giles, who is a very clever man. There were also top internationals like Billy Bremner, Norman Hunter, Eddie Gray, Peter Lorimer, Mick Jones, Allan Clarke, Frank Gray, Gordon McQueen, Terry Cooper and Joe. They were never going to take that. It was the worst approach.

You can have the maximum impact by waiting for an unexpected moment. It was hard to believe what happened on the final day of the 2015–16 Premier League season when Tottenham, who had another golden opportunity to finish above Arsenal for the first time since 1995, were beaten 5–1 by Newcastle United. Newcastle were already relegated and also went down to ten men during the game. What does Mauricio Pochettino do? He thought about how he would react and waited until they were all back at pre-season training two months later. The players probably thought they had got away with it but he gathered them together and did not hold back. The edited version is that he told them that if he'd had the opportunity to kill them, he would have killed all of them.

I'll also always remember seeing Sir Alex Ferguson when Aberdeen won the Scottish Cup in 1983 still letting his players have it because they had not reached the level of performance he expected. They can't have seen that coming and it would have been a real jolt. 'We're the luckiest team in the world,' he said. 'It was a disgrace of a performance. Winning Cups doesn't matter. Our standards have been set long ago and we're not going to accept that from any Aberdeen team. No way should we take any glory from that.'

Having a firm word is not just for those who might step out of line. Sometimes it is a way to encourage more from the very best professionals. Gareth Bale has a very strong character. He has proved that time and again in his life but I think there was a period at Tottenham when a harder line was better for bringing that out than just simply encouragement. Early on in my time at Tottenham, it felt like Gareth would get a little knock pretty much every day in training and be limping off on one leg with the physio running over. He would also be messing about with his hair, wetting it and putting his clips in. Eventually I did lose a bit of patience:

'Stop messing about with your barnet and just get on with it.' I also told the physio to leave him if he went down unless it was obviously serious. Watching him at Euro 2016 was so enjoyable, not just for his brilliant performances but for his on-field bravery and the manner in which he was such a leader for Wales, inspiring them all the way to the semi-finals. He gets kicked a lot and, while you could hardly compare the physicality of past eras to today, there is something of the George Best in the way that he is never discouraged and keeps running at people and getting back up for more. Gareth was only young when he was at Spurs but he had everything in terms of technique and ability. He was truly amazing at times on the training ground with the way he could suddenly beat two or three players and produce a moment that would make my whole day. He has toughened up and grown into an amazing footballer. The way he has handled the move to Real Madrid has also been impressive. I was worried that he might get overawed and just go into his shell a little bit, what with moving to Spain at the age of 24 for a world-record fee and Cristiano Ronaldo already there. That was the one question I had. Would he stand up and say, 'I'll take the free-kick'? My concerns were unfounded. Two Champions League finals later, it's clear there is steel running through him that should not be underestimated. It came out again even more in the Euros and I think he is right up there now with Lionel Messi, Cristiano Ronaldo, Luis Suárez and Neymar among the greatest players in the world. I love watching him play. He is probably the best footballer I have managed.

# CHAPTER SIXTEEN

. . . . . . . . . . . . . . . . . . . . . . . . . . . . . . . . . . . . . . . . . . . . . . . . . . . . . .

# HANDLING
# THE SPOTLIGHT

If there is one evening in the calendar that underlines how football's accompanying spotlight has so brightened in the past 30 years, it is transfer-window deadline day. You never even used to have television cameras at every top-flight game let alone dozens of them stuck outside each and every Premier League ground for a day when a football is not even kicked. Quite often, they are not even reporting on any players being signed. I know I became synonymous with the pantomime that is now screened live on three separate television channels. The sight of me talking to someone from Sky Sports News through the window of my car really wasn't some calculated gesture on my part. It's just that I was brought up not to ignore someone if they talk to me. The TV guys are usually stood outside from 7am on deadline day and they have a job to do. They are decent lads and so I would give them two minutes of my time. I was obviously not going to say if we had a big deal going on that could still be scuppered but, otherwise, it didn't do any harm to help them. When they were off air, I would also ask Gary Cotterill and the Sky cameramen if they wanted to pop in for a cup of tea and a biscuit. In January they'd have been stood out in the freezing cold all day and I felt sorry for them. I found it hard to walk or drive straight past someone. I am the same if I go out of my front door and a bloke is doing some painting work down the road. It doesn't cost anything to give someone a minute of your time.

I never had any strategy whatsoever with the media and I never planned what I was going to say before a press conference. I know that a lot could be made of what managers like Sir Alex Ferguson and José Mourinho might say ahead of a match and there is always this accusation of 'mind games'. My own feeling was that it was overblown and it was a lot less calculated than some people thought. Fans and journalists over-analyse and definitely overestimate managers. They actually think that we are much cleverer than most of us really are. I tried to answer media questions honestly. I think that those managers who just relentlessly use clichés and tell you how fantastic everything is lose credibility after a while. The man in the pub is not stupid and can see straight through it. So can the players, but you still see so much crap being spoken after a game. 'We got beat 4–0 but there are a lot of positives to take. We did this well and that was good.' Excuse me? I don't know if sometimes they are trying to convince themselves or the public. If you have obviously had a shocker, why not just say it? 'We were rubbish and we need to put it right next week.' You can't keep coming out talking nonsense as a manager if you have not performed. I have no regrets about criticising the performance of any player but they have become more sensitive souls. The problem is not just that so many players now take themselves more seriously but they have also got an agent, friends or maybe even some teammates who are indulging the more precious side of their character.

One of the most famous examples for me was at Tottenham with Darren Bent, although I can now reveal a happier ending to the story. It was in January 2009 that Darren missed an open goal with a late header that would have given us a win against Portsmouth. I was asked about it after the match and so said what everyone else was thinking. 'My missus could have scored it.' That was all I said. It was meant as a joke but, like most jokes, there was an element of truth: Sandra could have nodded that one in; Darren was about a yard off the goalline. It was a terrible miss and, with the match live on TV, there would have been two million blokes sitting at home watching that game saying, 'Cor, bleeding hell, my old woman could have scored that.' What was I supposed to say? 'Darren was unlucky. It somehow skimmed off his head because the wind maybe caught the ball'? Darren did not take it well. He got the needle with me and his agent called the chairman to say that he wanted to leave. He joined Sunderland later that year for £16.5 million. Darren was then one of the very first people I saw on my first morning at Derby County seven years later in 2016. He scored a wonderful top-corner volley from 30 yards during that training session. It was an amazing goal and so I shouted out across the pitch to him. 'Benty, my old woman couldn't have scored that one.' We both laughed this time.

I thought the situation with Darren was funny and it was the sort of thing that, a few years ago, the player would have just laughed at as well. The others would have joined in, taken the mickey a bit and it would all have been forgotten the next day. As it was, they probably got together and took it all very seriously. It would have been, 'He's out of order, he shouldn't say things like that to you.' That's how it got with players. People were constantly saying that you shouldn't criticise a player or a team in public, but I didn't really care. What was the Liverpool manager supposed to say when Ronny Rosenthal went around the goalkeeper in 1992 and missed one that a little two-year-old could have scored? You can't wash a flannel over that. My attitude to the players was, 'Get on with it and let your football answer me back.' I liked Darren. He got loads of great goals for us, including 17 in that 2008–09 season at Tottenham, and I would always be the first one to praise him and say, 'Cracking goal.' At the same time, if someone has played crap, I'll tell him and might make some comment about how 50 grand a week should at least get you someone who can pass to their teammate. I think it is better just to say it as it is and, if people don't like it, unlucky.

I know clubs have tightened their access for the media, but that was not something that affected me. People knew who I was and no chairman or press officer ever tried to tell me, 'Don't say this or don't talk to this person.' They might tell you that a certain issue was a bit delicate and not to bring it up but, in the main, I was left to handle things in the way I always have. I took the same attitude with players. I would not try to control what interviews they gave. You might try to protect a very young player but, generally, I took the view that the players were adults, and that far too much importance could be attached to what they did or didn't say. I liked the attitude of Roy Keane on the occasion he was accompanied by a PR representative who had pre-prepared the questions that she thought a group of journalists should ask. Once she had left the room, he screwed up the piece of paper and said to the journalists, 'Ask me what you like. If I don't like the sound of a question, I won't answer it.'

The best interview I ever saw was Don Revie and Brian Clough going at it on live television two hours after Clough had been sacked by Leeds United in 1974. Can you imagine something like that now? The PR people would never allow it. Clough and Revie hated each other. Revie would have wanted Clough to fail, and Clough would have known that – yet you still had the two of them agreeing to appear together live on television at such a raw moment.

I do think that some people now take themselves much too seriously, including managers. Some get to the stage where they can hardly accept criticism. I think José Mourinho got more like that during his second spell at Chelsea. I have the highest regard for José and, first time around, he was really loved and like a breath of fresh air. He came back and there was still great affection but, second time, people did start to get a bit fed up with it. It's much easier, though, when you are winning, and I know that it is definitely a lot easier to have some perspective from the outside. I've flown off the handle about something fairly minor plenty of times after a game and, when you have lost, all the media demands that you now have are one of the worst parts of the job. You can feel so down, angry and aggrieved, but you probably have 45 minutes of interviews to conduct straight away. Previously, you just came off the pitch, went in the dressing-room or your little office. You might have had a couple of pressmen waiting to speak to you outside. It changed completely when the Premier League launched. You now have a press conference. There is also a series of radio and television interviews, all in different rooms, as well as different newspaper briefings. As I have said, I am usually pretty straight-talking, but there are obviously moments when you simply cannot say exactly what you think after a game. If you said what you were actually feeling half the time, there would be murders. You would lose the dressing-room in about one week.

Look at the situation for Brendan Rodgers with Raheem Sterling at Liverpool, for example. He couldn't say what he must have thought when Sterling was stalling on a contract and agitating to leave. He was saying, 'We have a good relationship,' but really he must have hated what was happening. He had given him a chance at Liverpool and suddenly he was pushing for a move.

Jamie would tell me not to be too critical of the QPR players when he knew I was angry at some of them. A funnier example of me not saying what I really thought was when

Paolo Di Canio caught the ball against Everton in 2000. He could have scored after their goalkeeper, Paul Gerrard, had gone down injured, and it seemed the whole world was praising Paolo for his honesty. The scene inside our dressing-room was a bit different. Stuart Pearce marched in and said, 'Where is he? I'm going to kill him.' I was, 'No, Stuart, I'm going to kill him first.' Anyway, I went out to speak with the TV and the interviewer started off by saying, 'What a fantastic day for football. What sportsmanship.' I had no option but to go along with it: 'Yeah, yeah, fantastic. Yeah, really proud.' Paolo won some FIFA sportsmanship award for it as well, and was doubly excited because it was presented by the Kemp brothers and he is a massive Spandau Ballet fan.

I have had plenty of other moments in front of the camera that people seem to remember. Mostly it is the one where the ball hit me at Portsmouth's training ground during an interview which I'm told has been watched more than a million times on YouTube. People always ask, 'Who did it?' But the truth is that it wasn't one of the first-team players. It genuinely was one of the reserves and, although we have had a joke about it since with a spoof golf video, the kid really could have done me some damage that day.

Media relations were all very different previously. When I was a player with West Ham, the newspaper guys and photographers would regularly socialise with us. Nothing that happened on a night out would get reported. Nigel Clarke from the *Daily Mirror* would be there and maybe Ian Wooldridge from the *Daily Mail*. They would be out after the game in the same pubs and clubs as you and, next day, you knew they wouldn't write about it. They were part of the lads. I remember Wooldridge was once out with Jimmy Greaves and a group of players and suddenly claimed that he could outrun most footballers. Before you knew it, there were six press people in an impromptu race down the street. They were all the worse for wear but Wooldridge could not see what he was doing and ran straight into a spiked chain across the road. He had to be carried back to the nightclub by all the other lads, including Greavsie. I remember the photographer, Kent Gavin, coming over to the United States with us and a reporter to take pictures of Bobby Moore and Frank Sinatra. Nigel was friends with most of the West Ham lads and Bobby gave him the badge of his England shirt. There are new faces but still a few laughs. Tony Banks from the *Express* once wrote that I was wearing a suit that looked like it had been bought from Romford Market and how Arsène Wenger, by contrast, was a picture of elegance on the touchline. Bloody cheek. That suit was Armani and I have never let Tony forget it.

You could control things a bit more when I started out as a manager. I remember us once having the cameras and fans in at West Ham training on a day when there was sleet and rain. There were puddles all over the pitch. Kit would be dished out in the morning and I think John Moncur had got there a bit late. Anyway, we were waiting to start training when he came sprinting out naked with just his boots and socks on asking to know where the kit was. I was able to persuade the television guys not to run the footage. Now someone like Jack Wilshere has only got to have one puff on a cigarette, one little argument in the street, and you can guarantee that the footage will soon be everywhere. We were far more accessible to the fans back in those days and would all socialise in the East End where we all grew up. I love seeing the old pictures of Tommy Lawton clambering on the bus with the fans to get to a game. We would mix with our community at West Ham. Bobby Moore would get the most attention and always had people looking at him but he loved a night out and could let himself go. He was quite shy. I think he almost needed a drink to enjoy himself, but I never heard him say a bad word about anybody and he was the last person to get involved in any serious scrapes. He was a proper star, though, in a way that would transcend football. He would go to parties with the Beatles and Sean Connery.

Most footballers back then did not especially attract attention and we would be out at all the local pubs on a Saturday night. It was a time when the East End was buzzing. You would get some underworld figures attaching themselves to the group but no one really bothered us. The Blind Beggar pub in Whitechapel was my local almost every Saturday night and it was right at the time when it became famous for Ronnie Kray shooting George Cornell. I had just turned 19 when that happened in 1966. Obviously, a huge mystique has since grown around the Kray brothers but they would never bother you. They were not like, 'Who are you looking at?' They didn't do that. The only aggravation was in their own world. They had no problem with the football players and it was a great time for us. We always had the same group of lads following us around at West Ham.

The East End of London was a very safe place for the normal person back then, and there was always a party going on. Old ladies didn't get mugged, no one was walking around carrying knives, and we could enjoy ourselves without any fear. I lived two minutes from the Blind Beggar, and it was owned by Patsy and Jimmy Quill, who I still get a card from every Christmas. Jimmy was an ex-boxer and it was one of a dozen pubs like that in the East End that we would go out to. They were nearly all owned by ex-boxers, who could handle themselves and would look after their regulars and not want any aggravation.

It was more peaceful for footballers back then when they were out and about. Nowadays everyone has a phone and, once a player stops, suddenly there are 50 people around them all saying, 'Can I have a picture?' The new mobile phones are probably the worst thing that has ever happened for footballers who just want a quiet life. It's just cameras, cameras, cameras. If you met a footballer even as recently as the late 1990s, you didn't get anything without a bit of paper or a pen for an autograph. Everything went to another level after the Premier League was launched in 1992 – everybody's wages as well as the level of global interest. We have gone from no football live on television – except the FA Cup final then *The Big Match* on a Sunday afternoon in the 1980s – to the point now where 168 Premier League games are shown live in the UK and 380 are televised across the world. It is extraordinary. It sounds daft but I can go to Asia or America and still sometimes have people shouting, 'Harry,' if they see me. It goes without saying that did not happen before. You see replica kits on every continent.

The only people who had a West Ham shirt when I started out were the players. The crowd was just people in flat caps; there were no team colours because the shops did not sell them. No one thought about it. At Christmas, you got a pair of boots or a football. Nobody even thought about advertising. You look now at the wonderful footage of the 1950s. You would just have the commentator saying, 'It's the 1953 Cup final. It's Bolton versus Blackpool.' And then they'd show you the crowd all stood there. They were all wearing shirts and ties, even the kids, and everyone had a rattle.

I know it is easy to look back nostalgically on past eras but probably the biggest thing that upsets me today is to see how the mentality of some fans has changed. OK, there were no real facilities for supporters at grounds in the way that there are now, but there was also no need for segregation and none of the anger you see these days. My dad and I would go to watch matches around London and it was no big deal if we were at Arsenal one week, Tottenham the next and West Ham the one after. My dad would save up all week and we would get on the buses. We would take a flask of tea and we would talk to the people next to us. If Preston were in town, we would always want to go because my dad loved Tom Finney. He always said that he was better than Stanley Matthews, while Bill Shankly rated him as the best footballer of all time. We would chat to the Preston fans. These were the days before the M1 had even been built. It would be, 'How long did it take to come down?' They would be, 'Oh, nine hours. We left at 4am,' and then my dad would offer them a drop of tea. There was a bit of banter and humour but punters were not aggressive or nasty. People were very different in those days. Supporters just stood respectfully next to each other without any bother.

It upsets me now to hear some of the filth that comes out of the mouths of people at football matches. It is the worst thing about the modern game. It gets to be more about hating another club than supporting their own club. I think that quite a lot of the people who go to football now have no real love or feeling for the history of the game. They have not played the game at school or been interested in the history of the game. It's just a way of being one of the crowd, chanting abuse and having what they think is a good day out. I mean, you see someone like Arsène Wenger, after everything he has given to Arsenal, being angrily abused by people who claim to support the club and you just wonder what is going on in their heads. It's only the minority but it is a vocal, nasty element in football that any manager will tell you has grown. I have obviously experienced it, especially when I left Portsmouth the first time. Fans found out where I lived and even got hold of my mobile phone number. I would have crazy abuse shouted at me for agreeing to work at another club down the road. When we went back for a game at Fratton Park with Southampton, there were six SAS men to protect us in the dugout and they had helicopters flying above the team-bus. The team were too scared to play and we got battered 4–1.

The silly thing is that most supporters – even the abusive ones – are fantastic if you meet them on your own. I never get any aggravation on the street. People just like to have chat, which I enjoy, but put them in a stadium and some of them lose their mind completely. They are so busy shouting that you wonder how much they have actually seen of the game. It was in the 1970s and 1980s that the culture seemed to change and we went through a horrendous spell with violence around football. We often used to travel by train and you could get caught up in it as all the fans might be travelling at the same time. You would stop somewhere, say, Birmingham, and then have a mob getting on from another club and there could be a lot of trouble.

I should also stress that I have shared many laughs with fans and I know that the brilliant majority are what makes football. As well as the loud West Ham fan I famously brought on during a pre-season game at Oxford, who was slagging Lee Chapman off, we also once had a young guy turn up at Bournemouth from Liverpool and tell me he should be playing for us. 'Harry, I've been watching your team and I'm better than your players,' he said.

'Well, that's your opinion,' I said.

'Yeah, I'm a different class. I'm miles better than them. Why don't you give me a trial?' he said.

'Who do you play for?'

'Well, I'm not playing for anyone at the moment but I'm a good player,' he said.

He wouldn't go away. I couldn't get rid of him. In the end, I told him, 'Be here at ten o'clock tomorrow and I'll take a look.' He was, 'Oh, brilliant, Harry, I'll be there.' I was firm: 'Ten o'clock we start. Be here at ten o'clock.'

The next day, he turned up, out of breath, just before 12. We had finished. We didn't train for so long on a Friday. I looked at him and said, 'I told you to be here at 10. It's nearly 12 now. Go home. You're wasting my time.'

He had a good answer. 'No, you don't understand. I had to wait for the post office to open so I could cash my giro and buy these boots.' So I took pity on him and started kicking some balls towards him that I wanted him to trap and then pass back to me. The first one bounced off him. The next two he kicked like he had never seen a ball in his life. They went like a banana and were heading back towards the car park.

I said, 'Stop. Don't kick the ball any more.'

He said, 'Why?'

I said, 'Look, let's give those boots a wipe down. Take them straight back to the sports shop and get your money back.'

We had another guy who would turn up at West Ham every day. He wanted a trial. He lived in East Ham after coming to England from Nigeria. Every morning he would be at the training ground. I would stop at first, have a chat, try to help and be nice to him. I admired his persistence. 'Look,' I would say. 'I'm sorry but I am here to work with these other players today. The best thing is to go and find somebody who will look at you down the road. A club in one of the London or Essex leagues. We can put you in touch with some people.' But he wouldn't leave it alone. He kept turning up and coming in. Eventually we had to say, 'Look, you're not allowed in.' But still he kept turning up to the point where he was aggravation. He just wouldn't take no for an answer. We had an old car-park attendant called Charlie who was in the Parachute Regiment. He had more medals than I have ever seen in my life and was as hard as nails. He was a lovely old cockney character who we all loved to bits. He asked this kid to leave one day and he ended up having a go back at Charlie. We had to call the police in the end to stop him coming down.

Everyone thinks they can play. Even now I get them. I was getting a taxi in London just after Euro 2016 and the driver spent the whole journey telling me all about how he could have played for Manchester United but his dad wanted him to be a car mechanic. I've heard the stories so many times. 'I could have played with Arsenal but I did my ankle.' Or, 'My mum wanted me to do my exams.' They could have all played for someone.

Tim Sherwood is another who seemed to enjoy the interaction with fans. I know from experience that there were a few behind the dugout at Tottenham who were not shy about telling you what they thought and, in one game, he invited the fan in with him. I think he also ended up with Tim's gilet. Micky Quinn once had a pie chucked at him during a match at West Ham. Chicken and mushroom. What did Micky do? He managed to catch half and promptly ate it. Before another game at St James' Park, he bought 50 pies and was dishing them out to fans in the Gallowgate.

I have still tried to never lose that affinity with the fans and I am a sucker for any event that people ask me to help out with. Even when I was manager of Tottenham, I used to do things at working men's clubs and be thinking, 'I don't think Arsène

Wenger would be here.' Players no longer mix in the same way as we did with the fans, and it can be an effort to get some of them to talk to the man in the street. A lot of them live now in a world of their own, they keep among themselves and live in houses that are isolated. I know there is more demand on them now, especially with the camera phones, but there is a real danger if they are put on a pedestal and only mix in their own circles that they lose that connection with the people who pay their wages. It would be unhealthy for everyone. Most of the players are fantastic with fans but it does my head in when I see someone brush past supporters and not even spare a few seconds to stop for an autograph. It could be their kid one day and, if we stop and think about it, we can all remember when we have been on the other side of the fence. I still recall waiting outside Cassettari's Café when I was about ten for the West Ham players to come out and then getting John Bond and Kenny Brown's autographs. It was great.

I have always tried to remember my roots and be down to earth. You are no different or better because you are a football player or manager. The fans pay your wages and you can make someone's day by giving them a bit of time. I've seen lots of people on the way up get big-headed and carried away with themselves and then, when they have finished playing and have fallen on harder times, suddenly want to be a nice person. Be nice to people on the way up because you'll meet them on the way down. That was the first bit of advice I was ever given and, while we all might have our moments, I've always said that and tried to stick to it.

# CHAPTER SEVENTEEN

. . . . . . . . . . . . . . . . . . . . . . . . . . . . . . . . . . . . . . . . . . . . . . . . .

# WINNING
# AND LOSING

There is one certainty as a football manager. There will be some terrible lows. Yes, if you are fortunate and do well, there will also be some unbelievable highs, but the only real guarantee is those awful downs. The manager carries the weight of 30,000 supporters on his shoulders and it is impossible to over-emphasise the responsibility you feel and what that can do to you. I remember sitting in the dressing-room with Jamie at the end of the final game of the season against Manchester United with Southampton in 2005. Defeat had confirmed our relegation. It was just me and him. I cried. It was a fucking horrible feeling. It is scary how low I could get throughout my career about losing football matches. It is something I find difficult to explain and, even though I know it is ridiculous in the cold light of day, the best I can do is say that it feels like someone has died. You don't want to see anybody. You feel like the whole world is laughing at you. You think of those

30,000 people trudging out of the ground and you feel like you are completely responsible for their ruined weekend. I have been a player, coach, assistant and director as well, but the feeling when you are the manager does not even compare. Defeat just does you in completely.

You always do take it home with you. You try not to but I am yet to meet another manager who doesn't constantly carry that sick feeling around in their stomach if they have just lost. For a big setback, like a relegation, the process of getting over it can take weeks. Even after what you might call a normal defeat, it would usually take me several days to get my perspective back. The aim, really, would be to pick yourself up by the Monday morning so that you do not waste preparation time for the next game. Even so, I did often still feel very hollow on a Monday and it could be a struggle to get myself back on an even keel. That is when you most need good people around you. I was lucky to be able to go back home to someone like Sandra, who is not especially interested in football. Yes, she enjoys it in small doses, but she rarely comes to games and it is not what she wants to talk about. I would always look forward to a Saturday night and trying to get home in time to go out for a bit of pasta and a glass of red wine with Sandra. If we had won, it was the perfect way to end the week. If we had lost, she wouldn't bother saying much. She would know I had got the hump even if there would never be so much as a cross word between us. We would always go out regardless of the result. I could never make arrangements to meet anyone else on a Saturday night in case we had lost. I would hardly be able to talk and be of no use to anybody.

Christmas was also a difficult one. It is the busiest time of the year for football and so the chances of at least one setback are high. It meant that I was rarely up for a sociable or even happy Christmas. The teams would always train on Christmas Day and, if we had been beaten a few days earlier, I would be miserable. We've had some crap Christmases. The job does consume your life and, most of the time, it is very hard to think about anything else. You would hear your wife or your family talking to you about something else, but you would very often find that you had not listened to a word they had said.

It is similar for the vast majority of managers. Damien Comolli tells a story about Arsène Wenger and how, in the season he was relegated with Nancy in 1987, he actually shut himself away from friends and family over Christmas following a defeat. There was a mid-season break in France but Arsène literally just wanted to be on his own for the entire two weeks. I am sure that will sound crazy to some people, but I can understand that completely. That is how it gets to you. Arsène can also apparently be physically sick after a defeat. You have to find ways to move on and rationalise everything. Neil Warnock took to going out on his mountain bike and riding through Richmond Park when he was the manager of Queens Park Rangers. He once cycled out to a remote point in the park and started talking football to a grazing deer. When Gordon Strachan was Coventry City manager, he tried to get a defeat out of his system by going for a walk. He'd ended up 17 miles from home when he called his wife to collect him. He would say that being a football manager was like diving into a freezing cold sea. His point was that, although your experience might tell you exactly what was coming, nothing could completely prepare you for that sensation of the icy cold water once you had taken the plunge.

Results had a huge impact on my sleep and also, I think, my health. Your mind is going all over the place, especially when the team is struggling, and entire sleepless nights were not uncommon for me. I also heard Brian Clough say that, in the season he was relegated with Nottingham Forest, he was not sleeping for four or five nights of the week over a period of months. One way he would attempt to relax was by putting up a 'do not disturb sign' on the door of his office while he listened to Frank Sinatra.

There were times when the health aspect did worry me. I had a minor heart procedure while I was at Tottenham when I felt some pain in my chest while running, but that was very common for someone in their sixties and no big deal. There were moments, though, during my career when I could look at myself in the mirror and know that, as well as not feeling right, I did not even look right. My body would ache and my chest would feel tight. I did sometimes also find myself getting a bit more tired and would stay in London more rather than drive up and down every day to training from Bournemouth. Add in all the scouting I would do and my annual mileage reached 70,000 in most years of my career. I could be leaving

at 4am and regularly find myself parked up and waiting outside
the training ground for them to open at 7am while I was sat
listening to the radio. Whatever I might have lacked, it was
never resilience, stamina or enthusiasm, but defeats would
temporarily deplete me. You see other managers and you can
often sense a physical difference in them according to whether
they have won or lost.

The aim, of course, is to try to stay level and maintain
perspective through all the ups and downs. You have to tell
yourself that you are going to have these low moments and
you can't win every game, even if that doesn't usually make
it any easier to take. Managers can't all be successful all of
the time. Even among what I would term the 'big six' clubs
presently in England – those who have the most money and
highest profile managers – two are certain to not make the
Champions League each season and be classed as failures. You
accept the ups – and the salary – and you have to find a way of
absorbing the downs.

I was interested to read how Eddie Howe at Bournemouth
has used some of the teachings of the old American basketball
coach John Wooden to try to do this. Wooden's theory
was that you worry only about your preparation and the
performance of the team. You have to accept that the result is
ultimately out of your hands, but that it is within your control
to make sure you have done your very best. Eddie finds that
this outlook stops him wasting energy on issues he cannot
control, and he has also tried very hard to organise his time
so that he sees enough of his young family. He has a grid up

on his desk reminding him of when he should be at home and when he is supposed to be at work each week. It sounds great but it is funny when he talks about how he is actually getting on in practice. He says that his phone is usually pinned to his ear when he walks through the front door at night and that, for all his good intentions, he finds it almost impossible to switch off from football.

That's how, if you care, it does get to you – and the vast majority of managers really do care. There is one big difference, however, for those managers at the top end. By and large they are not facing anything like the same financial pressures personally as those lower down. Yes, there might be more spotlight and attention on their work but, whenever I speak to the guys in the lower leagues, and reflect on my own experiences earlier in my career, I remember that this is still where the deepest stress lies. I've been lucky to manage at the top level, where there is good money, over the last 20 years. I was still as desperate to succeed but it does at least give you a bit of independence in some of your decisions. There is usually a big difference for a young manager at a club in the lower divisions. They have probably played football all their lives and don't know anything else. You are also adapting to a completely different job when you move into coaching or management. As a player, you were finishing at 1pm and only had yourself really to think about but then, suddenly, you are at the training ground all day and the last one to leave at night.

Unless you can survive and work towards managing at the top end, it's really not such a great profession. Many of these guys lower down are hanging on by the skin of their teeth every week, thinking, 'What am I going to do if I lose? I've got three kids and a mortgage. I need to win on Saturday otherwise I could get the sack. If I get the sack, where am I going to find another job?' Just imagine that pressure of standing on the touchline knowing that, if you get beat, the chances are you're going to get sacked, and then the chances are you're not going to get another job in football. It's horrendous.

The added difference for those lads lower down, who are probably very good managers, is that they have not been earning the big money that some people think exists throughout football. They have probably been lower-division players and they are living week to week. They have got themselves on the ladder in football management but, should they fall, they do not have a job, a trade or any skills to fall back upon. What are they going to do with the next 35 years of their lives? What can they do? I spoke to a couple of ex-players in the summer of 2016 who had gone for a manager's job in one of the lower leagues. It was a decent opportunity at a good club but this job was paying £35,000 a year and really offered no long-term security. I have so much respect for those guys in the lower leagues. They know they will probably never get a chance to manage a Premier League club, and the game for them is trying to hang in there as long as possible. It is often a test of how long you can avoid the inevitable and it is not until you meet some of them that you properly appreciate what their life can be like.

It is the same when you have a chat to those who are out of work. It gives you a taste of real life outside the Premier League. You say to them, 'What are you up to?' They will be, 'Nothing, Harry. I lost my job 18 months ago. I have been doing a little bit of scouting and I have been applying for other jobs.' But it's so hard because there are still 40 or 50 people wanting that 35-grand-a-year job.

I certainly experienced that financial fear of 'How are we going to cope?' when we were living in a little house in Christchurch and I was driving up and down to Oxford and then working with Dave Webb at Bournemouth. Both jobs paid about £100 a week. Before that, I can still picture Sandra, with two young kids around her ankles, giving my battered old Marina a push-start one winter morning on my way to training during a very brief period at Brentford in 1976. They were certainly the scariest days of my career and I did often think, 'What would I do if it doesn't work out? What can I do?' I'd never been to work and I had never been out of football. Sandra had been a hairdresser since she left school and, when she was pregnant with Jamie and I was still playing, she worked so we had some extra income. She used to go out carrying one of those big hairdryers with a big hood that they used to put on over the customer's head. She had a list of old girls around Bournemouth who she would go and visit. She charged £1.50 for a set just to keep us going with a bit of extra income.

I was interested, then, to read Brian Clough say that, in spite of everything that went wrong for him at Leeds

United, the £98,000 pay-off was actually transformative in his career. That was a huge sum in 1974 and meant that he approached the job at Nottingham Forest without any financial concerns hovering over him. In his own mind it gave him the freedom to follow his instincts and hunches without worrying about the consequences of failure. Some of the guys who have lost their jobs at Liverpool, Manchester United, Chelsea or Manchester City in recent years have had huge pay-offs that, financially at least, have set them up. I can understand how having that bit of security would help ease some of the worry, but the truth is that you are still just as desperate to win once the whistle goes. I have experienced life at both ends and, when it actually gets to 3pm on a Saturday, I know that Pep Guardiola will still be feeling the same as John Still of Dagenham & Redbridge. I certainly did whether it was a Champions League quarter-final against Real Madrid or a trip to Scunthorpe with Bournemouth. I also know that if I agreed to manage Poole Town tomorrow, I would still come home in the same terrible state on a Saturday night if we got beat.

So what is it that keeps most football managers coming back for more? For some it is all that they know and a way of making a living, but football does also have an undoubted addictive quality. It does not take long before you miss it. The excitement from winning is incredible but it is also strangely fleeting, and most managers will tell you that it is almost impossible to savour one victory for more than a few hours before your mind has already switched to the next target. My mind would always turn to the challenges of the next season, and how we kept on moving forward, even after a big success.

The first really big victory for me in management was when Bournemouth won what until recently was known as the Johnstone's Paint Trophy during my first season in 1984. It was the only year that the final has not been held at either Wembley or the Millennium Stadium. We were playing Hull City, but the Horse of the Year show had been held a few days earlier on the Wembley pitch and ruined it. We eventually played at Hull's ground but still won 2–1. My main memory of the celebrations was stopping at the motorway services on the way home and all the team having egg and chips with the trophy proudly displayed on the greasy table.

Winning promotion to the old Second Division with Bournemouth at Fulham in 1987 was also unforgettable, especially as the day ended with Jimmy Hill throwing half of our directors out of the boardroom at Craven Cottage. Bournemouth had never been up past the third tier in those days and there was this daft theory in the town that the football team would somehow never be permitted to play at such a high level. With about 12 games to go, I would meet these doubters and have the strangest conversations. Someone would say, 'Well done, Harry, but Bournemouth won't go up.'

I would say, 'What do you mean?'

They'd reply, 'Well, the council won't let us.'

'How are they going to stop us?'

'They will. They don't want it down here.'

'They don't want what? What are they going to do? Come into the dressing-room and tell us to lose?'

'Well, I don't know what they will do, but they won't let you go up.'

I had this nonsense everywhere I went. What Eddie Howe has since achieved is on another planet but Bournemouth had been almost a hundred years outside the top two divisions at that time so, to actually get promoted, was especially sweet.

We were owned at the time by a local company called Macbar Construction. Rodney Barton was the chairman and he was a sailing man, but his partners were two Irish boys from Galway called Jimmy Craven and Peter McDonagh. They were great guys, who loved a drink. They had come up the hard way and come to England digging up roads. They ended up owning a big company building roads. We clinched our promotion and the Division Three title by beating Fulham 3–1. Jimmy and Peter got in the bar after the game to celebrate and drunk Fulham dry. I loved Jimmy Hill. He was one of football's all-time greats and also the chairman at Fulham at the time as well as the *Match of the Day* presenter. He ended up telling them to leave. We then travelled back down to Bournemouth and a little steak house 200 yards from the ground for some food and a glass of wine.

People assume that there is always some huge party in the West End if a football clubs wins something, but it is not really like that – well, it can be like that for the players maybe, but not the manager. At Portsmouth, when we won what is now the Championship to get promoted to the Premier

League, we simply went to a little Italian pizza house near the stadium. The players were there, as well as the staff and the chairman Milan Mandarić. Apart from an unwanted soaking by the players live on Sky Sports, there were no great wild celebrations either when we clinched Champions League qualification for Tottenham by beating Manchester City. We just flew home that night and I think I got a 'well done' from the chairman Daniel Levy. It was the first time Tottenham had qualified for the Champions League. People often ask, 'What did you do that night?' after a big victory, but I am usually one for getting home if I can. Sometimes there is just so much relief after all the pressure and build-up that you really just need to sit down and try to take it all in. You have almost lost all of your energy and you just want to have a glass of wine and a bit of grub. I am not a big drinker and so it is not as if I would go out celebrating all night anyway.

The day at Wembley after promotion to the Premier League with QPR was the same. I was dropped off back at Loftus Road, where they were having a celebration upstairs. I went in there for ten minutes, poked my head through the door, and then disappeared back to the hotel, where I had a bit of dinner on my own as I had to stay up in London. Even after I was cleared of tax evasion at the High Court in February 2012, all I wanted to do was get back home to Sandra. I went to the hotel and there were lots of people there – friends, neighbours and people who had supported me – but I needed to get back to Bournemouth. I just said, 'Look, I don't feel great,' and I jumped in my car and drove home.

The FA Cup final day with Portsmouth was strange too. It was a fantastic feeling on the final whistle but it was quite surreal and almost felt like it wasn't really all happening. Since becoming a manager, the dream was always to lead a team out at Wembley. It certainly made me remember my dad and us watching the FA Cup final at home – that was the highlight of the year for him. It was the only game that was televised live, and our big day. We had a nine-inch black and white television and I always remember that we would have a three-inch magnifying glass strapped across the back to make it 12 inches for the Cup final. The only channel was BBC. At 12 noon on Cup final day the streets were deserted. Those who did have TVs had it on; those who didn't would go around the house of someone who did. We would watch the whole build-up to the game: the teams arriving on the coach, the man in the white suit singing 'Abide with Me' and 100,000 joining in at Wembley. I can recall Cup final moments like Ray Wood playing on with a fractured jaw in the 1957 final and Bert Trautmann breaking his neck but still finishing the match a year earlier.

I did think how special it would have been for my dad to have lived to see me managing a winning team on that stage. The parade on Southsea Common the next day with 200,000 people was also extraordinary. To see so many Portsmouth people turn out and be so happy, genuinely happy, is what it was all about for me. As managers, that is what you are there to do.

But it's not always the more famous victories that give you the most satisfaction. Winning with a late goal is always especially sweet, and I can remember many times just being in my car on my own or with a friend, and singing or shouting 'yes' over a result we'd just had. Brian Clough was once asked for the best part of the job. He said it was, 'When we've won away from home on a midweek night. We've stopped for a bag of chips and then we're having a sing-song on the coach, with all of us having a day off tomorrow. It is almost as good as still playing.' I would agree with him on that – there is a buzz from winning that is just irreplaceable.

Yet that is still only part of what drives us on through the harder times. For me, it was not so much the victories that were the main enjoyment but just being around the training ground every morning with fantastic footballers. Arsène is another who talks about management in terms of 'an addiction' and how he now feels afraid of packing it in. Bill Shankly once described the word 'retire' as the stupidest in the world. 'You retire when they put the lid down on your coffin with your name on top,' he said. I am not so sure about that – and I do know that Sir Alex Ferguson has thoroughly enjoyed his time since standing down as manager of Manchester United. I never stopped caring desperately about the outcome. If I had, I knew it would be time to stop. But every game still always felt like life and death, and that terrible overbearing pressure of wanting to be successful has never left me.

# CHAPTER EIGHTEEN

# MOVING ON

The statistics get scarier by the year. There were 56 sackings and 70 changes of manager through the 92 English professional clubs during the 2015–16 season. In England, on average, a manager survives between one and two years in his job and, most alarming of all, more than half of managers never get a second chance. Malcolm Allison would always say that, 'You're not a real manager unless you've been sacked,' and it is something that even the greats generally experience at least once in their careers. There is a certain gallows humour about it within the profession, even if the personal consequences, especially in the lower leagues, can be utterly devastating. It is hard to think of a more precarious profession. The League Managers' Association has almost 400 members in this country and they are largely competing with each other for fewer than 100 jobs. Factor in all the other managers from abroad who are desperate to work in England and you don't have to be a genius to see that your odds of being out of work are actually higher than those of having a job. This excess of supply over demand also encourages some chairmen to behave like they are at a casino. They can gamble on one manager and, if it does not work, they still know that good applications for the vacancy will soon come flooding in.

Frank Burrows used to work with me at West Ham United and also managed all over the country in a career that spanned almost 30 years. He got to the stage where he would say that he kept a big cardboard box at the end of his desk just so that he was ready. There was also the joke among managers that you could judge your life expectancy by whether they bothered with a plaque outside the door. You really knew that you were in trouble when they only wrote the manager's name up on the door in chalk with a bucket and sponge beside it.

There were five managers who had been at their clubs for more than five years when the Premier league was launched in 1992–93, but that was down to just one by 2016–17, and it is increasingly hard to see there being another Arsène Wenger. The pressure and analysis that surrounds every match is huge. Factor in the rewards that are on offer in the Premier League and you can see why the kneejerk reaction has become the norm. When I started out, it was not unusual to meet managers who had been at their club for a decade or more. Even relegation rarely resulted in the sack. If the club thought you were a good manager, you could go down but then have the chance to come back up with the same team. Relegated managers now can count themselves lucky to even get a few games at the start of the next season. Crowds are so much more restless and no one can survive when the fans really turn. It rarely makes sense for an industry where stability and team building can be so beneficial, but the increased churn at just about all the big clubs is the same.

Take Manchester United. They are on their third manager since Sir Alex Ferguson after finishing seventh, fourth and fifth in the first three seasons without him. But where did they finish in their first four full seasons under him? Second, eleventh, thirteenth and sixth. It was absolutely right that the directors didn't flinch back then – and Alex certainly inherited a more difficult job than those who came after him – but it is impossible to imagine a manager getting that sort of time at a club like Manchester United now.

Every manager is constantly only five or six games from the sack. The biggest change is that chairmen previously were not surrounded by this constant soundtrack of opinion through television, radio phone-ins and now social media. Turn any sort of device on and you will hear the same rants every week when a team gets beat: 'They were useless. The manager has got to go. He has lost the plot. He doesn't know what he is doing.' It can come after only one game of the season. A good proportion of those offering their opinions do not even go to the games but they still contribute to a tension that directly influences clubs. I am lucky to have never had the crowd shouting for me to be sacked but, in my last season at Queens Park Rangers, I did start seeing stories in newspapers that were saying I was under pressure. I had never had that before and, after only seven games of the season, it is not nice. A lot of the chairmen are on Twitter and are constantly exposed to all this background noise and some of the more extreme views. They want to be pals with the fans and they react to what they are hearing.

There was a definite change when radio phone-ins started in the early 1990s and you suddenly had people moaning away on national BBC Radio on a Saturday evening. I had a little bad spell where we lost a few games at West Ham and suddenly David Mellor, who was the host of the Radio 5 *606* phone-in from 1992 until 2001, started on me. I knew someone who worked there and I was told that he wouldn't take any positive calls about me. They said he was only taking negative calls. I'll never forget going to Chelsea one winter's night and seeing him on my way back from getting a cup of tea at half-time. I was in the row behind and, honestly, I thought about making out I had tripped so that I spilt this cup of tea all over his head. I was with someone and they said, 'Don't get involved with him, he's an idiot.' I think he got the hump because I came out and said, 'Don't listen to him, hasn't he just been caught in bed with a Chelsea shirt on?' Anyway, that's how it got. We had people like him, who had probably never kicked a ball in his life, hosting debates with fans about whether managers should get sacked. The only programme about football used to be *Match of the Day*. Now you can catch people debating football every time you turn on a television, radio, computer or even a mobile phone.

John Barnes and Jason McAteer certainly found that out at Tranmere Rovers in 2009. John had just held his press conference on the Friday before a match when he was summoned to see the chairman to be told that they had both lost their respective jobs as manager and assistant just 11 games into the season. It meant that the television cameras and photographers were still there when John and Jason were clearing their stuff and preparing to leave. John had cycled in but Jason told him not to ride his bike home. He could see the 'On your bike' headlines already if the photographers took a picture and so offered to drop John off at his house. Jason, though, was struggling to fit the bike into the boot of his car – whichever way he turned it there seemed to be a part still sticking out. This had been going on for a few minutes when Jason's phone went off. It was his mate who just said, 'You need to turn the wheel the other way and then push the saddle in.' The bike went straight in. Jason thought his mate must have turned up at the training ground and would be just walking across the car park. He looked around but could not see him, so he said, 'OK, thanks, where are you?' His mate just replied, 'No problem. I am watching you live on Sky Sports News.'

Timing was also hardly Simon Jordan's strong point when he delivered the news to Trevor Francis at Crystal Palace in 2003. It was Trevor's 49th birthday. Simon later claimed that Trevor just sat there and simply said, 'But it's my birthday,' as he received a P45 rather than a card from his boss.

Sometimes just about everyone else seems to know before the manager. Martin Jol suffered that at Tottenham when, after officials had been photographed meeting Juande Ramos, news of his departure began spreading around the ground during a

European match against Getafe in 2007. It was similarly messy for Louis van Gaal at Manchester United in 2016 when, just as he was literally guiding the club to an FA Cup win over Crystal Palace at Wembley, journalists were breaking the news that he would be replaced the following season by José Mourinho.

One of the most brutal sackings I can remember was that of John Lyall at West Ham. He had won the FA Cup twice. He had led West Ham to a European final and their highest ever league position of third. At 15 years, he was the longest serving West Ham manager of the post-war era. Even before that, he had worked as a youth coach at Upton Park after his career was cut short at the age of just 23 by a horrific knee injury. After then joining the groundstaff in 1965, John had been at the club for 34 years when he was called in to be given the news in 1989. Details of his dismissal are not well known but he did once speak about it to other managers when he gave a talk on the subject of loyalty, or the lack of, in football. He said that he got called up into the West Ham boardroom when they delivered the news and then said, 'Could we have your car keys?' Straight away. They did not say, 'John, you have been our manager for 15 years and an employee here for 34 years. Give yourself a few weeks to sort the car out. Arrange for us to pick it up one day.' They just asked straight out for the keys. Not only did he have to clear his car out – and he probably had a boot full of stuff – but he also still had to find a way to get home. He told us that he just threw his keys on the table and left. John said that he never went back; he was to die of a heart attack in 2006 when he was only 66.

They named the main gates after him at Upton Park, but that was three years later. It was similar with Bobby Moore. When he died, they made a statue of him at Wembley and Upton Park. They also named a stand after him but what did they do when he was alive? That's how the game is, unfortunately. When you're gone, you're gone. A lot of people don't want to know what you've done or who you are.

That could hardly have been more evident than with the man who oversaw the greatest triumph in the history of English football. Sir Alf Ramsey was sacked as England manager in 1974, but there is an extraordinary story about the day he lost his job. On the way back from Wembley, he bumped into Ted Phillips, an old striker of his at Ipswich Town, at Liverpool Street station. Ted had been working in London and was travelling back to Essex while Alf, whose 11 years as England manager had come to an abrupt end, was heading home to Ipswich. Alf suggested that he buy Ted a drink, which was very unusual. They talked and then went their separate ways. Yet it was not until the next day, when Ted was making his way back into London on the train, that he read that Alf had been sacked. It must have happened just a few hours before they had their drink together and yet Alf did not mention it. That was how it was in those days. There was no fuss. If you had not seen the six o'clock news, you would not know that the England manager had been sacked until you got a paper the next day. Now, of course, it would be on Sky Sports News every minute. There would be people ringing in, messages on Twitter. In those days, there was nothing. Like Bobby, Alf was pretty much ignored in his later life. There was a campaign for all the substitutes to get a medal for the 1966 World Cup but the Football Association did not give Alf anything, and there was nothing at Wembley in his name until after he died. The only time I ever met him was at a coaches' course at Lilleshall, but he did seem aloof. He came from Dagenham and so probably spoke like me when he was younger, but had taken the elocution lessons by that point. He was very, very quiet when we met him at Lilleshall and he really just kept himself to himself.

My own departures have come at different times and for different reasons. I know people thought there was something more to it when I left Queens Park Rangers in February 2015, especially as it was the day after the transfer window closed, but there was no row. I really do have a huge amount of time for the chairman, Tony Fernandes, but I was struggling very badly with my knees and I had stopped enjoying it. The situation had been on my mind for several months. It got to the stage where I had to make sure I would not have to walk more than about a hundred yards if I was going somewhere. I was in pain all the time and could barely stand to watch a match, let alone take anything approaching a hands-on role in training. My mind was pretty much made up the weekend before I left, when I had to go back to my car to sit down after about five minutes of watching my grandson play. I did not sleep a wink on the night I finally made my decision and I called Tony just before 6am to let him know. I just felt that it would be best to give somebody else a crack at it who could give more physically to the job, and I wanted to leave enough time to give them a decent shot. I thought that we still had as good a chance to stay up as the five or six other clubs at the bottom. There was nothing in it and, although we had not been getting the results, the performances against teams like Liverpool and Manchester City had made me certain that we could put a run together.

Once I had left, I felt that they should really have given the job to Glenn Hoddle. They had an ex-England manager working with them, who still has a huge amount to offer, but Les Ferdinand had come to the club and I think he wanted to get Chris Ramsey more involved.

I did not leave because of any issues about transfers. We had tried to get Emmanuel Adebayor during the January transfer window but the deal was not possible financially. I respected the limitations we had, even if I did have concerns about the squad from the moment we went up in the play-off final of 2014. When I was stood on the pitch at Wembley after we beat Derby County, my mind was already turning to the Premier League and what it would take to stay up. I was thinking, 'There are probably only two players here that I really want next year in my team.' I felt that we needed to get a virtually new team if we were going to have a chance of surviving. Unfortunately, two weeks before the season started, I pretty much still had the group that I was looking to change. I remember a meeting with the owners where they outlined the limitations. I warned them that I felt we seriously risked relegation with that squad. I was being encouraged to play younger players from the academy, but they were not ready. If we'd had the kids to do the job, I would have played them – just as I did at West Ham. At QPR they put some of them in the first team after I left and they got slaughtered because they weren't good enough at that time. That doesn't do kids any good in the long term because their confidence gets drained.

Even so, nine of the team that started on the final day of the season with Chris in 2014–15 had been with us when we got promoted the previous year through the play-offs after finishing well behind Leicester City and Burnley. Quality was the main issue. But all that said, I really don't look back on my time at Loftus Road with any bad feelings. Given the issues we had with the squad and the sort of players they had brought in previously, it really was a good feat to get promoted in 2014. Bobby Zamora's goal in the play-off final was a moment I will never forget and, although we were fortunate on the day, it was something that the QPR owners and fans truly deserved for all their commitment to the club.

I did not see it coming on either of the two occasions I have been sacked. As I have already said, I probably brought the West Ham situation on myself to an extent, but it was still sudden and completely out of the blue. The chairman, Terry Brown, had been talking about a four-year contract and Mick McGuire from the PFA was doing that deal on my behalf. It was dragging but it was there to be signed for about three months and I just never got round to doing it. Then Mick rang me one day and said, 'What's happening?' I said, 'I don't know, why?' He said, 'I don't know but I just spoke with Terry Brown and he's always, "Harry this, Harry that and Harry's going to be running it for the next ten years" but I had said about coming in to sign the contract and he said, "I don't know if there is a contract now."' He got upset about something I said about him in a fanzine and that was it. I was gone.

It is a very strange feeling to be sacked. I had a year remaining on my contract at Tottenham in 2012 when I left. I was very happy, and we had also talked about extending it. We had finished in the top four twice in three seasons. We should have finished third that year but were decimated by injuries and I had felt that we should strengthen in January when we were already in great shape. Even so, I was sure that we had the basis of a team that could genuinely challenge to win the Premier League over the next few years. My faith would never be tested. I met the chairman Daniel Levy in London, where he delivered the news and, by the time I had left the offices with him and the club solicitor, it was about 4am. I'll never forget it because there were no taxis outside and so I was walking through London in the dead of night knowing that I had lost my job. A Spurs-supporting taxi driver eventually happened to pick me up and took me to the hotel but, with him talking excitedly about the coming season, I did not have the heart to tell him what had just happened. I got to the hotel and just wanted to drive home to Bournemouth rather than stay in London. As I was heading down the M3, at what must have been about 5am, my phone went. It was Daniel. 'I just want to say that I hope we can remain friends,' he said.

I was, 'Yeah, no problem, Daniel, that's life.' Whether it was Daniel or whether it was the owner Joe Lewis who made the decision, I don't really know.

It obviously did not help that we'd lost our Champions League place when Chelsea somehow beat Bayern Munich in the 2012 final. We would also have qualified by finishing third if Márton Fülöp had not had one of the worst games I have ever seen, on the final day of the Premier League season when West Bromwich Albion lost 3–2 against Arsenal.

There were no fallouts with anyone at Spurs and I felt that I got on well with Daniel, but they then obviously went in a different direction and down the road of having more of a coach with a director of football. That was the structure they had before me as well, with Damien Comolli, but they moved away from everything they had been trying to do, really, when they went for me and brought a manager in. As soon as I went, they appointed Franco Baldini as technical director and, although I was surprised to hear that Paul Mitchell was leaving his post as head of recruitment and analysis in August 2016, they seem to have kept a similar sort of structure.

I didn't get any sleep on the night I was sacked by Tottenham and just ended up playing golf the following morning. It actually happened in between England's group games at Euro 2012 against France and Sweden but, if the bookmakers were to be believed earlier in the year, it would have been me leading the national team that summer. I was 10–1 on and Roy Hodgson was 10–1 against after I was cleared in the High Court. At that time, I was being given the impression that I would be able to pick between the jobs. People were not asking whether Tottenham or England wanted me. The repeated question was, 'Which one are you going to choose?' It felt like it was a done deal and it was not just the bookmakers or journalists. It was people from high positions in football telling me that it was my job. To this day, I don't know what happened. Something happened. Something must have happened because the information was coming from the right places. The FA did not even speak to me, but one thing that I did subsequently discover after leaving Tottenham was that I had a very lopsided contract.

The move from Portsmouth to Tottenham in 2008 had happened very quickly. We were travelling back from Braga on the team-bus on the Thursday after a UEFA Cup match when I was first called. In less than three days it was all agreed and the contract was signed. I did not read that contract. Daniel Levy just said, 'I'll give you x amount of pounds a week. This is your bonus if you get in the Champions League.' Like an idiot I said, 'Yeah, fine,' and I just signed it. I'm absolutely useless like that. Tottenham paid compensation to Portsmouth for me but, in the contract, there was also a clause that, if I went anywhere else, the people who came in for me would have to pay back the compensation. They would also have to pay back all the wages I had earned at Tottenham. I am sure that if the FA had approached Tottenham, and I don't know if they did, they would have just said, 'Well, this is the deal.' I don't know whether that was the reason for not getting the job, but I did then also leave Tottenham within a couple of months.

It was a double whammy, but I was never one for getting bitter. I have seen enough in football to have some perspective about the inevitable ups and downs. There are a lot worse things happening than me not getting the England job and then getting the sack at Tottenham. I can also appreciate just how fortunate I have been. So much of your path in management comes down to luck and having people who believe in you and give you a chance. Few jobs in management end with the sort of fairytale Sir Alex Ferguson enjoyed in signing off with a 13th Premier League title, but that does not stop the vast majority wanting to come back for more.

Not many know this but, when I retired from playing, my plan was simply to buy a taxi in Bournemouth. I thought, 'I'll be my own boss.' That was all I had in my mind. I looked into it. The taxi plates were £14,000 and, once you had them, it was like you had bought yourself a livelihood. Our house at the time was only worth £15,000 and we just couldn't raise the money. I would think, 'What am I going to do? What can I do? I can't do anything.' But then I got my opportunities. I would have been prepared to move wherever there was work earlier in my career, but I was ultimately very lucky that my six clubs were either in London or on the south coast and so a move was never forced upon us. The families of football managers and coaches generally have to put up with an enormous amount of upheaval in their lives.

Even so, when I lost that first game at Bournemouth 9–0 and had already been making plans for an alternative career as a taxi driver, I could never have imagined that I would be here now sharing experiences of almost 35 years in professional football management. I am told that my tally of nearly 1,400 games puts me in the top ten for most matches and the top five of those to have managed in England's top flight. I am proud of all that but it is really not the records and statistics that matter most. It is not even the victories and defeats. It is the people I have met, the laughs I have shared, the great moments I have witnessed and the stories I have heard. Former players do become special to you. If one of my lads from that first Bournemouth team ever asks me to do anything, I could never say no. Without them, I would not have had the career I did.

Yet it really all started for me with my dad's love of football. We would be as happy watching a parks team play on Hackney Marshes as getting a ticket for the FA Cup final at Wembley. I feel no different now, whether I am at a big Premier League match, helping out as a director at Wimborne Town in the Southern League, going to Bournemouth (where I am a season-ticket holder) with my mate Mervyn or simply watching my grandchildren play. My dad just loved the game in the purest sense. He passed that on and, if I have done the same for some of the players, fans and people I have worked with, that will do me nicely.

# PHOTO CREDITS

**First plate section:** Page 1 (top) ©Colorsport/REX/Shutterstock, (bottom) ©PA Images. Page 2 (top) ©Allsport UK/Allsport, (bottom) ©Phil Cole/Getty Images. Page 3 (top) ©S&G and Barratts/EMPICS Sport, (middle) ©The private collection of Ernie Gregory, (bottom) ©George W. Hales/Fox Photos/Getty Image. Page 4 (top) ©Bob Thomas/Getty Images, (bottom) ©Liverpool FC via Getty Images. Page 5 (top) ©Javier Garcia/BPI/REX/ Shutterstock, (bottom) ©Michael Steele/Getty Image. Page 6 (top left) ©Paul Gilham/Getty Images, (top right) ©Michael Steele/EMPICS Sport, (bottom) ©KHALIL MAZRAAWI/AFP/ Getty Images. Page 7 (top) ©John Peters/Man Utd via Getty Images, (bottom) ©Michael Fresco/Evening Standard/Hulton Archive/Getty Images. Page 8 (top) ©David Price/Arsenal FC via Getty Images, (middle) ©Jasper Juinen/Getty Images, (bottom) ©GLYN KIRK/AFP/Getty Images.

**Second plate section:** Page 1 (top) ©Local World/REX/ Shutterstock, (bottom left) ©BBC, (bottom right) ©Colorsport/ REX/Shutterstock. Page 2 (top) ©Plumb Images/Leicester City FC via Getty Images, (bottom) ©Matthew Peters/Manchester United via Getty Images. Page 3 (top) ©Mike Hewitt/Getty Images, (bottom) ©RossKinnaird/Allsport. Page 4 (top) ©Justin Goff/UK Press via Getty Images, (bottom) ©Colorsport/REX/ Shutterstock. Page 5 (top) ©Nick Potts/PA Archive/Press Association Images, (bottom) ©IAN KINGTON/AFP/Getty Images. Page 6 (top) ©ITV Studios Ltd, (bottom) ©BNPS. Page 7 (top) Paul Gilham/Getty Images, (bottom) ©Ben Radford/Getty Images). Page 8 (top) ©Michael Regan – The FA/The FA via Getty Images, (bottom) ©Action Images.